Conducting Environmental Impact Assessment in Developing Countries

Prasad Modak and Asit K. Biswas

160201

United Nations University Press

TOKYO · NEW YORK · PARIS

United Nations University Press
The United Nations University
53-70, Jingumae 5-chome,
Shibuya-ku, Tokyo 150-8925, Japan
Tel: +81-3-3499-2811   Fax: +81-3-3406-7345
E-mail: sales@hq.unu.edu   http://www.unu.edu

UNU Office in North America
2 United Nations Plaza, Room DC2-1462-70, New York, NY, 10017
Tel: +1-212-963-6387   Fax: +1-212-371-9454   E-mail: unuona@igc.apc.org

United Nations University Press is the publishing division of the
United Nations University.

Cover design by Andrew Corbett

Printed in the United States of America

UNUP-965
ISBN 92-808-0965-2

Library of Congress Cataloging-in-Publication Data
Modak, Prasad.
Conducting environmental impact assessment in developing countries /
Prasad Modak and Asit K. Biswas.
      p. cm.
   Includes bibliographical references and index.
   ISBN 9280809652 (paper)
   1. Environmental impact analysis-Developing countries.
I. Biswas, Asit K. II. Title.
   TD194.68.D44   C66   1999
   333.7′14′091724—dc21   99-6139
                                                  CIP

Contents

v

Preface

The process of environmental impact assessment started at the beginning of the 1970s. During the following years, general interest in environmental management has steadily increased in both developed and developing countries. During this period, the awareness of the importance of environmental protection and our knowledge of the complex and dynamic interrelationships between environment and development issues has improved significantly as well.

Neither developed nor developing countries form homogeneous groups in terms of their approaches to environmental management or the progress they have made in managing their environment. Generally speaking, formal assessment as an integral part of national efforts to manage the environment properly is less advanced in developing countries compared to the Western nations. The environmental conditions in many countries in transition are also different. Overall, most countries now require an environmental assessment of all major development projects. However, the actual implementation of this policy varies significantly from one country to another, and some times even from one part to another within the same country. Furthermore, it should be noted that whereas some developing countries, such as the Philippines, required environmental impact assessments of major development projects as early as in 1977, a few important industrialized countries, such as the Federal Republic of Germany, institutionalized similar requirements only about a decade later.

Numerous developing countries have already made EIA mandatory for clearance of projects. Organizations such as the World Bank and Interamerican Development Bank currently insist that proper environmental assessments must be carried out so that the projects will be eligible to receive loans. Thus, numerous EIAs have been carried out in developing countries in recent years because of national and international requirements. My own personal estimate indicates that the Asian developing countries alone have already carried out more than 15 000 environmental impact assessment studies. Unfortunately, however, no objective evaluation has been conducted on the overall quality of these assessments, and/or to what extent they have managed to protect and enhance the environment. The few evaluations that are available are of limited use because of their academic and abstract nature.

On the basis of my own personal experience as a Senior Advisor to 17 developing countries and all major development-oriented international institutions, it is clear that EIA has often become a mechanistic process. The "means", that is EIA, is receiving almost exclusive attention, and the "end", that is implementation of EIA to improve the environment, is often not getting appropriate consideration. Analysts often have no clear idea as to what type of information is needed by environmental managers to make rational and timely decisions. Furthermore, too much emphasis is often given to data collection, and not enough on their analysis, interpretation, and their overall environmental implications.

Another major problem stems from the fact that monitoring and evaluation of the actual environmental impacts of projects are mostly conspicuous because of their absence. Unquestionably, monitoring and evaluation are absolutely essential to ensure that the compliance measures agreed to are properly carried out within the agreed timeframe. Equally, only regular monitoring and evaluation would give a clear picture not only of the accuracy of environmental assessment techniques used, but also would provide actual post-project environmental conditions. Thus, absence of proper monitoring and evaluation is now a major handicap for rational environmental management in developing countries.

Faced with these constraints, the United Nations University decided to develop a text which emphasizes the EIA requirements of developing countries. The present text is the direct result of this effort.

The project could not have been started or completed without the strong support and encouragement of Dr. Juha I. Uitto, Senior Programme Officer of the United Nations University. I am also most grateful to my co-author, Dr. Prasad Modak, who is one of India's leading environmental scientists and who did a lion's share of work for this book. I am thus most grateful to Dr. Uitto and Dr. Modak for making this text possible.

Asit K. Biswas
Project Coordinator, UNU
Mexico City

Abbreviations

ADB	Asian Development Bank
AfDB	African Development Bank
AI	artificial intelligence
AMDAL	Analysis Mengenai Dampak Lingkungan (Indonesian EIA)
AsDB	Asian Development Bank
BAPEDAL	Badan Pengendalian Dampak Lingkungan (Indonesian Environmental Impact Management Agency)
BKPM	Investment Coordination Board (Indonesian)
BLEVE	boiling liquid expanding vapour explosion
BOD	biological oxygen demand
CBA	cost-benefit analysis
CEA	cumulative effects assessment
CEO	chief executive officer
CEQ	Council for Environmental Quality
CFC	chlorofluorocarbon
CGOSD	Cairo General Organization for Sewerage and Sanitary Drainage
CIDA	Canadian International Development Agency
CIM	component interaction matrix
COD	chemical oxygen demand
COPP	Country Operational Program Papers
CWO	Cairo Wastewater Organization

DG	director general
DMP	disaster management plan
DOE	Department of Environment
EA	environmental assessment
EARP	environmental assessment and review process
EBM	environmental base map
EBRD	European Bank for Reconstruction and Development
ECA	environmentally critical areas
EcoRA	ecological risk assessment
ECP	environmentally critical projects
ED	environmental design
EES	environmental evaluation system
EHIA	environment health impact assessment
EIA	environmental impact assessment
EIS	environmental impact statement
EIU	environmental impact unit
EMP	environmental management plan
EPA	Environmental Protection Agency
EPM	environmental protection measures
ERA	environmental risk assessment
ESP	electrostatic precipitator
FEARO	federal environmental assessment and review office
FINNIDA	Finnish International Development Agency
FMEA	failure modes and effects analysis
FMECA	failure modes, effects, and critical analysis
FS	feasibility study
GIS	geographical information systems
HAZID	hazard identification
HAZOP	hazard operability study
HC	hydrocarbons
HHRA	human health risk assessment
HSI	habitat suitability index
IA	initial assessments
IDB	Interamerican Development Bank
IEE	initial environmental examination
IS	international standard
ISA	irrigation service area
KA	terms of reference (Indonesian)
LCA	life cycle analysis
LPG	liquefied petroleum gas
MATS	multi attribute tradeoff system
MEIP	Metropolitan Environment Improvement Project
MOI	Ministry of Industry

NEPA	National Environment Policy Act
NORAD	Norwegian Agency for Development Cooperation
ODA	Overseas Development Administration
ODS	ozone depleting substances
OENV	Office of Environment
OM&R	operations, maintenance, and replacement
PIC	public information and consultation
PIU	parameter importance unit
PMC	project management consultant
PPC	Project Processing Committee
PR	public review
PU	Department of Public Works (Indonesian)
RKL	environmental management plan (Indonesian)
ROW	right of way
RPL	environmental monitoring plan (Indonesian)
SEA	strategic environmental assessment
SIA	social impact assessment
SOP	standard operating practices
SPM	suspended particulate matter
TAFR	total accident frequency rate
TDS	total dissolved solids
TOR	terms of reference
TSP	total suspended particles
TSS	total suspended solids
UNEP	United Nations Environment Programme
USAID	United States Agency for International Development

1

Introduction

1.1 The environmental movement

Perhaps one of the first and most influential warnings about the degradation of the environment was *Silent Spring*, a book about the use of pesticides, written by Rachel Carson and published in 1962. In the early 1960s, however, public opinion had shown no great awareness of environmental problems. By the mid-1960s, some scientists in the USA were sounding warnings about the possibility of climate change due to increased carbon dioxide levels in the atmosphere resulting from the burning of fossil fuels.

By the end of the 1960s, warnings, conferences, legislative initiatives, and media attention had created a dramatic change. The phenomenon was paralleled in other western countries, setting the stage for legislation, environmental institution building, and the rise of proactive citizen groups – the non-governmental organizations.

In the United States, this climate of thought and innovative legislators produced a law that represented a landmark in environmental management – the National Environment Policy Act (NEPA) of 1969. NEPA is considered a watershed in environmental legislation because of the manner in which it dealt with cross-sectoral issues, and because NEPA launched environmental impact assessment and environmental impact statements into worldwide use.

NEPA directs all federal agencies to use a systematic, interdisciplinary approach that will ensure the integrated use of the natural and social sciences and environmental design in planning and in decision making. Another salient feature of NEPA was its emphasis on providing the public with an opportunity to influence the implementation of a development project. The act also specified that the project's proponents must provide information on any adverse environmental effects of the proposed action, alternatives to the proposed action, and information on any irreversible effects. NEPA was enacted with the intention of producing changes in the diverse internal planning and decision-making processes of the federal agencies. NEPA is therefore frequently known as the Magna Carta of environmental law, not only in the USA but also worldwide.

If the latter half of the 1960s can be called the period of environmental awakening, then the 1970s was an era of response and action. Prior to 1970, many countries had enacted legislation to control specific problems such as air or water pollution or soil erosion. A feature of the 1970s and 1980s was the introduction of broad spectrum environmental legislation, an indicator of widening concern and of the need for action at the national and international level. The most influential responses were the United Nations Conferences on the Environment (1972), Population (1974), and Human Settlements (1976).

Appropriately, the United Nations Conference on the Environment, held in Stockholm in June 1972, dates back into the "environmental awakening" period. The objective of this conference was to provide a framework for the comprehensive consideration of the problems of the human environment. This framework was required to focus the attention of governments and public opinion on the importance and urgency of this question. The agreed agenda was to cover:
- planning and management of human settlements for environmental quality;
- environmental aspects of natural resources management;
- identification and control of pollutants and nuisances of broad international significance;
- educational, informational, social, and cultural aspects of environmental issues;
- development and environment;
- international organizational implications of action proposals.

As a result of the 1972 conference, the United Nations Environment Programme (UNEP) was set up, together with a fund to finance major projects. A 26-point declaration of environmental principles was adopted, calling for commitments by countries to deal with environmental problems of international significance.

1.2 Tracing the history of environmental impact assessment

In parallel with, and following, the Stockholm Conference, there was a surge of policy making and institution building in the developed world. In the 1970s, many governments introduced environmental legislation, established agencies with environmental responsibilities, or grafted these into existing departments. Others moved more cautiously, with "pilot" policies that could be elaborated after experience had been gained. In such a scenario, the environmental impact assessment (EIA), the discipline that could steer decision-making towards allowance for environmental factors, was introduced in some countries.

EIA was conceived as a policy and management tool for both planning and decision-making. It was expected to assist the identification, prediction, and evaluation of the foreseeable environmental consequences of proposed development projects, plans, and policies. Often regarded with suspicion as an unnecessary impediment to legitimate developmental objectives and progress, EIA took a decade to be acknowledged as a tool that could actually produce projects superior both in quality and value.

Two significant pieces of environmental legislation, one at the beginning of the period (1969) and one at the end (1990), both of a trail blazing character, are illustrated here. The National Environmental Policy Act (NEPA) of the United States was the first piece of legislation that dealt with cross-sectoral issues and it launched EIA into worldwide use. The second, the Resource Management Act of New Zealand, enacted in 1990, was the first legislative statement of the principle of sustainability.

Between these two pieces of legislation, several countries have either developed specific amendments to legislation on EIA or modified existing legislation by the introduction of rules and guidelines. Some of these are chronologically outlined in Table 1.1.

Two major observations may be made from Table 1.1. Firstly, more countries introduced EIA in the 1980s and 1990s than in the 1970s and 1980s. This indicates a widespread acceptance of EIA. Secondly, EIA has been introduced fairly early in some of the developing countries, such as Malaysia and the Philippines. A trend of moving EIA from project level to plans and policies may also be observed. These trends are discussed in more detail in Section 1.3 (below).

Governments were not the only institutions to take action. In 1971, the World Bank established an environmental section to analyse environmental reconnaissance of hydro projects because of the importance of environmental management. It was recognized that the environmental context of development proposals should be a base within which planning could proceed with proper reference to potential impacts.

The Asian Development Bank (ADB) set up an environmental unit in

Table 1.1 EIA legislation in various countries worldwide

Country	Year of introduction of EIA	Comments
Sweden	1969	EPA 1969: 387 (with later amendments) describes general EIA requirements
USA	1970	National Environmental Policy Act
Canada	1973	Environmental Assessments Review Process (EARP)
Australia	1974	Environmental Protection (Impact of Proposals) Act, 1974
Malaysia	1974	EIA required under Section 34 A, Environmental Quality Act, 1974
France	1976	National Environmental Assessment Legislation
Philippines	1978	As per Presidential Decree No. 1586
Japan	1984	Environmental Assessment implemented *vide* a cabinet resolution
UK	1985	Town and Country Planning (Assessment of Environmental Effects) Regulations 1988 (Sl. No. 1199)
Indonesia	1986	AMDAL (EIA) process established by law through Government Regulation No. 29 of 1986
Netherlands	1986	Environmental Protection (General Provisions) Act transformed into Environmental Management Act of 1993
New Zealand	1986	Environmental Act of 1986 and Resource Management Act of 1991
Sri Lanka	1988	National Environmental Act No. 47 of 1980 was amended to include *inter alia* provision to include EIA
CEC	1988	EU Directive on Environmental Assessment for 12 Member States
Norway	1989	Under the Planning Act of 1989
Germany	1990	National Environmental Assessment Legislation
Thailand	1992	Sections 46 & 47 under National Environmental Quality Act 1992
Nepal	1993	In the form of National EIA Guidelines issued by National Planning Commission Secretariat
India	1994	Before January 1994, obtaining Environmental Clearance from Central Ministry was only an administrative requirement intended for mega projects but from 1994 the EIA notification was issued

Note: In all the countries indicated in **bold letters** a law or notification has been specifically enacted for EIA whereas in the other countries only guidelines have been provided with no regulation specifically enacted for EIA.

Sources:

1. Towards Coherence in Environmental Assessment results of the Project on Coherence of Environmental Assessment for International Bilateral Aid Vol. III. Summary of Country Policies and Procedures submitted by Canada to the OECD/DAC working party on Development Assistance and Environment, 1994.

2. The Canadian Guide to Environmental Assessment by W. J. Couch, Federal Environmental Assessment Review Office, 1993.

Table 1.2 EIA guidelines in bilateral agencies

Agency	Year	Comments
USAID	1975	USAID asked to implement the intent of NEPA for assessing development aid projects. More general guidelines by Executive Order 12114 specifying EIA for specific projects
CIDA	1986	Document "Policy to Practice" produced, providing guidance on operationalizing EARP Guidelines Order of 1984 for EIA; Adoption of "Policy for Environmental Sustainability" in 1992 for integration of environmental considerations into CIDA's decision-making activities
NORAD	1988	Adopted a system for EA of development aid projects. No specific legislation
FINNIDA	1989	Document on "Guidelines for EIA in development assistance"
JICA	1993	The Basic Environmental Law recognizing "environmental considerations" (synonymous with EA) in areas of international cooperation. JICA and OECF guidelines used for EA of projects

1987, which in 1990 became the Office of Environment (OENV). This office was set up to provide a focus within the Bank for the review of the environmental aspects of projects and for the promotion of awareness and institution building in regard to environmental issues. This office is involved in the project cycle at the important stages of project preparation, appraisal, approval, implementation, and post-evaluation.

The ADB recognizes need for EIA or IEE (initial environmental examination), depending upon the type of project. Development projects have been categorized into three categories:

category A – projects with significant environmental impacts;

category B – those with adverse environmental impacts but of lesser degree and/or significance than A;

category C – projects unlikely to have any adverse environmental impact.

This categorization of projects is used as a basis to determine the type of assessment, IEE or EIA, that is required for a project.

A number of bilateral agencies also have prescribed guidelines for environmental assessments of projects for which they provide financial assistance. Table 1.2 lists the guidelines adopted by some of these agencies.

1.3 Changes in the perception of EIA

Tracing the environmental movement from its origin in the 1960s to the present day appears to be a fitting backdrop on which to weave the evo-

lution of the process of EIA. In essence, it appears that as the understanding of the environment and its multidimensional interdependent
nature matured, so did the size and scope of environmental legislation.
The philosophical birth of the environmental movement in the 1960s has
grown into the concrete laws and regulations of the 1990s, which today
has encompassed both the developed and developing world. The mean-
ing of the "commons" and *Our Common Future* (see below, Secton 1.3.3)
is becoming clearer, as is the understanding that the assessment of effects
of development activities needs to be conducted from the policy level
down to the project level. The effect of development on social issues as
well as on human health is being considered as a crucial area of study and
public participation, strongly emerging as a crucial force in influencing
decision-making. In this section, an attempt is made to highlight such a
gradual process of evolution in EIA.

1.3.1 EIA at the project level

In many countries in the world where EIA is in place, developmental
projects such as construction of highways and expressways, ports and
harbours, hydropower projects, manufacturing industries, mining projects, etc., undergo an environmental examination prior to being given
clearance to establish and operate. The EIA study then recommends appropriate mitigation measures or monitoring and management plans in
the project itself. Examples of such modifications include:
• change in the alignment of a highway;
• establishment of oil spill emergency operations for a port;
• reducing the height of a dam;
• providing for resettlement of affected people;
• recommendation for change in the fuel for a power-generating project;
• suggestion to use a cleaner manufacturing technology which over a
  long run can accrue more profits or returns;
• reduction in the chemical storage of a petrochemical plant on the reasons of safety;
• developing soil conservation and a compensatory green belt of specified width and height around a mining activity.

At the project level, based on some of these recommendations, the
project developers make further modifications in the project size, design,
technology, and operation if this is found to be necessary.

1.3.2 From project level to regional EIA

Another significant turn of events during the late 1970s was the emergence of a multidimensional character in project level EIA by the inclu-

sion of social dimensions to the process. Social impact analysis and risk analysis were incorporated into the process of EIA. This was presumably an outcome of the increased recognition and understanding of the interdependence of the various components of the environment.

It was also realized at this point that the effects of environmental contamination did not respect country boundaries anymore. Air pollution was affecting the forests and lakes of Europe and North America. The major cause of this was the burning of fossil fuels. In the twentieth century, global emissions of sulphur dioxide grew by an estimated 470 percent and emissions of carbon dioxide grew tenfold. Emissions of nitrogen oxides in the USA have increased nine times over the same period. Given suitable atmospheric conditions, sulphur dioxide and nitrogen oxides can be transported long distances and transformed into acids. Acid rain affects not only lakes and streams but also crops and vegetation.

It was then realized that the scope and level of EIA need to be expanded further when regional plans and developments are to be considered. An EIA can thus be performed at various levels depending on the scale of a development activity. In a large industrial estate, for example, while the individual industrial emissions may be within tolerance limits, the cumulative effects of the emissions can lead to a serious deterioration of the regional air quality. Similarly, the chemical storage placed in the vicinity, although physically in different industrial units, can raise the overall risk potential due to the possible "domino" effect.

Planning agencies developing satellite urban conurbations need to address environmental impacts on a regional or cumulative basis and must not be limited to individual projects. Here, the cumulative impacts of changes in land use due to activities such as housing, transportation, water supply, and waste disposal can lead to a significant regional impact and need to be managed by speculating the impacts on a region-wide scale.

Cumulative effects assessment (CEA) is a fairly recent extension of impact assessment which investigates the combined effects of multiple activities rather than the effects of specific developmental projects. Examples of development plans meriting such a cumulative or regional level EIA are:
- development of long coastal areas for exploiting aquaculture;
- development of a water resources basin;
- development of a regional transportation network;
- development of regional level hazardous waste management facilities, etc.;
- development of urban area improvement projects such as the Metropolitan Environment Improvement Project (MEIP), supported by the World Bank, or the Mega Cities project of the ADB.

An outcome of the understanding of the concept of regional impacts was the recognition and emergence of environmental health impact assessment (EHIA) as a necessary part of a study. This aspect was always considered in environmental assessment (EA) but its significance was usually diluted as it was mentioned in passing as part of the text of the EIA report.

1.3.3 Policy level strategic EIA

In 1987 the World Commission on Environment and Development published *Our Common Future*, the outcome of over three years of travel, hearings, and study. From an urgent call by the General Assembly of the United Nations, the Commission was set up in 1983 to find effective strategies, define long-term issues, propose new forms of international cooperation, and raise levels of understanding and commitment. Among the various problems discussed in the report was a problem long clear to the International Union for the Conservation of Nature – loss of species and threats to ecosystems which had become a major economic and environmental hazard. *Our Common Future* then discussed management of the "commons" (the ecosystems used by all people) – oceans, the atmosphere, outer space, and Antarctica.

In 1974, there was a prediction that chlorofluorocarbons (CFCs), used in refrigeration and as propellants for aerosols, could damage the stratospheric ozone layer. Eleven years later, in 1985, this was confirmed. The ozone shield over the Antarctic was thinning and a "hole" had developed. Unprecedented international action led, by 1987, to a world action plan. The main components of this plan were global monitoring to estimate the impact of changes in the ozone layer on radiation, skin cancer, ecosystem and regional climate, and collecting data on production and emissions. While the world action plan was developing, an international convention was being hammered out. The Montreal Protocol, providing a framework for action by each country, was agreed in 1987. Officials from most of the CFC producing/using countries agreed to a 50 percent reduction by 1999. But new scientific evidence indicated that the situation was more serious than it had been thought. The Helsinki Declaration of 1989 stated the intention of 80 countries to phase out CFCs completely by the year 2000.

Another major global concern of the 1980s and 1990s was the increasing concentration of carbon dioxide (CO_2) in the atmosphere and the potential for global warming. Data showed increasing concentrations, not only of CO_2 but also of nitrogen oxides (NO_x), methane (CH_4), and specific CFCs. Both global warming and ozone depletion could contribute to serious environmental degradations.

The global scale of the ozone and climate change problems was a confirmation that environmental deterioration was accelerating, in spite of the international initiatives set in motion, initially by the Stockholm conference of 1972, and then by subsequent international forums.

Clearly, the impetus to the generation of projects and large-scale development plans has always been the policies. By the late 1980s and early 1990s, experience of EIA over projects and regional plans led to the recognition that EIA of policies should be conducted on a strategic level.

A strategic environmental assessment (SEA) makes an inquiry into the likely environmental changes (both positive and negative) resulting from the development produced by existing, new, or revised developmental policies, plans, and programmes. SEA can be applied both at the level of broad policy initiatives, and to more concrete programmes and plans that have physical and spatial reference.

If the policies at a generic level are evolved on an environmentally sound basis, then the associated regional plans and projects are expected to cause least conflict between the regional and local environmental priorities and issues. Examples of SEA are:
- policy of industrializing coastal belts;
- policy of depending on hydropower rather than on thermal power on a national basis;
- policy of reducing the tax structure on the import of clean or environmentally friendly manufacturing technologies;
- policy of allowing the use and manufacture of only selected biodegradable fertilizers;
- phasing out of ozone depleting substances (ODS) from the aerosol industry.

These examples show that the issues discussed in a SEA embrace national as well as international boundaries and can yet, in some cases, overlap EIA of plans on a regional level. At a policy level, therefore, the EIA study can become quite complex, i.e., difficult in scope, and may need a consideration of the sociopolitical as well as macroeconomic factors. Whilst there is much current debate on the subject, there is limited practical experience, particularly at the policy level. Current SEA processes vary considerably. They may be formal or informal, comprehensive or more limited in scope, and closely linked with or unrelated to either policy or planning instruments.

The changing perception of EIA since the introduction of NEPA in the USA in 1969 thus moves from project level to strategic level with an expansion into areas such as the social impact assessment, environmental health assessment, risk assessments, etc. This process of evolution is summarized in Box 1.1.

Box 1.1 The evolution of environmental assessment

Date and phase	Trends and innovations
Prior to 1970, Pre EA	Project review based on engineering and economic study, e.g., cost-benefit analysis; limited consideration of environmental consequences
1970–1975 Methodological development	EA introduced in some developed countries; initially focused on identifying, predicting, and mitigating biophysical effects; opportunity for public involvement in major reviews
1975–1980 Social dimensions included	Multidimensional EA, incorporating SIA and risk analysis; public consultation as integral part of development planning and assessments; increased emphasis on issues of justification and alternatives in project review
1980–1985 Process and procedural redirection	Efforts to integrate project EA with policy planning and follow-up phases; research and development focusing on effects of monitoring, on EA audit and process evaluation, and on mediation and dispute resolution approaches; adoption of EA by international aid and lending agencies and by some developing countries
1985–1990 Sustainability paradigm	Scientific and institutional framework for EA begin to be rethought in response to sustainability ideas and imperatives; search begins for ways to address regional and global environmental changes and cumulative impacts; growing international cooperation on EA research and training
1990–present	Strategic environmental assessment (SEA) of policies, programmes, and plans introduced in some developed countries; international convention on transboundary EA; UNCED places new demands on EA for expanded concepts, methods, and procedures to promote sustainability (e.g., through sustainable development strategies)

Source: A Directory of Impact Assessment Guidelines, after B. Sadler, *Proposed Framework for the International Study of the Effectiveness of EA*, 1994.

FURTHER READING

1 Environmental Impact Assessments, USEPA, EPA/600/m-91/037, March 1992.
2 Environmental Impact Assessments in Development Co-operation, Directorate-General for International Co-operation, Dutch Ministry of Foreign Affairs, February 1993.
3 Directory of Impact Assessments Guidelines, after B. Sadler, *Proposed Framework for the International Study of the Effectiveness of EA*, 1994.

2

Introduction to EIA

2.1 What is EIA?

Environmental impact assessment (EIA) is a policy and management tool for both planning and decision-making. EIA assists to identify, predict, and evaluate the foreseeable environmental consequences of proposed development projects, plans, and policies. The outcome of an EIA study assists the decision maker and the general public to determine whether a project should be implemented and in what form. EIA does not make decisions, but it is essential for those who do.

Environmental assessment (EA) refers to an understanding of the present status of environmental impacts and a study of how to manage them. An environmental impact statement (EIS) is the final step of an EIA/EA exercise where the conclusions of the assessment are put out in a communicable form to the concerned developer or authority. There is thus a distinction between the terms EIA, EA, and EIS.

A frequent opinion is that an EIA should usually only examine or look into the possible negative consequences of a project on the environment. Any positive issues emerging from the development are taken as stated by the project proponent or the developer. However, EIA is not restricted or biased to the examination and mitigation of negative impacts alone. EIA can also look into the possible positive issues due to the developmental projects and explore or suggest ways of enhancing them further by carrying out modifications in the project.

Box 2.1 Definition of EIA for developing countries

1 The EIA may be defined as a planning tool which is used, together with the project feasibility study (FS), to ensure that the project plan is the optimal economic-cum-environmental plan, that is, that the plan is environmentally as well as economically sound and thus represents the best approach to planning for development projects in order that continuing economic development will be sustainable. The essential message of the famed U.N. Brundtland Report of 1987 is that the only sustainable development is economic-cum-environmental development.

2 The EIA is not intended to disrupt nor to impede economic development. A protect plan which is economic-cum-environmental will have a higher benefit/cost ratio than a plan which is not responsive to environmental needs, especially when long-term as well as short-term effects are considered.

3 The role of the EIA is not just to identify and describe environmental hazards which a proposed project will likely cause if no EPM (environmental protection measures) are included in the project. Rather the EIA should specify the necessary EPM and ensure that these EPM are included in the overall project plan as delineated by the feasibility study.

4 Environmental protection measures mean more than "mitigation". EPM include (i) mitigation measures to reduce adverse effects, (ii) measures for offsetting unavoidable adverse effects, and even (iii) measures for environmental enhancement.

Source: Guidelines for Impact Assessment in Development Assistance, Finnish International Development Agency, FINNIDA, Draft, 1989.

EIA is thus a multifaceted decision-making process. The process is structured to anticipate, analyse, and disclose the consequences associated with proposed activities with respect to established public policies for protecting and enhancing the natural and anthropogenic environment. The definition of EIA and its elaboration by FINNIDA (Finnish International Development Agency) specifically for developing countries is shown in Box 2.1.

EIA is essentially an early warning process. The aim of EIA is to balance the environmental interest in the larger scheme of development issues and concerns. The primary objective of EIA is to ensure that potential problems are foreseen and addressed at an early stage in the project's planning and design. To achieve this objective, the assessment should provide information on the environmental, social, and economic benefits of proposed activities, which should then be presented clearly and systematically to decision makers. Having read the conclusions of an EIA, the project planners and engineers can then shape the project so that its expected benefits can be achieved and sustained without causing inadvertent environmental impacts. An EIA process, for instance, can greatly influence where and how a project is sited, the size of the facilities to be built, the technologies employed, and the area served or affected by the project.

Specifically, an EIA:

- identifies the sources of impacts from the project activities and recognizes the environmental components which are critical to the change or the impacts;
- predicts the likely environmental impacts of projects on the identified environmental components either using quantitative, qualitative, semi-quantitative, or hybrid methods;
- finds ways to reduce unacceptable impacts and enhance the positive contributions of the project by recommending mitigation measures or by exploring a change in the capacity, technology, or design or even by evaluating alternative sites;
- presents to decision makers and other concerned agencies the results of impact identification, prediction, and assessment with options of suggested measures of mitigation and monitoring.

One of the purposes of EIA is to ensure that both public and private enterprises consider the environmental effects of the decisions they make with regard to implementation of the project or programme. The process of EIA is well defined and practiced today in a number of developing countries also with appropriate customization. In Chapter 3, the EIA process is introduced in detail.

2.2 Who is involved in the EIA process?

EIA is generally the responsibility of the project proponent and is often prepared with the help of external consultants or institutions, i.e., the EIA practitioners. In some cases, an independent commission is responsible for ensuring quality control throughout the implementation of the impact assessment, for setting appropriate terms of reference, and/or for the external review. The EIA study should be carried out by a multi-disciplinary team comprising civil engineers, water supply and sanitation engineers, planners, chemists, life scientists, and socio-economists.

The agency responsible for receiving the impact assessment report and taking any subsequent action, i.e., the implementing agency, will usually indicate how the study is to be carried out and how the results should be used in the decision-making process. The institutional structures and agencies responsible for the management and implementation of EIA vary amongst countries, reflecting different political, economic, and social priorities. Mostly, they include local government agencies, NGOs, research institutions, and affected groups feeding into a specialist environmental unit within the implementing agency.

Apart from all these agencies, the general public is also involved in the

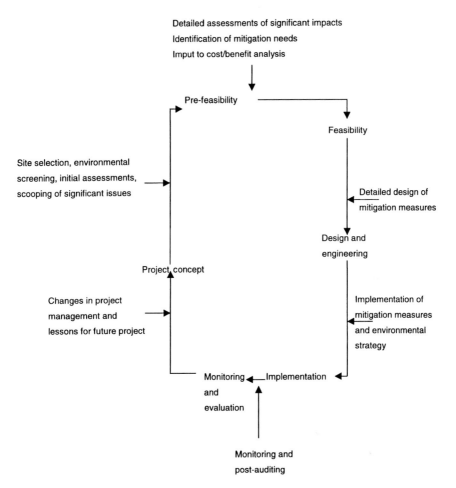

Figure 2.1 EIA and the project cycle

process of EIA. Ideally public opinion should be solicited through public hearings arranged for the purpose of discussing the impacts of the project. Public participation as a component of EIA is practiced as a requirement in only a few countries, such as Canada. However, this trend is increasingly evident in EIA practice in a number of other countries.

2.3 When should the EIA be undertaken?

The EIA needs to be managed so that it provides information to decision makers at every stage of the project planning cycle. Figure 2.1 shows the various options for conducting EIA vis-à-vis the project.

Sequential

Note: There are two teams working sequentially on engineering/economic planning first, followed by studies on environmental aspects

Concurrent

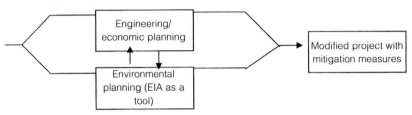

Note: There are two teams working concurrently on engineering/economic planning and environmental aspects with continuous interaction

Integrated

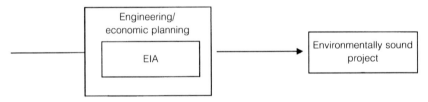

Note: There are two teams working on both engineering/economic planning simultaneously considering environmental issues

Figure 2.2 Integrating EIA into the planning process

EIA can be done sequentially, i.e., it may be conducted after the engineering/economic planning stage in the project cycle. The resultant EIA report would provide the required mitigation measures in order to implement the project in an environmentally sound manner. The second option is to conduct environmental planning (which includes the EIA study) and engineering/economic planning concurrently to emerge with a suitable project alternative together with requisite mitigation measures for project implementation. The goal, however, is to integrate the environmental aspects in the project cycle, as shown in Figure 2.2, considering EIA as a management tool on a par with engineering studies and economic planning. Such an integration of EIA into the project cycle would probably maximize its effectiveness and minimize delays in project implementation.

The major benefit of using EIA in project planning is to prevent avoidable losses of environmental resources. A feature often overlooked by various developers is that a well-prepared EIA incorporated into the planning and design of a project can save the developer and regulatory agency valuable time and expense. If the EIA is performed early enough to be considered during the decision-making phase, delays in construction and operation owing to government regulatory procedures can be minimized. Improper planning or design that will lead to unacceptable levels of environmental deterioration may require costly rectification, remediation, or replacement.

EIA should therefore be initiated as early as possible and should also include a provision to cover the monitoring of project implementation and operation and eventually an audit of the project. In some cases, e.g., nuclear power projects, it will also be important to include project decommissioning within the scope of EIA.

2.4 Effectiveness of EIA

Mere promulgation of laws and regulations is not sufficient to ensure that the benefits of EIA are maximized. To ensure an effective EIA some conditions should be fulfilled and some of these are summarized below.

2.4.1 Legal regulations

EIA must be promulgated by law in an unambiguous regulation, leaving no misunderstanding about the interpretation of the obligation to carry out EIA.

2.4.2 Rational and open decision-making

EIA performs best in a model of rational decision-making, in which one designated authority (i.e., the competent authority) makes a crucial decision based on factual information and rational arguments. Experience shows that it is crucial to start an EIA procedure in an open way; there should be enough room to consider alternatives and to absorb new information.

Usually, the main reason for an ineffective EIA is lack of an open approach. When the decisions are already made, EIA is used as a defence-in-retrospect and is guided to this result. Possible new information is "argued away" and can at best be used in a future decision-making process.

2.4.3 Project EIA sustained by strategic EIA

Sometimes, the room for decisions is restricted by earlier decisions at national level. In that case, EIA should be applied to these strategic decisions as well. An example could be that of the policy of industrial development in rural areas. This overall policy needs to be subjected to EIA rather than examining each industrial project separately. The policy EIA may bring forth land use as well as standard mitigation guidelines which may lead to the promotion of environmentally sound individual industrial projects.

2.4.4 Room for public participation

Public participation proves to be important in EIA in several ways. EIA provides objective information about an activity to the people involved. Local residents or NGOs often possess information that can be useful for EIA. In some cases public participation leads to the formulation of new alternatives.

2.4.5 Independent review and central information

Appointment of an independent body to prepare draft guidelines for the preparation of EIA reports and to review these reports after publication, etc., may further strengthen the process. If this body is independent from the government agency then it could provide impartial judgement on the desirability of an activity. This body need not have formal legal power: its role could be advisory in nature. Moreover, this body could function as a central EIA information desk, with a complete EIA library. This could improve the overall performance of EIA.

2.4.6 Scoping in EIA

Good scoping produces an effective EIA process. Scoping is the process which helps in understanding the extent of environmental impacts and identifies significant environmental issues for further analysis. Scoping will be discussed at greater length in Chapter 3.

2.4.7 Quality of the EIA

Sound decision-making should be based on good EIA, containing at least:
- information on the environmental impact of the proposed activity and its alternatives, including an environmentally friendly alternative;
- comparison of all (relevant) alternatives;
- comparison of impacts with environmental objectives and standards and (implicit) evaluation of the latter;
- survey of gaps of knowledge.

A good presentation of the EIA report is important, as it enables a proper use by all participants.

At the heart of the EIA is the development and comparison of alternatives in regard to the environmental impacts. Constructing a (realistic) environmentally most friendly alternative is the most interesting and most creative part of EIA, containing possibilities for breaking new ground. As long as the influence of environmental measures does not suffice to counteract the increasing deterioration in quality of the environment, conducting an EIA is justified.

2.5 EIA and other environmental management tools

EIA was one of the first specific management tools developed for the analysis and management of environment effects. However, a number of other tools which constitute the "tool-kit" of processes/techniques for environmental management include:
- environmental audits (audit);
- life cycle analysis (LCA);
- economic assessment, usually through cost-benefit analysis (CBA);
- environmental design (ED).

Rather than being comprehensive, self-contained procedures, these tools are really aids which can be adapted to various situations. Legislative and bureaucratic frameworks for environmental management differ considerably between various countries. The use of these tools therefore varies from country to country. The methods listed above contribute to decision-making procedures. In practice they must be used in a flexible way, rather than as "cookbook" solutions.

The tools shown in Table 2.1 may be used at various stages of the project, as indicated. LCA encompasses the "cradle to grave" analysis of the products and services and has an in-built impact assessment step to

Table 2.1 Illustration of how each tool might be used in an industrial project

Stage	EIA	CBA	Audit	LCA
Initial investigation	▓	▓		
Planning	▓	▓		
Concept development	▓	▓		
Comparison of options	▓	▓		
Selection of an alternative	▓	▓		
Construction	▓	▓		
Plant installation	▓	▓	▓	
Commissioning	▓	▓		
Production	▓	▓		▓
Monitoring	▓	▓	▓	
Decommissioning	▓	▓		

assess the impacts at the resource level. EIA and CBA may be integrated into the project cycle while audit may be conducted during project construction/plant installation and post-project monitoring.

3

EIA process

3.1 Introduction

The structure of an EIA process as it is practiced today has evolved from and is dictated primarily by the need to accommodate all the key issues discussed in the preceding chapters. Prior to describing the process of EIA, however, it is necessary to understand the basic principles in the management of EIA that ensure its effectiveness.

3.2 Principles in managing EIA

Important principles in managing an EIA may be summarized as:
1 focus on the main issues;
2 involve the appropriate persons and groups;
3 link information to decisions about the project;
4 present clear options for the mitigation of impacts and for sound environmental management;
5 provide information in a form useful to the decision makers.

3.2.1 Principle 1: Focus on the main issues

It is important that an EIA should not try to cover too many topics in too much detail. At the outset, the scope of the EIA should be focused on only the most likely and most serious of the possible environmental impacts. Large verbose, complex reports are unnecessary, and can be counter-productive, as the findings from the EIA may not be in a form readily accessible and immediately useful to decision makers and project planners. When mitigation measures are being suggested, the focus of the study should be only on workable, acceptable solutions to the problems. Finally, the conclusions of the EIA should be communicated in a concise form, preferably including a summary of information relevant to the needs of decision makers. Supporting data should be provided separately.

This activity of focusing on the significant issues typically constitutes the scoping exercise of the EIA process.

3.2.2 Principle 2: Involve the appropriate persons and groups

Another equally important point to be considered is selectivity when involving people in the EIA process. Generally, three categories of participants are needed to carry out an EIA:
- those appointed to manage and undertake the EIA process (usually a coordinator and a staff of experts);
- those who can contribute with facts, ideas, or concerns to the study, including scientists, economists, engineers, policy makers, and representatives of interested or affected groups;
- those who have direct authority to permit, control, or alter the projects, that is, the decision makers – including, for example, the developer, aid agency or investors, competent authorities, regulators, and politicians.

The key issue of this principle is ensuring public participation in the process of EIA whereby involvement of all the stakeholders in the project is ensured.

3.2.3 Principle 3: Link information to decisions about the project

An EIA should be organized so that it directly supports the decisions that need to be taken about the proposed project. It should start early enough to provide information to improve basic designs and should progress through the several stages of project planning. As stated in Chapter 2, EIA should be handled concurrently and in an integrated way, as shown in the project cycle (see Fig. 2.2).

In a typical sequence:
- when the developer and investors first broach the project concept, they consider likely environmental issues;
- when the developer is looking for sites or routes, environmental considerations are used to aid the selection process;

- when the developer and investors are assessing the project's feasibility, EIA should be initiated to help in anticipating any concerns or problems;
- when engineers are designing the project, the EIA identifies certain standards for the design to meet;
- when a permit is requested, a complete EIA report is submitted, and published for general comment;
- when the developer implements the project, monitoring or other measures provided for in the EIA are undertaken.

The central idea of this principle is that it is essential to integrate the process of EIA into the project cycle by incorporating it right from the project-planning stage.

3.2.4 Principle 4: Present clear options for the mitigation of impacts and for sound environmental management

To help decision makers, the EIA must be designed so as to present clear choices on the planning and implementation of the project, and it should make clear the likely results of each option. For instance, to mitigate adverse impacts, the EIA could propose:
- pollution control technology or design features;
- the reduction, treatment, and/or disposal of wastes;
- compensation or concessions to affected groups.

To enhance environmental compatibility, the EIA could suggest:
- several alternative sites;
- changes to the project's design and operation (e.g., clean technology);
- limitations to its initial size or growth;
- separate programmes which contribute in a positive way to local resources or to the quality of the environment.

To ensure that the implementation of an approved project is environmentally sound, the EIA may prescribe:
- monitoring programmes or periodic impact reviews;
- contingency plans for regulatory action;
- involvement of the local community in later decisions.

This principle thus focuses on the evolution of the environmental management plan as well as a post-project monitoring plan.

3.2.5 Principle 5: Provide information in a form useful to the decision makers

The objective of an EIA is to ensure that environmental problems are foreseen and addressed by decision makers. To achieve this objective, information should be presented to decision makers in terms and formats that are immediately meaningful.

- Briefly present hard facts and predictions about impacts, comments on the reliability of this information, and summarize the consequences of each of the proposed options.
- Write in the terminology and vocabulary that is used by the decision makers and the community affected by the project.
- Present the essential findings in a concise document, supported by separate background materials were necessary.
- Make the document easy to use and provide information visually whenever possible.

3.3 Framework of environmental impacts

EIA is based on understanding how the natural world functions, and how social, technological, and economic forces interact with the environment and resources issues. An understanding of the natural process allows the prediction of the consequences of development, which is the essence of EIA.

Any simplification of the EIA system, such as neglect of an important component, could lead to inaccurate assessment prediction and inaccurate identification of mitigation measures. For example, in assessing a proposal to clear a wetland, it could be noted that a mangrove forest may protect a shore area against storm surges, thus assuring an ideal habitat for fish spawning. Partial or incomplete assessment should be avoided. For example, an oil-fired thermal generating plant would require oil transport and storage. Sewage treatment also means sewage sludge disposal, in addition to the disposal of treated wastewaters.

Impacts may be considered as interactions between the project and the environment. Impacts are essentially changes to the environment. In other words,

$$[\text{Project}] + [\text{Environment}] \rightarrow \{\text{Changed Environment}\}$$

Predicting the likely environmental changes, given the project setting and the site description, is the task of EIA. One of the approaches to understand project–environment interactions is to follow the principle of decomposition. The idea here is to decompose the project into activities and the environment into components. Generally, the environmental components may consist of a large number of terms which may enable the description of any site to a reasonable extent.

Project activities, on the other hand, may be rather specific to the project type. (More discussion on the setting up of the activity–component framework is described in Chapter 4.)

As the project consists of a number of activities and the environment consists of several components, we may make following representations. Since:

$$[\text{Project}] = (\text{Activity})_1, (\text{Activity})_2, \ldots (\text{Activity})_n$$

and

$$[\text{Environment}] = (\text{Component})_1, (\text{Component})_2, \ldots (\text{Component})_n$$

the impact relationship becomes,

$$(\text{Activity})_i (\text{Component})_j \rightarrow (\text{Impact})_{ji}$$

where $(\text{Impact})_{ji}$ denotes the impact on the jth component due to the ith activity. $(\text{Impact})_{ij}$ is essentially an *issue* requiring a further inquiry or examination.

To illustrate this concept, let us consider project–environment interactions for a thermal power plant proposed near a coastal area. In this case, the activity component description may take a form such as:

[Thermal Power Project] =
   (site acquisition), (site clearance), (construction of plant including utilities), (movement of equipment and construction materials), (erection and commissioning trials), (power generation), (fuel transport), (fuel rejection), (waste heat release), (waste emission release), (solid waste release), (employment), (power distribution), (power tripping and plant shutdown and start up).

[Coastal Environment] =
   (coastal water quality), (marine life, e.g., fisheries), (coastal recreational use), (mangroves), (terrestrial vegetation), (coastal air quality), (land use and landform), (employment), (per capita income), (societal risk).

The typical impact interaction elements of the activities and components listed above are essentially $(\text{Impact})_{ji}$ elements. An activity such as waste emission release may be *associated* with the environmental component of coastal air quality to *speculate* an impact. Another example could be that of the activity of waste heat release, which may be associated with an impact on the environmental components of coastal water quality. Marine life or fisheries may be affected by the discharge of the waste streams and thus the income of fishermen who depend on the fisheries may change. On the positive side, power generation may be considered as an activity leading to employment benefits and an increase in the per capita income.

In the case of a positive impact issue, efforts need to be made to further enhance the benefits or at least ensure that the benefits are realized by evolving management systems. However, in the event of an undesirable impact issue, it becomes necessary to assess the significance of the issue and look for suitable mitigation measures or even alternative project plans, technologies, and locations.

A wide range of measures are proposed to prevent, reduce, remedy, or compensate for each of the adverse impacts evaluated as significant. Possible mitigation measures include:

- changing project sites, routes, processes, raw materials, operating methods, waste disposal routes or locations, or engineering designs;
- introducing pollution controls, monitoring, phased implementation, landscaping, personnel training, introducing social services, or public education;
- offering (as compensation) restoration of damaged resources, money to affected persons, concessions on other issues, or fit site programmes to enhance some other aspects of the environment or quality of life for the community.

All mitigation measures cost something, and this cost must be quantified too. Because of the imposition of the mitigation measures, the "impact equation" becomes:

$$(\text{Activity})_i (\text{Component})_j \rightarrow (\text{Impact})_{ji} \rightarrow (\text{Prediction and Assessment})$$

$$\rightarrow \text{Mitigation Measures} \rightarrow (\text{Residual Impact})_{ji}$$

Assessment evaluates the predicted adverse impacts to determine whether they are significant enough to warrant mitigation. Prescription of the mitigation measures in many cases leads to either add-on systems or in some cases a major reformulation of the project. The cost of the project also escalates.

There are the following possibilities in such an analysis:

- impacts are impossible to assess considering state of the art (alternatives need to be assessed at the project and location level);
- impacts are difficult to assess as more information and/or skills are needed (specific and detailed studies around the identified issue need to be carried out);
- impacts can be assessed but the available mitigation measures do not

lead to total alleviation of impact, so the residual impacts are still at a non-acceptable level (either more studies are needed to understand the impact and its mitigation or additional mitigation measures need to be sought or both);
- impacts can be assessed and fully mitigated (adequate specification and translation of the mitigation and monitoring systems needs to be evolved).

Thus, an activity–component framework helps to prepare a sound impact framework for further analysis. To achieve effectiveness in the practice of EIA the impact framework, described above, has been translated into a formal and structured process of "tiers".

3.4 EIA process in tiers

EIA is generally conduced in tiers. In most countries, EIA processes fall into four tiers, explained in Figure 3.1.
- **Screening**: decides whether the EIA process is applicable at all to the development project. Screening should basically "clear" all those projects where there are no major negative impact issues.
- **Scoping**: helps in understanding the extent of environmental impacts and identifies significant environmental issues for further study. In the activity–component framework, this would mean that scoping should assist in the identification of impacting activities and impacted environmental components for all major negative impact issues.
- **Initial environmental examination**: assesses the severity of the significant issues and finds ways to mitigate or enhance environmental impacts by considering the available information from past experience or the standard operating practices (SOPs; standard mitigation measures).
- **Detailed or comprehensive EIA**: carries out a detailed examination of impacts by conducting relevant surveys. Studies are monitored by applying more rigorous impact evaluation/prediction tools where necessary and ensuring the effectiveness of the mitigation and enhancement measures. Detailed EIA thus focuses on impacts which are critical but not fully understood.

In a tiered EIA process, such as that above, the relevant regulatory agency decides whether there is nothing to be concerned about, or that the evaluation should proceed to the next tier.

Conducting EIA in tiers helps optimize the resources as well as to increase the effectiveness of the exercise by maintaining a better focus. Another advantage of a tiered approach is that the extent of the inquiry or examination expands with the advancing development of the project

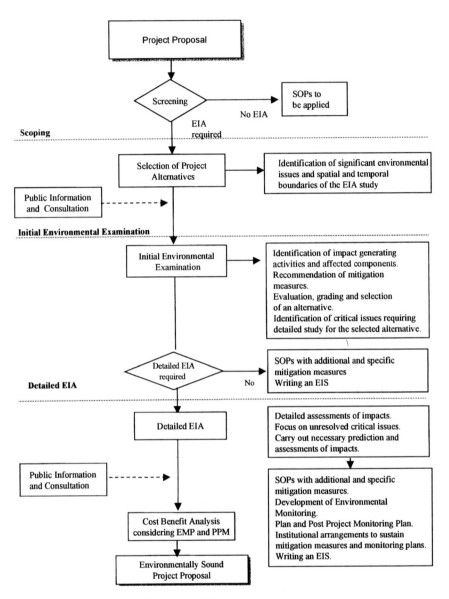

Figure 3.1 EIA process in tiers

plans. Such a tiered process is most suited for developing countries which are in the rapid phase of development.

In the above EIA process, screening should be done when the project is only a rough concept. Later, when the project is under more general discussion, a preliminary assessment, called the initial environmental examination (IEE), can look deeper into alternative sites and project variations. Finally, just before the preliminary stages of feasibility and design work get underway, a detailed EIA study, also called comprehensive EIA, can commence, so that it can influence the detailed decisions yet to come.

Such a concurrent approach ensures that impacts are examined at a very early stage in the project planning, and not later when sites or designs are already decided by other factors. The EIA process thus gets truly integrated with the development process if EIA is conducted in tiers as described above. However, one significant point that needs to be understood is that in concept and reality, EIA is an iterative process. The relationships between the various elements is shown in Figure 3.2.

The tiered system can have variants in different countries. In some countries, only two tiers, such as screening and detailed EIA, are used in the EIA process. There are also instances where no screening is performed but instead the EIA process starts with a preliminary assessment, followed by a detailed assessment if required.

As illustrations of typical tiered processes, examples of EIA procedures and systems in Indonesia, Malaysia, and Canada are presented at the end of this chapter (Section 3.6).

3.4.1 Screening

Screening is the decision whether or not to perform an EIA. In some cases, screening would help to decide which tier of the EIA process should be used, that is, IEE or a detailed EIA. In this example, the process of screening extends to scoping.

Screening criteria generally involve the specification of the *location*, *type*, and *size* of the project. In the case of some countries such as India, the size of the project is defined in terms of the economic investment undertaken. Some countries establish a list of types and sizes of projects that must always have an EIA. Others apply guidelines on a case-by-case basis.

Over a period of time, the following development activities justifying an environmental assessment have emerged from both approaches:
- large industrial and manufacturing plants;
- large construction projects – deep draught ports, highways, airports;
- water resources structures – dams, irrigation systems;
- electric power plants;
- mining and minerals processing;
- hazardous chemicals manufacture, handling, storage;
- sewerage and sewage treatment plants;
- municipal wastes and hazardous wastes;
- new human settlements;

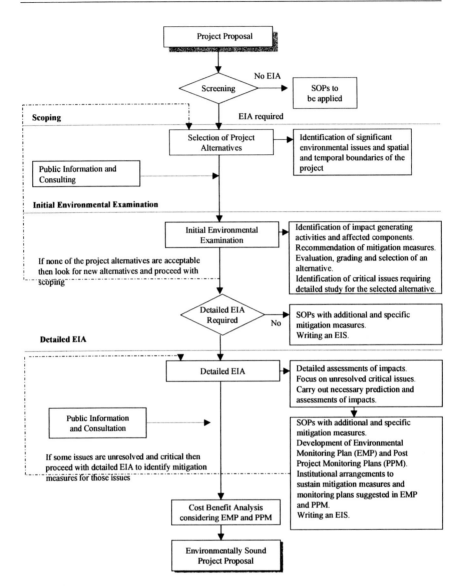

Figure 3.2 Iterative nature of the EIA process

- large-scale intensified forestry, fisheries, or agriculture;
- tourism facilities;
- military facilities;
- large-scale changes in land use.

However, the importance of an environmental consequence may be out of proportion to the size of a project. For example, a rural road can make pristine forest land accessible, or a small tannery or metal plating shop can release hazardous amounts of toxic chemicals.

It is not a good idea to place a quantitative limit of some measure of project size below which no EIA is ever required. This might provide an unreviewable exemption that could be taken advantage of by unscrupulous developers. For example, in one country, hotels with less than 80 rooms did not require an EIA; as a result, 79-room units were constructed in large numbers and substantial environmental impacts occurred.

In the final analysis, common sense and discretion must be exercised in deciding whether a proposal triggers the need for an EIA. Some small projects may have more adverse effects than some larger projects and the "threshold" value judgement must always be applied on a case-by-case basis.

3.4.1.1 Illustrations of screening

Screening thresholds are generally set considering the project type, size, and location. The project type and size are used to estimate the extent of the impacts while the thresholds of the project size depend on the project type. Information on the project location is used to assess the sensitivity or fragility of the neighbourhood environment. In practice, a combination of project type, size, and location is used. Some examples of different screening models are illustrated below. Clearly, there is no screening criteria which could be considered as the "best". The criteria depend on the context and are to be examined or updated each time new information comes in or the understanding of the impacts improves.

(i) Project type and location
In the Philippines, projects are screened based on the type of project, whether it is a heavy industry, infrastructure project or whether it is based on resource extraction (Box 3.1 below). The other criterion considered is the location of the project in sensitive areas, regardless of the type. The two aspects are therefore mutually exclusive.

(ii) Project type and size
The screening process in Indonesia is governed by the type and size of the project. The Decree of the Minister of State for the Environment No. KEP-11/MENLH/3/94, as of 19 March 1994, specifies the following activities which require an EIA before project approval. (As per the Decree of the Minister of State for the Environment Number: KEP-14/MENLH/3/1994.) (See Box 3.2, page 33.)

(iii) Screening by categorization across tiers
In the above two cases, examples of screening systems were given wherein the criteria of type, size, and location are used at the national

Box 3.1 Screening criteria adopted in the Philippines

Prescribed activities requiring an EIS in the Philippines

The EIS system in the Philippines was established by PD 1586 in June 1978. PD 1586 defines the scope of the EIS system and broadly defines environmentally critical projects (ECP) and environmentally critical areas (ECA) that are included in the EIS system. PD 2146 specifically defines ECPs and ECAs and lists the types of projects and areas covered by the EIA system.

   Lists of ECPs and ECAs are shown below.

Environmentally critical projects

Projects defined as environmentally critical and requiring an EIA based on type, regardless of location.
- Heavy industries: non-ferrous metal industries, iron and steel mills, petroleum and petrochemical industries, smelting plants.
- Resource extractive industries: major mining and quarrying projects, forestry projects, fishery projects.
- Infrastructure projects: major dams, major power plants, major reclamation projects, major roads and bridges.

Environmentally critical areas

Projects that require a project description but may require an EIA are those located in environmentally critical areas, regardless of type. (The concept of "project description" in the Philippines is similar to an IEE.)
   Environmentally critical areas are:
- national parks, watershed reserves, wildlife reserves, and sanctuaries;
- potential tourist spots;
- habitat for any endangered or threatened species of indigenous Philippine wildlife (flora and fauna);
- areas of unique historical, archaeological, or scientific interest;
- areas traditionally occupied by cultural communities or tribes;
- areas frequently visited and/or hard-hit by natural calamities;
- areas with critical slopes;
- prime agricultural lands;
- recharge areas of aquifers;
- water bodies.

level. Financial institutions also have specific guidelines for screening projects to ascertain whether an EIA is required or not. The system adopted by the ADB is shown in Box 3.3 (page 37) as an illustration.

   The categorization by the ADB of each proposed programme or project is made according to its type, location, sensitivity, scale, the nature and magnitude of its potential impact, and the availability of cost-effective mitigation measures. The screening method is thus linked to the other tiers of the process of EIA. The screening process in the ADB not only tells "whether an EIA is required: but also what level of EIA is required."

Box 3.2 Screening threshold for EIA in Indonesia

No	Type of activity	Size
I	Mining and energy sector 1 Mining area during exploitation phase, for production of: • coal • primary ores • secondary ores • non-metallic minerals, sand and gravel (Golongan C), radioactive materials, including mining, processing, and purification 2 Transmission lines 3 Electricity generating stations: diesel, gas, steam, and combined cycle 4 Hydroelectric generating stations of all types and sizes, except mini-hydro and direct current types 5 Geothermal electricity generating stations 6 Other types of electricity generating stations 7 Oil and gas exploitation 8 Oil and gas processing (refinery) 9 Oil and gas pipelines	$\geqslant 200$ ha and/or $\geqslant 200{,}000$ ton per year $\geqslant 60{,}000$ ton per year $\geqslant 100{,}000$ ton per year $\geqslant 300{,}000$ m^3 per year $\geqslant 150$ kV $\geqslant 100$ MW $\geqslant 55$ MW $\geqslant 5$ MW $\geqslant 25$ km
II	Health sector 1 Class A hospitals producing basic drug materials 2 Other hospitals which are equivalent to Class A or Class I 3 Other hospitals 4 Hospitals with full/comprehensive specialist services 5 Pharmaceutical industry facilities producing basic drug materials	 $\geqslant 400$ beds
III	Public works sector 1 Construction of dams and embankments 2 Irrigation area development 3 Tidal swamp area development 4 Coastal protection in large cities 5 River improvement works in large cities 6 Canalization/flood control facilities in large cities 7 Canalization other than item 6 above (coastal areas, swamps, etc.) 8 Construction of toll roads and fly-overs	height $\geqslant 15$ m or impounded area $\geqslant 100$ ha irrigated area $\geqslant 2000$ ha area $\geqslant 5000$ ha population $\geqslant 500{,}000$ population $\geqslant 500{,}000$ population $\geqslant 500{,}000$ length $\geqslant 5$ km or width $\geqslant 20$ m length $\geqslant 25$ km or width $\geqslant 50$ m

Box 3.2 (cont.)

No	Type of activity	Size
	9 Highway construction	length ⩾25 km
	10 Arterial and collector road construction and upgrading outside of large cities and metropolitan areas	length ⩾5 km or area ⩾5 ha
	11 Garbage disposal using incineration	⩾800 ton/ha
	12 Garbage disposal using controlled landfill or sanitary landfill systems	⩾800 ton/ha
	13 Garbage disposal using open dumping systems	⩾80 ton/ha
	14 Drainage systems using canals in large cities and metropolitan areas, primary canal length	⩾5 km
	15 Wastewater treatment:	
	Construction of wastewater treatment facilities in urban areas	area ⩾50 ha
	Construction of sewerage systems	service area ⩾2500 ha
	16 Public housing and settlement construction	area ⩾200 ha
	17 Urban renewal projects	area ⩾5 ha
	18 Construction of multi-storied and apartment buildings	height ⩾60 m
IV	Agricultural sector	
	1 Shrimp/fish culture	area ⩾50 ha
	2 Development of rice fields in forested areas	area ⩾1000 ha
	3 Plantations	area ⩾10,000 ha
	4 Cash crop farms	area ⩾5000 ha
V	Tourism sector	
	1 Hotels	size ⩾200 rooms or area ⩾5 ha
	2 Golf courses, recreational parks, tourism resort areas, or estates	⩾100 ha
VI	Transmigration and forest resettlement sector	
	1 Proposed transmigration settlement construction	area ⩾3000 ha
VII	Industrial sector	
	1 Cement (made through production of cement clinker)	
	2 Pulp and paper industry	
	3 Chemical fertilizer (synthetic)	
	4 Petrochemical industry	
	5 Steel smelting	

Box 3.2 (cont.)

No	Type of activity	Size
	6 Lead smelting 7 Copper smelting 8 Alumina production 9 Blended steel smelting 10 Aluminum ignot production 11 Production of metal pellet and sponge products 12 Production of pig iron 13 Production of ferro-alloys 14 Industrial estates 15 Ship building 16 Aircraft production 17 Integrated plywood production 18 Production of weapons, ammunitions, and explosives 19 Battery production	vessels ≥ 3000 DWT including associated facilities
VIII	Communications sector 1 Railway construction and associated facilities 2 Subway construction 3 Construction of Class I, II, and III harbours and associated facilities 4 Construction of special ports 5 Coastal reclamation projects 6 Marine dredging 7 Port handling areas 8 Airports and associated facilities	length ≥ 25 km area ≥ 25 ha volume ≥ 100,000 m³
IX	Trade sectors 1 Trading/shopping centres (relatively concentrated)	area ≥ 5 ha or building area ≥ 10,000 m²
X	Defence and security sector 1 Construction of ammunition storage facilities 2 Construction of naval bases 3 Construction of airforce bases 4 Construction of battlefield training centres/shooting ranges	 classes A, B, C classes A, B, C, or equivalent area ≥ 10,000 ha
XI	Nuclear energy development sector 1 Nuclear reactor construction and operation, and energy production reactor, and research reactor	≥ 100 kW

Box 3.2 (cont.)

No	Type of activity	Size
	2 Construction and operation of non-reactor nuclear energy facilities Nuclear materials fabrication Radioactive waste treatment facilities Radiation source materials Radioisotope production	production $\geqslant 50$ fuel elements per year all facilities source $\geqslant 1850$ TBq (5000 Ci) all facilities
XII	Forestry sector 1 Safari park construction 2 Zoo construction 3 Forest concessions (HPH) 4 Sago palm forest concessions 5 Industrial forest concessions (HTI) 6 Establishment of parks, including national parks, nature reserves, hunting preserves, marine parks, wildlife preserves, biosphere preserves	$\geqslant 250$ ha $\geqslant 100$ ha $\geqslant 1000$ ha $\geqslant 1000$ ha $\geqslant 5000$ ha $\geqslant 5000$ ha
XIII	Toxic and hazardous materials management 1 Construction of toxic and hazardous (B3) waste treatment facilities	
XIV	Integrated/multisectoral activities Businesses and activities comprised of related activities in a single ecosystem type, which require an EIA individually and which are under the authority of more than one government agency	

Screening systems discussed above use guidelines but do not include details of the project and the environment. A quantitative and higher order screening system based on questions and a rating system is described in Tables A and B of Box 3.4 (page 38). This system essentially "grades" the projects into high, moderate, and low impacts and this classification could be potentially used to decide on whether EIA is required, as well as the level of EIA.

3.4.2 Scoping

If screening does not automatically clear a project, then the developer may be asked to undertake a scoping exercise. Scoping involves sufficient research and expert advice to identify the project's key impacts on the local environment in terms of impact issues and to evaluate briefly the

Box 3.3 Environmental categorization of projects at the Asian Development Bank

The ADB's Office of the Environment (OENV), in consultation with staff from the projects departments, categorizes all projects listed in Country Operational Program Papers (COPP) and/or Project Processing Committee (PPC) notes, and sub-projects covered by the program, sector, or financial intermediary lending, according to their anticipated environmental impacts. Based on OENV's screening, projects are assigned to one of the following three categories:

Category A: Projects with significant adverse environmental impact as predicted by the IEE. An EIA is required.

Category B: Projects with adverse environmental impact but which are of lesser degree and/or significance than category A impact. Although an EIA may not be required, an IEE is required for these projects.

Category C: Projects unlikely to have adverse environmental impact. No EIA or IEE is normally required.

Illustrative examples of categorization of projects

Category A projects/sub-projects
  (i) Forest industries (large-scale)
  (ii) Irrigation (large-scale with new source development)
  (iii) River basin development
  (iv) Large-scale power plants
  (v) Large-scale industries
  (vi) Surface and underground mining
  (vii) Large water impoundments
 (viii) New railways/mass transit/roads (near or through sensitive areas)
  (ix) Ports and harbours
  (x) Water supply (with impoundment and/or river intakes)
Category B projects/sub-projects
  (i) Agro-industries (small-scale or no wet processing)
  (ii) Renewable energy
  (iii) Aquaculture and mariculture
  (iv) Rehabilitation, maintenance, and upgrading projects (small-scale)
  (v) Industries (small-scale and without toxic/harmful pollution discharges)
  (vi) Watershed projects (management or rehabilitation)
  (vii) Water supply (without impoundments or new river intakes)
 (viii) Tourism projects
Category C projects/sub-projects
  (i) Forestry research and extension
  (ii) Rural health services
  (iii) Marine sciences education
  (iv) Geological and mineral surveys
  (v) Education
  (vi) Family planning
  (vii) Capital market development study
 (viii) Securities ltd.

Box 3.4 Screening questions and project rating

Project Screening Questions. Twelve project screening questions in Table A (below) have been developed to categorize potential project impacts according to project characteristics. The questions cover a broad range of major environmental impacts associated with the construction projects. These questions are answered either by "yes" or "no" or by "high", "medium", or "low". Determination of an answer is based upon response rating criteria.

Response Rating Criteria. Specific criteria were developed to determine the answer to each project screening question. Such criteria prescribe what is meant by a "high", "medium", or "low" (or "yes" or "no") rating for a particular question.

Example rating criteria presented in Table B (below) for each screening question were developed by use of informed professional judgement and were meant to apply to construction projects. Suggested response rating criteria shown in Table B would have to be modified to apply to other types of projects as experience in their use shows shortcomings.

Project Screening Criteria. Each response rating from Table B is assigned a score of 10, 5, or 0. For each "yes", a project gets a score of 10; for each "no", the score is 0; for "high", "medium", or "low" ratings, scores assigned are 10, 5, and 0, respectively.

Possible total scores for all combinations of various construction projects range from 0 to 120. Within this range, the following three levels of projects are defined:

Level I:	small-impact projects	scores 0–60
Level II:	medium-impact projects	scores 60–100
Level III:	high-impact projects	scores >100

Typically, level I projects may not be subjected to an EIA and may be left without prescription of SOPs. Level II projects may be asked to do an IEE, while level III projects need a comprehensive or detailed EIA.

Table A Screening questions

No	Question	Rating	Score
1	What is the approximate cost of the construction project?	high medium low	10 5 0
2	How large is the area affected by the construction project?	high medium low	10 5 0
3	Will there be a large, industrial type of project under construction?	yes no	10 0
4	Will there be a large, water-related construction activity?	yes no	10 0
5	Will there be a significant waste discharge (in terms of quantity and quality) to natural water?	yes no	10 0

Box 3.4 (cont.)

Table A (cont.)

No	Question	Rating	Score
6	Will there be a significant disposal of solid waste (quantity and composition) on land as a result of construction and operation of the project?	yes no	10 0
7	Will there be significant emissions (quantity and quality) to the air as a result of construction and operation of the project?	yes no	10 0
8	How large is the affected population?	high medium low	10 5 0
9	Will the project affect any unique resources (geological/historical/archaeological/cultural/ecological)?	yes no	10 0
10	Will the construction be on floodplains?	yes no	10 0
11	Will the construction and operation be incompatible with adjoining land use in terms of aesthetics/noise/odour/general acceptance?	yes no	10 0
12	Can the existing community infrastructure handle the new demands placed upon it during construction and operation of the project (roads/utilities/health services/vocational/education/other services)?	no yes	10 0

Table B Example of response rating criteria

No	Criteria	Rating
1(a)	The construction is less than or equal to $1 million	low
1(b)	The construction cost is >$1 million but <$20 million	medium
1(c)	The construction cost is >$20 million	high
2(a)	The area affected by construction is less than or equal to 10 acres	low
2(b)	The area affected by construction is >10 acres but <50 acres	medium
2(c)	The area affected by construction is >50 acres	high
3(a)	An industrial-type project costing more than $1 million is involved	yes
3(b)	Otherwise	no

Box 3.4 (cont.)

Table B (cont.)

No	Criteria	Rating
4(a)	The large water-related construction project consists of one or more of the following: a dam; a dredging operation of 5 miles or longer and disposal of dredged spoils; a bank encroachment that reduces the channel width by 5 percent; filling of a marsh slough acres; continuous filling of 20 or more acres of riverine or estuarine marshes; a bridge across a major river (span: 400 feet).	yes
4(b)	Otherwise	no
5(a)1	At least one of the following waste materials is discharged into the natural streams: asbestos PCB heavy metals pesticides cyanides radioactive substances other hazardous materials (specify)	yes
5(a)2	Rock slides and soil erosion into streams may occur because: no underpinning is specified for unstable landforms; no sluice boxes/retention basins are specified for excavation and filling	yes
5(b)	Otherwise	no
6(a)1	At least one of the following solid wastes is disposed of on land: asbestos PCB heavy metals pesticides cyanides radioactive substances other hazardous materials	yes
6(a)2	The solid waste generated is greater than 2 pounds/capita/day	yes
6(b)	Otherwise	no
7(a)1	If there are to be: Concrete aggregate plant – EIS does not specify dust control devices	yes
7(a)2	Hauling operations – EIS does not specify use of dust control measures	yes
7(a)3	Road grading or land clearing – EIS does not specify water or chemical dust control	yes

Box 3.4 (cont.)

Table B (cont.)

No	Criteria	Rating
7(a)4	Open burning – EIS does not specify disposal of debris	yes
7(a)5	Unpaved roads – EIS does not specify paved roads on construction sites	yes
7(a)6	Asphalt plants – EIS does not specify proper dust control devices	yes
7(b)	Otherwise	no
8(a)	Less than 20 persons are displaced by the project	low
8(b)	From 20 to 50 persons are displaced by the project	medium
8(c)	More than 50 persons are displaced by the project	high
9(a)1	A rich mineral deposit is located on the construction site	yes
9(a)2	A historical site or building is located at or near the construction site	yes
9(a)3	An existing or potential archaeological site is located near the construction project	yes
9(a)4	A rare or endangered species is resident on the land proposed for construction	yes
9(b)	Otherwise	no
10(a)	The construction project is on a 100-year floodplain	yes
10(b)	Otherwise	no
11(a)1	No visual screening is specified in the EIS for the construction site	yes
11(a)2	No progressive reclamation of quarry and/or disposal sites is proposed	yes
11(a)3	No permissible noise level specifications are stated for vibrators	yes
11(b)	Otherwise	no
12(a)	The projected demand for community services exceeds existing or planned capacity. These services include: water supply wastewater treatment/disposal electric generation transportation educational and vocational facilities cultural/recreational facilities health services safety services, fire, flood, etc.	yes
12(b)	Otherwise	no

"Otherwise" implies that none of the previously mentioned situations are applicable to the project.

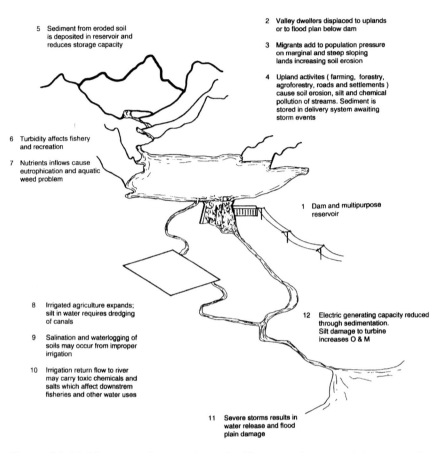

5 Sediment from eroded soil
   is deposited in reservoir and
   reduces storage capacity

2 Valley dwellers displaced to uplands
   or to flood plain below dam

3 Migrants add to population pressure
   on marginal and steep sloping
   lands increasing soil erosion

4 Upland activites (farming, forestry,
   agroforestry, roads and settlements)
   cause soil erosion, silt and chemical
   pollution of streams. Sediment is
   stored in delivery system awaiting
   storm events

6 Turbidity affects fishery
   and recreation

7 Nutrients inflows cause
   eutrophication and aquatic
   weed problem

1 Dam and multipurpose
   reservoir

8 Irrigated agriculture expands;
   silt in water requires dredging
   of canals

9 Salination and waterlogging of
   soils may occur from improper
   irrigation

10 Irrigation return flow to river
   may carry toxic chemicals and
   salts which affect downstrem
   fisheries and other water uses

12 Electric generating capacity reduced
   through sedimentation.
   Silt damage to turbine
   increases O & M

11 Severe storms results in
   water release and flood
   plain damage

Figure 3.3 Multipurpose dam project: significant environmental issues to be examined in scoping

importance of the critical issues to the various stakeholders apart from the decision makers.

Setting the boundaries of the assessment is the most important step of the entire EIA. Too narrow a scope will likely leave out an important factor or effect, but too broad a scope may make the analysis unwieldy or take too long a time. Other aspects of scoping are to choose the important issues to be resolved and to agree on responsibilities for performing the EIA.

Setting the correct geographic boundary for analyses is essential. Consider, for example, a multi-purpose dam and reservoir project in a large upland watershed (refer to Fig. 3.3). A narrow financial analysis might include just the costs of the dam and hydroelectric generator and just the benefits of the power delivered to an electric grid. From the standpoint of society, however, many related effects on natural systems would be important.

In the case of industrial projects, the scope should include reasonably important factors (e.g., transport of raw materials and products, worker housing, and pollution or waste discharges) extending beyond the site. Highly imaginative indirect effects may be mentioned but need not be evaluated (e.g., civil unrest, price fluctuations in distant markets, rare natural calamities).

All time phases of the project (i.e., construction, operation, and decommissioning maintenance) should be covered. The more important question, however, is how far into the future predictions should be taken. Although their accuracy falls off rapidly with time, predictions of effects out to the expected lifetime of the project or facilities should be attempted. Instances where some sort of perpetual management is necessary (e.g., hazardous waste or radioactive materials) should be noted. If dismantling of a facility is necessary, the impacts of that activity at a future time should be covered.

In addition to geographic and time boundaries, the scoping team should agree on the alternatives and major issues to be addressed. Others may be added during the assessment, i.e., initial environmental examination, by using tests of significance, urgency, and irreversibility.

In particular, the scoping exercise should involve the following steps:
- review all written materials on the purpose, need, or prospectus for the project;
- perform field reconnaissance of the desired site or sites for the project;
- interview local residents and affected communities that use resources;
- consult with other agencies that have expertise, jurisdiction, or influence on the decision to approve, design, or site a project;
- consult with local or regional scientists at colleges, universities, institutes, or field stations;
- visit local political leaders where the project may be sited.

The first task of the study team is to conduct a "scooping" meeting. The aim of scoping is to ensure that the study addresses all the impact issues of importance. A "map" of the project (in the form of a neat sketch) at about 1:10,000 scale on a large piece of paper can be used to organize the discussion. All participants are encouraged to add items to the sketch and to propose alternatives and issues to be assessed. Flows of materials, energy, and people are indicated on the sketch map. Impacts are tentatively predicted. Ecologically sensitive areas (e.g., steep slopes, flood plains, wetlands) are located. Later, a fresh version of the map should be prepared. First, the study team's outlook is broadened (by discussions with the project developers, decision makers, the regulatory agency, scientific institutions, local community leaders, and others) to include all the possible issues and concerns raised by these various groups. Then the study team selects primary impacts (where the project activities affect directly the environmental components) for the EIA to focus on, making their choice on the basis of magnitude, geographical extent, significance to decision makers, or because of special local sensitivities (e.g., soil erosion, the presence of an endangered species, or a nearby historical site). Next, brief speculation is done on any significant secondary impacts (where the activities affect the environmental components in an indirect manner).

The scoping exercise can be used to assist early in the planning of a project (for instance, to narrow the discussion of possible sites) and it can serve as an early warning that the project may have serious impact issues. Scoping is thus an activity in the developer's interests.

In the framework of environmental impacts introduced earlier, scoping assists in the identification of all possible related impact issues. Box 3.5 illustrates how to grade the issues related to impacts in the scoping exercise of a fertilizer complex.

3.4.3 The initial environmental examination

IEE is a process of further inquiry into the impact assessment, taking clues from the exercise of scoping. There is, however, a fairly thin dividing line between scoping and an IEE when it comes to identification and gradation of the impact issue. Some of the discussion and inferencing shown in Box 3.5 could also be done at an IEE level.

Scoping, however, lays an emphasis on the identification of issues and on the boundaries of the analysis. IEE attempts to examine the issues in more detail by carrying out an exercise of prediction and assessment to identify required mitigation measures. In this manner each alternative is assessed. Later, these alternatives are analysed to rank them and find the alternative which may be either cleared or taken to the next tier of detailed EIA.

IEE focuses on the assessment of impacts and identification of obvious mitigation measures. This is generally done by conducting baseline information and by collecting any available secondary data. The issues are assessed by carrying out a prediction exercise by using informal judgement, the opinion of experts, or in some occasions by using screening level mathematical models.

The idea of assessment is to grade the impacts in terms of significance. Significance of the impact is expressed in terms of "highly significant" or "of minor significance", or in terms of additional descriptors such as "reversible", "irreversible", etc. The idea of assessing the significance is

Box 3.5 Illustrates a possible generation, reduction, and gradation of the impact issues in the scoping exercise of a fertilizer complex

In the case of a fertilizer project, for instance, a number of issues were placed in the scoping meeting. These issues emerged as the project description was presented by the developer to the group of local residents, NGOs, consultants, and government officials. A scoping meeting was also organized internally by the developer by inviting staff and consultants to improve on the understanding of the impact issues. Typically, the issues identified were as follows:

- land acquisition leading to displacement of nearly 5000 local residents;
- fear of air pollution in terms of strong odours – these odours may be expected to keep the tourists away some 6 km downwind on a beach;
- fear of air pollution affecting the crops, especially the sulphur and nitrogen oxides which may seriously affect the farmers growing cane sugar in the nearby fields;
- deterioration of the receiving water quality caused by the discharge of effluents – this is expected to affect the fisheries in the zone 30 km downstream;
- nuisance of noise levels caused by the operation of the plant;
- possible urbanization due to the setting up of the plant – the local residents feel that most of the employees would be shifted from the urban centres located in a 100–120 km radius, resulting in an imbalance in the local setting;
- likely increase and subsequent congestion of road traffic due to frequent transport of raw materials and the chemicals/fertilizers produced;
- potential risks of hazard during transportation of chemicals and storage. A discussion on the impact issues led to the following results.

(a) Most critical issues

- Land acquisition leading to displacement of nearly 5000 local residents
It was suggested that the developer should specify on the map the alternative location to be provided. It was also suggested that the IEE exercise to follow should look at the resettlement package carefully, include the alternative site in the baseline study and study the effect of relocation on the receiving population. Two other sites near to the proposed site were identified as "alternatives" where the issue of relocation is rather minor.
- Deterioration of the receiving water quality caused by the discharge of effluents
This issue was debated extensively as the stakeholders included not only the fishermen but the residents of a small township and two industries located between 8 to 10 km downstream of the proposed effluent discharge. The impact on the fisheries at such a long distance was considered to be not so critical. One of the scientists, however, expressed a concern on the long-term discharge of spent catalysts and biocides in the cooling water discharge. The effluent treatment suggested was expected to result in residual impacts which may still be significant over a long run. Ways to minimize effluent strength and volume were required to be considered by upgrading the technology. Alternative locations of the disposal point, especially downstream of the intake works, was discussed by laying a

Box 3.5 (cont.)

pipeline. NGOs are little sceptical as it was feared that the pipeline maintenance could itself be a task. IEE is expected to examine the available data on the water quality and quantity downstream of the location to the fishing zone. Examination of the present water quality data at the intake works was considered in the scope. The need for a multi-parameter and ecological water quality model was expressed at the detailed or comprehensive EIA level.

• Potential risks of hazard during transportation of chemicals and storage
The developer was asked to prepare an inventory of the hazardous substances as well as to study all the major transportation routes carrying hazardous substances and identify any sensitive receptors around the same. A possibility of reducing the containment of chemicals on the site and a consequent analysis of some of the critical storage was considered essential in the further tiers of assessment.

Moderate issues

• Fear of air pollution affecting the crops
This issue was considered moderate only because of the strict emission controls proposed by the developer. The local office of the pollution control was requested to exercise even stricter emission standards to ensure a pressure on the developer. An emergency power supply was suggested to ensure no abnormal situation. In order to enable study of the impacts, however, scoping recommended a baseline study of the crops, crop type, yield, and cover. An agricultural expert was requested in the developer's study team conducting the IEE.

• Possible urbanization due to the setting up of the plant
It was difficult to assess the level of this impact issue unless the scoping boundary was extended over a longer period of time. An examination of the current levels of infrastructure and resource availability (especially water) was needed to be included in the scope to check the adequacy.

• Likely increase and subsequent congestion of the road traffic
Discussions were held to identify any alternatives, such as setting up a separate railhead. This possibility was expected to reduce the overall risk potential during transportation as well. For the construction of the railhead, however, routing was considered to be critical as some sensitive land acquisition is needed as well as tunnelling for a short distance. The scope was extended to include such a sub-project.

Minor issues

• Fear of air pollution in terms of strong odours
On discussion with the developer and the scientific experts, this impact issue was considered to be completely mitigable by better process control and in any case the odours were expected to disperse 2 km beyond the project site. The scoping exercises suggested that the tourist site located 6 km from the present site need not be covered in the IEE.

• Nuisance of noise levels caused by the operation of the plant
After study, this issue was considered as minor.

to identify suitable mitigation measures. The level of mitigation measures suggested is based on the understanding of the severity of the impacts.

Factual differences between alternatives may be better understood if the impacts are described and compared in a quantitative form: emissions to the air in mg/m^3, loss of vegetation in surface area, loss of biodiversity in the number of species, noise in dB(A), groundwater level changes in cm. By showing the impacts in this way, the information about the size of the effects remains intact. Even the use of percentages can sometimes be misleading. For example, in an area with an extremely high background concentration of SO_2 a fractional increase of 0.5% can mean a substantial emission increase.

In the framework of impacts, the IEE process can be expressed as:

$$(\text{Activity})_i (\text{Component})_j \rightarrow \text{Prediction} \rightarrow (\text{Impact})_{ji}$$

$$\rightarrow (\text{Assessment}) \rightarrow \text{Mitigation Measures}$$

$$\rightarrow (\text{Residual Impact})_{ji}$$

Any issues emerging from the IEE requiring further study are also identified and if a detailed EIA is required then the terms of reference to conduct the study are also prepared.

The IEE study thus results in the following:

- a brief description of the expected or predicted environmental changes due to the project;
- measures or procedures that could be implemented to avoid or reduce the impacts on the environment;
- examination of alternatives, including the proposed action and no action;
- additional study requirements, regulatory requirements, and other coordination requirements for the detailed EIA, if required.

Alternatives should be feasible and substantially different from each other. Sometimes alternatives are made up and used to place the preferred alternative in a favourable perspective. A comparison of alternatives, done at the IEE level, should answer several questions.

a How will the proposal change the environment?
- To identify the environmental consequences of the proposal, in comparison with the existing state of the environment.

b How serious are these changes for the environment?
- To compare the impacts to environmental standards and objectives.

c How can serious impacts be prevented?
- To compare the different possible solutions for the proposal, choose the best alternative, and present the arguments for it.

The following criteria can be used to check the selection of alternatives. Alternatives should:

- be feasible in practice (sense of reality);
- meet the objectives of the initiator, provided they are not defined too narrowly (problem solving capacity);
- be sufficiently different (discriminating potential).

3.4.4 The detailed EIA study

In the EIA process up to this stage, scoping identifies the significant environmental issues emerging from the project, while through the activity of IEE a preliminary study of the assessment of the various impacts is conducted. In addition, obvious mitigation measures are identified to meet regulatory requirements and any residual issues requiring further detailed study are identified.

The next tier involves detailed EIA. The study is broadly conducted along the lines of IEE, albeit in a more detailed manner. In the detailed EIA, all significant issues are examined once again in the formal framework of identification, prediction, and assessment, and all issues previously dealt in the IEE level are reassessed for adequacy. New issues, if any, are identified because of: (a) increased understanding of issues due to IEE; (b) project modifications; and (c) suggested mitigation measures.

An IEE often leads to either new information on the projects and its activities or the presence of a critical environmental component. This can lead to issues not identified earlier. For example, an IEE may focus on the normal emissions arising out of the stacks or well identified sources from an industry. However, additional information collected on the fill-and-draw of the storage tanks and emissions thereof, and properties of the chemical stored, can lead one to check the transient emissions as well. Similarly, possibilities of frequent start up and shut down of the plant (either due to process instability in the initial periods or due to power failure) may become a reason to include emergency or incidental emissions as an issue.

An exercise of IEE may ask for project modifications. These modifications would then need a scoping exercise (note the iterative nature of EIA) and in this process new significant issues may be identified.

In some cases, the mitigation measures themselves may require checks and balances as these are generally proposed in isolation at the IEE level. For example, for the mitigation of dust-laden emissions from an industry, a Venturi scrubber may be suggested. It becomes necessary then to ensure that the water (solvent) required for the purpose of scrubbing is shown in the overall water balance and that the scrubbed water is included in the overall effluent volume.

In the case of an industry discharging its effluents on a coastal area, an outfall into the sea may be suggested as mitigation. This measure can, however, lead to impacts during construction (e.g., noise and debris leading to disturbance to the marine ecosystem) as well as during operation (e.g., causing obstruction in the navigation pathways of the local fishermen). These issues arising out of the mitigations themselves need to be addressed in detailed EIA.

In detailed EIA, a systems approach is used in the identification of the significant issues.

The next step in detailed EIA is to classify issues which can be understood by available information and those which require additional information and inference. This leads to identification of the necessary surveys, prediction and assessment exercises, and appropriate mitigation measures. The final recommendations in the detailed EIA extend beyond the mitigation measures to include the necessary institutional set up for the support of the overall environmental management system.

It is possible that a few issues may be significant but not fully mitigable or only partially understood. These issues need to be communicated at the end of the detailed EIA through public information and consultation (PIC).

The essence and spirit of the exercises of prediction, assessment, and mitigation are described below in more detail.

3.4.4.1 Prediction

As far possible, prediction scientifically characterizes the impact's causes and effects, and its secondary and synergistic consequences for the environment and the local community. Prediction follows an activity–component relationship (e.g., discharge of liquid effluent as an activity and river water quality as an environmental component) and estimates the subsequent effects (e.g., such as reduced concentration of dissolved oxygen, reduced fisheries). Prediction draws on physical, biological, socio-economic, and anthropological data and techniques. In quantifying impacts, it may employ mathematical models, photomontages, physical models, sociocultural models, economic models, experiments, or expert judgements.

To prevent unnecessary expense, the sophistication of the prediction methods used should be kept in proportion to the "scope" of the EIA. For instance, a detailed mathematical model of atmospheric dispersion should not be used if only a small amount of relatively harmless pollutant is emitted. Simpler models are available and are sufficient for the purpose. Also, it is unnecessary to undertake expensive analysis if they are not required by the decision makers for whom the EIA is being done.

All prediction techniques, by their nature, involve some degree of uncertainty. So, along with each attempt to quantify an impact, the study team should also quantify the prediction's uncertainty in terms of probabilities of "margins of error".

A shortcoming of many detailed EIAs is that social and cultural impacts are not given the prominence they deserve in describing the extent of changes expected to result from a major development project. This has probably been due to the bias of physical and biological scientists against the comparatively younger disciplines of cultural anthropology and sociology. This is an unfortunate bias, since sociocultural impacts are the ones that would affect the local community in their everyday lives. A consideration of sociocultural impacts should be integrated, wherever possible, into every discussion of physical/biological change, and not just treated separately in a minor chapter or appendix. Several methods and analytical tools are available for this purpose; they are discussed in detail in Chapters 4 and 5.

3.4.4.2 Assessment

The next question addressed by the EIA – "Do the changes matter?" – is answered in the next step, assessment, so called because it evaluates the predicted adverse impacts to determine whether they are significant enough to need mitigation. This judgement of significance can be based on one or more of the following:
- comparison with laws, regulations, or accepted standards;
- consultation with the relevant decision makers;
- reference to pre-set criteria such as protected sites, features, or species;
- consistency with government policy objectives;
- acceptability to the local community or the general public.

3.4.4.3 Mitigation

If the answer to the previous question is "Yes, the changes do matter", then the EIA answers the fourth question – "What can be done about them?". In this phase, the study team formally analyses mitigation. A wide range of measures are proposed to prevent, reduce, remedy, or compensate each of the adverse impacts evaluated as significant. Possible mitigation measures include:
- changing project sites, routes, processes, raw materials, operating methods, waste disposal routes or locations, or engineering designs;
- introducing pollution controls, monitoring, phased implementation, landscaping, personnel training, involving social services or public education;
- offering (as compensation) restoration of damaged resources, money to affected persons, concessions on other issues, or fit site programmes

to enhance some other aspects of the environment or quality of life for the community.

Note that some mitigations have already been identified in the IEE exercise.

All mitigation measures have a cost, and this cost must be quantified.

3.4.4.4 Evaluation

At the end of the exercise of detailed EIA, an evaluation is performed considering all the project costs (including mitigation, compensatory, and enhancement measures) and project benefits (including no interruption due to compliance to regulations) to establish an overall cost-effectiveness of the modified project.

3.5 Resources needed for an EIA

Because of the EIA's acknowledged importance in planning a country's sustainable economic growth, EIAs are now undertaken throughout the world, even in places with very few resources. There are, however, certain minimum resources needed to perform EIAs that can successfully shape major projects.

- Qualified multidisciplinary staff. This includes a skilled manager (to coordinate the activities, communicate with decision makers, and motivate the study team), trained specialists (in fields such as environmental science, rural and urban planning, economics, waste and pollution control, process engineering, landscape design, sociology, and cultural anthropology) and a communications expert.
- Technical guidelines, agreed with the competent authority, for carrying out the various phases of the EIA process, especially screening, scoping, prediction, evaluation, and mitigation.
- Information about the environment (especially relating to the impacts being considered after "scoping") which can be sorted and evaluated.
- Analytical capabilities for doing field work, laboratory testing, library research, data processing, photomontage, surveys, and predictive modelling.
- Institutional arrangements, including a formal procedure for consultation with the decision makers and other interested groups, the authority to obtain the necessary information about the proposed project, and a formal process for integrating the EIA into the decision-making process about projects.
- Review monitoring and enforcement powers, to ensure that accepted mitigation measures are included in the development.

Among the resources needed to perform an EIA are money and time.

Regarding time, the following are averages for a sampling of recent EIAs; IEEs take between 2 to 10 weeks to complete; detailed EIAs may last between 3 months and 2 years. Regarding costs, officials often balk at some of the figures they hear, but developers and investors will realize that they represent only a very small percentage of the costs of any major development project – nearly always less than 1%. Indeed, it is a relatively small price to pay to prevent costly unforeseen problems, to promote development that can be sustained, to help prevent potentially ruinous environmental catastrophes, and to obtain approval and acceptance.

3.6 Some illustrations of EIA processes in various countries

Although EIA is currently practiced in many countries, no two countries have adopted the same processes for the preparation or implementation of EIA. However, the effectiveness of EIA as an environmental management tool will always be influenced by the political and economic philosophy of the respective country. Although many lessons have been learnt regarding issues such as appropriate EIA methodology, etc., an ideal approach to EIA does not currently exist.

The problems encountered with the substantive goals and procedural requirements of EIA vary only slightly between industrial and developing countries. There are a number of reasons mentioned by various experts in the field of EIA, about why the EIA experience cannot be repeated in developing countries:

- the conflict between pursuing environmental considerations and much needed economic development;
- the financial costs of conducting a full-blown EIA are too high;
- data for identifying and predicting potential impacts are not available at an appropriate level of detail;
- the expertise for conducting a comprehensive EIA is not available;
- EIA is a technology developed in first world countries and therefore includes cultural values that make the transfer of EIA to third world countries difficult.

Apparently a number of these reasons are also true for developed countries. However, it is important to note that the most appropriate EIA methodology for a project or plan must always be considered on a case-by-case basis, not by mimicing approaches adopted in other countries. Much of the EIA carried out in developing countries is not inferior to the work done in developed countries; it is simply a different approach.

Examples of EIA processes have been selected from both developed and developing countries. This is an attempt to provide a cross section of the priorities of various countries embarking on developmental projects.

3.6.1 EIA system in Indonesia

The EIA process in Indonesia known as AMDAL (Analysis Mengenai Dampak Lingkungan) is characterized by the absence of IEE. Screening is directly followed by detailed EIA. There is extensive saving of time. In Indonesia, due to the maturity of the system, some projects do not have to be assessed but must be implemented based on certain well defined SOPs.

The AMDAL process was originally included in law through Government Regulation No. 29 of 1986 (PP29/1986), promulgated under Law No. 4 of 1982, Indonesia's fundamental Environmental Law, which establishes the principle of sustainable development. The 1986 regulation was revoked in 1993 and replaced by PP51/1993. The subsequent guidelines issued by the Minister of State for the Environment were Kep-10/MENLH/3/1994 to Kep-15/MENLH/3/1994 and Keputusan Kepala BAPEDAL Kep-056/1994.

The most important parties involved in the implementation of AMDAL are:
- the government, through the responsible sectoral agencies and provincial governments, as well as the Environmental Impact Management Agency (Badan Pengendalian Dampak Lingkungan; BAPEDAL);
- proponents of businesses and development activities, both public and private sector;
- the AMDAL commissions which review and decide on AMDAL documents;
- consultants and technical staff of proponents and commissions who prepare AMDAL documents;
- the public at large, including community representatives and NGOs.

3.6.1.1 Responsibility for AMDAL

Overall coordination of the AMDAL process is the responsibility of BAPEDAL. BAPEDAL provides guidance and monitors implementation.

Authority for implementation of environmental management in general, and for AMDAL in particular, is currently assigned to the sectoral government departments and agencies at the central level, and to the governments of the 27 provinces and special administrative areas.

The government regulation concerning AMDAL (PP51/1993) establishes an AMDAL commission in each department, agency, or provincial government. The tasks of the commissions include the evaluation of the various AMDAL documents required. The membership composition and work procedures for the commissions are specified by BAPEDAL.

A "technical team" of departmental or agency staff may be formed to assist each commission.

3.6.1.2 Screening: determining which projects require AMDAL

The AMDAL process is targeted at those proposed business activities or projects which have the greatest potential to affect the environment significantly. Essentially, this covers large projects, those using dangerous processes or producing hazardous materials, and those located in or near to areas which require special protection (conservation areas or environmentally sensitive areas).

BAPEDAL is authorized to specify the criteria for deciding which proposed businesses or activities require AMDAL. These criteria are specified in KepMen 11/1994, which should be consulted for further details (see Box 3.2, page 33). Questions regarding the application of the criteria in specific cases can be referred to BAPEDAL for a decision.

Special provisions have been made in the 1993 revision of the AMDAL process for three types of AMDAL process.

i AMDAL Kegiatan Terpadu/Multisektoral is for multi-sectoral projects (several departments or agencies responsible for different aspects; i.e., integrated pulp and paper and forestry plantation). Such projects are handled by an AMDAL commission located within BAPEDAL, rather than in the various responsible government departments.

ii AMDAL Kawasan is for projects which are sited together in special areas (including industrial estates, tourism development areas, and special bonded import/export areas). All projects in these special areas would be assessed as a group, rather than requiring a separate AMDAL for each one.

iii AMDAL Regional is for regional impact assessments. This will cover regional development areas and will address the cumulative impacts of a number of different activities in an area. Guidelines for this type of AMDAL are under development.

3.6.1.3 AMDAL procedures

A general flow chart of the implementation of AMDAL is shown in Figure 3.4. The first point of contact for a project proponent is the responsible government authority at the national or provincial level, either:

a a sectoral department;
b a non-departmental government agency; or
c the Investment Coordination Board (BKPM).

Development projects generated internally in the various sectors of government and agencies are handled internally, and are referred directly to the relevant commission. Examples include irrigation projects, or road projects, which are handled by the Department of Public Works (PU). Some private sector projects which do not require foreign or domestic investment or other government privileges are also under the government department or agency which regulates or licenses their sector.

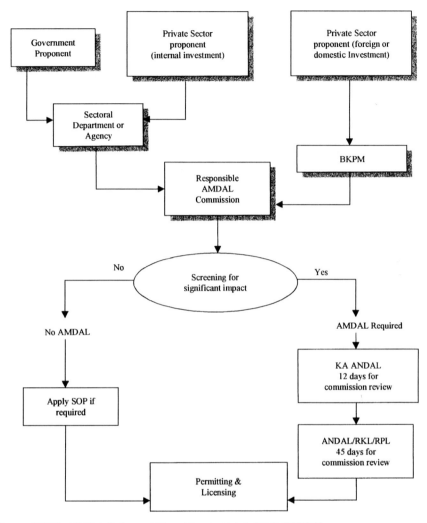

Source: AMDAL, A Guide to Environmental Impact Assessments in Indonesia, BAPEDAL
with EMDI, 1994.

Figure 3.4 Outline of AMDAL process in Indonesia

All other private sector development projects which require either foreign or domestic investment or other government privileges (i.e., duty-free import of equipment) must go to the BKPM. The BKPM's environmental division (stages) will screen the project, using BAPEDAL's criteria in KepMen 11/1994, and will direct the proponent to the appropriate government department or agency for further action.

The AMDAL commission in the department or agency concerned will review the proposed business or activity and decide on the requirement for AMDAL. It should be noted that businesses and activities which are not subject to AMDAL (because they are too small, or situated in non-sensitive locations, or for which technology is readily available to mini-mize impacts) are still required to be implemented in a way which mini-mizes detrimental effects. This is to be done through adhering to SOPs (known locally as UKL and UPL) to be specified by the department, agency, or provincial government responsible. BAPEDAL has issued general guidelines for the departments and agencies regarding the prep-aration of UKL and UPL. It falls under the general responsibility of each department to provide environmental management in the sector or disci-pline under its jurisdiction, and is not considered to be a part of AMDAL per se.

Businesses or activities requiring AMDAL must first prepare terms of reference, or KA, for the AMDAL study. The KA describes the scope of the study to be carried out, which must focus only on the major issues predicted to arise in the specific project. The KA also describes the data collection and analytical methods to be used. The KA is submitted to the commission, which then has 12 working days to review it and to issue a decision. Usually, the commission will meet with the proponent to discuss the KA and recommend additions or changes.

The proponent must then carry out the study as defined in the KA, and prepare the impact assessment in the form of the EIA document (known locally as ANDAL). The ANDAL is an in-depth study of the potential impacts of the proposed project. At the same time, the proponent pre-pares an environmental management plan (RKL) and an environmental monitoring plan (RPL). The RKL specifies all environmental manage-ment techniques which must be implemented to reduce or eliminate the predicted significant environmental impacts. This can include design changes, construction and operating procedures, and site rehabilitation measures, along with compliance standards and compensation plans. The RPL specifies the technical details of the monitoring that must be carried out to ensure that the environmental management procedures are indeed implemented and are effective in mitigating detrimental impacts. The ANDAL, RKL, and RPL documents are all submitted to the commission, which has 45 days to carry out its detailed review.

The commission may, at its discretion, approve the documents or may require further study or discussion by the proponent of controversial issues. It may also reject the proposed business or activity if it decides that the associated impacts are unacceptable, in which case the proponent may revise or abandon the proposal. Final decisions on projects reviewed at the national level are made by the sectoral minister or head of agency, on recommendation of the central AMDAL commission. Decisions on projects reviewed at the provincial level are made by the governor, on recommendation of the regional AMDAL commission.

3.6.1.4 Permits and licenses

Permit and license conditions provide the means by which environmental mitigation and monitoring requirements developed in the AMDAL process can be made legally enforceable in the event of non-compliance by the proponent. Once all of the AMDAL documents have been prepared to the satisfaction of the commission, the minister or head of the agency should then indicate to the relevant licensing or permitting agencies that the AMDAL documents have been approved, subject to specified conditions, and that they may issue the required licenses and permits. Although there are not currently any specific environmental permits or licenses in Indonesia, environmental conditions can be included in one or more of the investment, location, activity, or nuisance permits issued by various agencies.

According to Article 5 of PP51/1993, final operating permits (Izin Usaha Tetap) for an industrial facility should not be issued until after the RKL and RPL have been implemented. This provision is intended to ensure, for example, that waste treatment facilities have actually been put into operation.

3.6.1.5 Public participation in AMDAL

The AMDAL regulation requires the government department or agency concerned to inform the public about businesses or activities which require AMDAL. All AMDAL documents are to be open for public inspection. The public may also provide oral or written comments to the AMDAL commission before it issues a decision on any proposed business or activity.

General guidelines for the preparation of AMDAL documents also encourage the practice of involving local people.

3.6.2 EIA procedure and requirements in Malaysia

The EIA procedure adopted in Malaysia consists of three major steps. The steps in the EIA procedure, which are shown in Figure 3.5, are described below. The unique feature about the process of EIA in Malaysia is the integration of EIA in the project cycle.

Preliminary assessment relates to the initial assessment of the potential impacts. Preliminary assessment is the stage of the EIA procedure that should normally be initiated at the pre-feasibility study stage of the development of an activity. Project options are identified at this stage and

58

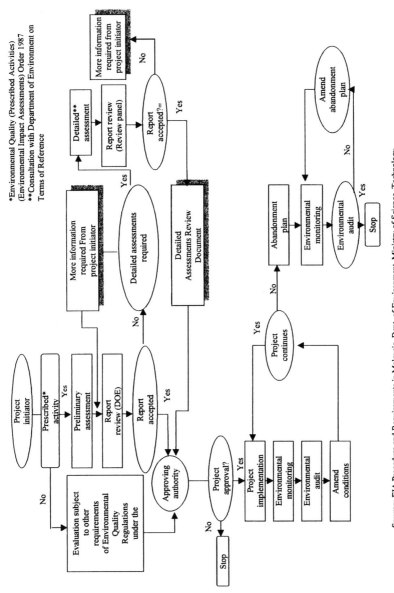

Source: EIA Procedure and Requirements in Malaysia, Dept. of Environment, Ministry of Science, Technology and the Environment, Malaysia, 1993.

Figure 3.5 Outline of EIA process in Malaysia

*Environmental Quality (Prescribed Activities) (Environmental Impact Assessments) Order 1987
**Consultation with Department of Environment on Terms of Reference

any significant residual environmental impacts are made known. The preliminary report that is prepared is reviewed internally by a technical committee in the Department of Environment (DOE). However, when expertise within the department is lacking, assistance from other governmental and non-governmental agencies may be sought.

Detailed assessment is undertaken for those projects for which significant residual environmental impacts have been predicted in the preliminary assessment. The assessment should ideally continue during project feasibility and the detailed EIA report be submitted for approval by the director general of environmental quality prior to the giving of approval by the relevant federal or state government authority for the implementation of the project. Detailed assessment is carried out based on specific terms of reference issued by an ad hoc review panel appointed by the director general, who chairs it.

Review of EIA reports is carried out internally by the DOE for preliminary assessment reports and by an ad hoc review panel for detailed assessment reports. Recommendations arising out of the review are transmitted to the relevant project-approving authorities for consideration in making a decision on the project. The normal period allocated for a review of a preliminary assessment report is 1 month while that for a detailed assessment report is 2 months. The DOE maintains a list of experts who may be called upon to sit as members of any review panel established. The selection of the experts depends on the area of environmental impact to be reviewed.

Other main features of the EIA procedure, as shown in Figure 3.5, include the following.

The approving authority is the government authority that has the task of deciding whether or not a project should proceed. The authorities include the following:
1 the National Development Planning Committee for federal government sponsored projects;
2 the regional development authorities;
3 the state planning authorities for state government sponsored projects; and
4 the Ministry of Trade and Industry or MIDA for industrial projects.

Recommendations arising from the review of the EIA reports are forwarded to the relevant project-approving authorities. At the completion of the review period for a detailed EIA, a detailed assessment review document is issued by the review panel. This document may include:
• comments on the detailed assessment report;
• recommendations to the project proponent and the project-approving authority including any specific conditions attached to the project approval; and
• recommendations for environmental monitoring and auditing.

3.6.2.1 Integrated project-planning concept

The EIA procedure in Malaysia is designed to follow the integrated project-planning concept, as shown in Figure 3.6. The features of the concept include the following:

1 at the outset, during the project identification stage, the need to conduct an EIA study is also determined;
2 if the project requires preliminary assessment, it is done in parallel with the pre-feasibility study for the project;
3 similarly, if detailed assessment is required, it is conducted as part of the feasibility study for the project;
4 the preliminary assessment and detailed assessment reports are reviewed simultaneously with the pre-feasibility and feasibility reports, respectively, before a final decision on the project is made;
5 during project construction and project operation, environmental monitoring is carried out.

The concept is recommended to be followed to minimize project delay and improve project planning.

3.6.2.2 How is EIA processed and approved?

(i) Organizational structure

Figure 3.7 illustrates the organizational structure of the EIA report processing and approval procedure. The organizational set-up is headed by the director general (DG) of environmental quality. The DG is responsible for approving or rejecting an EIA report. The DG is assisted by the director of the prevention division, the head of the evaluation section, and the EIA report processing desk officers. The functions of the director of the prevention division include the chairing of EIA technical committee meetings. The EIA technical committee is an in-house committee set up to examine preliminary reports. On receiving preliminary EIA reports, the desk officers prepare review documents to be tabled at the EIA technical committee meeting. The EIA technical committee then makes recommendations to the DG of environmental quality on the acceptability of the preliminary EIA report. The committee may also make recommendations to the DG requesting the project proponent to proceed with detailed EIA.

The detailed EIA review panel's main task is to critically review detailed EIA reports and formulate recommendations of the relevant project-approving authority. The detailed EIA review panel is established on an ad hoc basis specifically for a particular project. The panel comprises independent members of relevant disciplines, from different organizations such as universities and NGOs. Detailed EIA reports are also displayed at all DOE offices, as well as at public and university

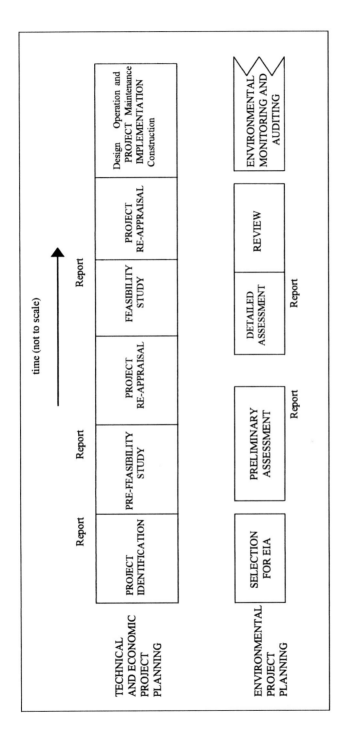

Source: EIA Procedure and Requirements in Malaysia, Dept. of Environment, Ministry of Science, Technology and the Environment, Malaysia, 1993.

Figure 3.6 Integrated project planning concept in Malaysia

61

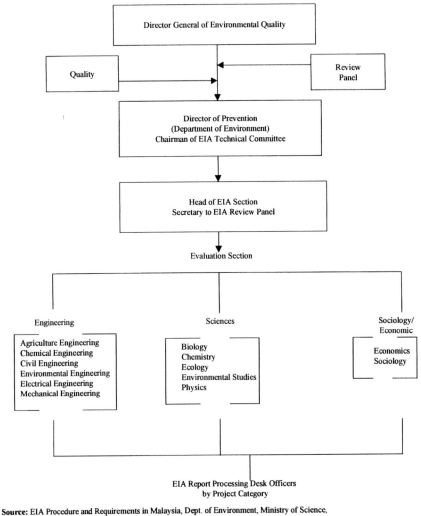

Director General of Environmental Quality

Quality

Review
Panel

Director of Prevention
(Department of Environment)
Chairman of EIA Technical Committee

Head of EIA Section
Secretary to EIA Review Panel

Evaluation Section

Engineering

Agriculture Engineering
Chemical Engineering
Civil Engineering
Environmental Engineering
Electrical Engineering
Mechanical Engineering

Sciences

Biology
Chemistry
Ecology
Environmental Studies
Physics

Sociology/
Economic

Economics
Sociology

EIA Report Processing Desk Officers
by Project Category

Source: EIA Procedure and Requirements in Malaysia, Dept. of Environment, Ministry of Science,
Technology and the Environment, Malaysia, 1993.

Figure 3.7 Organizational structure of EIA report processing and approval procedure in Malaysia

libraries, for public comments. The public is widely notified through the
mass media when and where the detailed EIA reports are available for
review and comment.

The EIA section comprises EIA report processing desk officers,
assisted by assistant environmental control officers. The desk officers are
trained in different disciplines including environmental engineering,

agricultural engineering, chemical engineering, civil engineering, electrical engineering, mechanical engineering, environmental sciences, biology, chemistry, environmental studies, physics, economics, sociology, and ecology.

(ii) Activities subject to EIA

The Environmental Quality (Prescribed Activities) Environmental Impact Assessment Order 1987 which is made under powers conferred by Section 34A of the Environment Quality Act, 1974 (Amendment) 1985, specified those activities that are subject to EIA. Twenty categories of activities are prescribed, included those related to: agriculture, airport, drainage and irrigation, land reclamation, fisheries, forestry, housing, industry, infrastructure, ports, mining, petroleum, power generation, quarries, railways, transportation, resort and recreational development, waste treatment and disposal, and water supply.

Many of the activities related to these 20 categories are defined in terms of project size (as area) and capacity (quantum), while others are not defined by an unit of measure. Hence, to assist project initiators or project-approving authorities to make quick decisions on whether a proposed activity is subject to the Act or otherwise, three simple checklists have been prepared as follows:

(a) activities defined by quantum;
(b) activities defined by project size; and
(c) activities not defined by unit of measure.

(iii) Classification of projects by timing of EIA report submission (project planning cycle)

In order to integrate the environmental dimension in the project planning or designing process, the timing of submission of an EIA report to the Department of Environment for approval is vital, so as not to cause any major disruption to the overall project planning cycle. The project initiator is encouraged to submit the EIA report as early as the project identification stage to enable recommendations on environmental changes or modifications to the project plan to be incorporated. On the other hand, submission of an EIA report towards the end of the project planning cycle will reduce the value of an EIA, and will possibly increase environmental costs or delay implementation of the project.

In order to guide project proponents, a classification system for EIA reports has been made in accordance with time of submission, as tabulated in Table 3.1. The timing of submission of an EIA report corresponding to the stage of project planning cycle has been divided into nine classifications. The nine classifications are ranked from "high distinction" to "failure". In addition, the corresponding environmental issues and

Table 3.1 Classification of EIA reports by timing of submission (project planning cycle)

Project planning cycle	Report classification	EIA issue	Environmental planning cycle	Project approval
Project identification	0	Is the project environmentally sound?	Exploring environmentally sound projects	Own approval or memorandum of understanding
Sourcing for technology or license	1	Is the technology most advanced and clean?	Assessments for environmentally sound technology	Business transactions, technology transfer, and license agreement
Prefeasibility/siting decision	2	Is the proposed site environmentally least sensitive?	Baseline study and submission of preliminary assessments report	DOE clearance
Feasibility/project design	3	Does the project design incorporate all the required pollution control and other environmental mitigating measures?	Extended cost/benefit analysis and submission of complete or detailed EIA report	EIA report to be approved by the director general of DOE, prior to license to be granted by relevant government agencies, or lease to be given, land conversion or change of ownership approval by state government
Contract	4	Are sufficient environmental and safeguard specifications in contract documents and agreements?	Submission of plans on pollution control and other environmental mitigating measures	
Detailed design	5	Is the design complying with all the specifications?		Budget approval

				Written permission
Tendering	6	Is there budget for environmental control and other environmental mitigating measures in the tender exercise and award?		
Development and construction	7	Are project development and construction closely supervised?	Environmental monitoring	Approval by land, resources, safety, health, environment, and local authorities
Commissioning	8	Does the project meet all set standards and conditions?	Monitoring and project auditing	Certification by safety, health, environment, and local authorities
Operation and maintenance	9	Is the project fully complying with the standards all the time?	Source and environmental monitoring	Approval by the relevant federal, state and environment authorities
Abandonment/end of project life	X	Are there significant residual environmental impacts?	Continued environmental monitoring	

Key classification
1 – high distinction; 2 – distinction; 3 – high credit; 4 – credit; 5 – simple credit; 6 – low credit; 7 – low pass; 8 – just pass; 9 – fail.

requirements for project approval have also been identified for the various stages of project planning. For example, the submission of an EIA report at the stage of project identification or sourcing for technology is classified as Class 1 and given "high distinction", whilst reports submitted towards the end of project construction or commissioning fall under Class 8 and are ranked "low pass".

An EIA report submitted at the commencement of the project identification stage will give an opportunity to project planners to exhaust environmental issues and to find solutions to them prior to project implementation. When undesirable significant adverse environmental impacts are identified, alternatives which are environmentally acceptable should be found. This exercise should be repeated until an acceptable solution is found.

(iv) Consultation

Although there is no requirement for notification and a project proponent is under no formal obligation to consult the DOE about his proposal before submission of his EIA report, there are practical reasons for doing so. The DOE and other relevant departments will often have useful information, in particular data on environmental quality or local problems, as well as knowing aspects of the project most likely to be of concern and requiring emphasis in the EIA report. It would be beneficial for all concerned if project approval authorities could advise potential project proponents as soon as a project is conceived to check with the DOE to confirm that EIA is required. By doing this, the issues of timing can be settled.

3.6.3 EIA in Canada

The cases described so far have been illustrations of the process of EIA in developing countries. It may be useful to look briefly at the process in a developed country, to understand the maturity of the process by virtue of their longer experience in the practice of EIA. The process of EIA as carried out in Canada is outlined here.

Canada introduced EIA as a planning tool in 1974, closely following the adoption of EIA in the USA. However, EIA did not have a legislative basis. The federal environmental assessment and review process (EARP) came into effect in 1974. The process was further strengthened in 1977 and in 1984 the EARP guidelines were issued by an order-in-council. These guidelines underwrite the EARP in Canada (Figure 3.8).

Briefly, these guidelines include:
- onus, documentation, instructions on how to do;
- duties of;

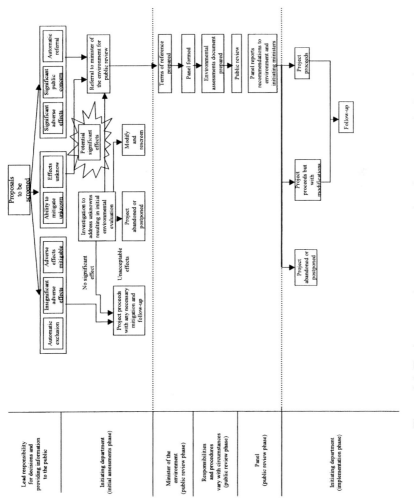

Figure 3.8 Environmental assessment and review process in Canada

67

- initiating departments, proponents, panels, and reviews;
- initial assessment categories, technical methods, information required, definition of effects, format considerations;
- public consultations;
- quantifying effects criteria (magnitude, risk, prevalence, etc.), thresholds of concerns, mitigation measures, monitoring and follow-up;
- activities which may need a referral to the public panel review stage;
- information to be included in the report to the Minister of the Environment.

The process, which has several stages, is applied to any undertaking for which the federal government has a decision-making role. The projects requiring EIA under Canadian law are defined in the form of two lists, a mandatory study list and an exclusion list. EA requirement does not apply to private sector projects or activities unless federal funding or federal Crown land is involved. The eventual decision on project approval or rejection resides with the Minister of the Environment. EARP also would apply to federal agencies providing aid in other countries, like the Canadian International Development Agency (CIDA), but the publishing of results depends on the consent of recipient countries.

The onus and authority for making the assessment rests with the government department that is undertaking the proposal or initiative. However, the Department of the Environment also becomes involved, because of the environmental assessment and review office which oversees the process.

3.6.3.1 The process

The Canadian federal government EIA procedure has two main phases – an initial assessment and a public review. The most noteworthy point about the Canadian EIA process is the strong element of public participation both at the scoping as well as at the detailed EIA stages. All project-related documents are made public. The scope of the EIA is determined by the terms of reference (TOR) and public input in the scoping process.

Initial assessments (IA) are a screening process to determine potential environmental impacts and directly related social impacts that a project could create. It is carried out by the initiating department early in the planning process. The assessments are documented and made available to all interested parties at the federal environmental assessment and review office (FEARO). Actions that could allay or avoid important environmental impacts identified in the initial assessment must be incorporated in any proposal that proceeds to the next step.

After IA, four courses of action become possible, as shown in Figure 3.8, depending on the potential effects identified. If insignificant potential environmental damage is discerned, or if effects can be allayed by known means, the proposal may proceed to implementation.

If significant potentially adverse effects are identified, or if public concern is high enough, the initiating minister must refer the proposal to the Minister of the Environment for an independent panel review. In cases where adverse environmental impacts are unknown, the initiating department must undertake an in-depth study, or initial environmental evaluation, and then decide if the proposal needs a public review. In the final alternative, where potential adverse environmental effects identified by the initial assessment are not acceptable, the initiating department must either modify and reassess, or abandon the project proposal.

Proposals with identified significant environmental effects are subject to a public review which entails a detailed examination of potential environmental and direct social effects. This review is carried out by an independent, ad hoc panel appointed by the Minister of the Environment and composed of mainly non-government people. The terms of reference can include general socio-economic and technological assessments but the main responsibility is to investigate potentially adverse environmental effects of a proposal, the scope, and public views.

The second phase, that is, public reviews (PR), is very important because they provide a neutral forum for consultation and eventually lead to improved coordination and delivery of government services. Public participation in development project proposals establishes the major issues involved and helps ensure that environmental and socio-economic concerns are involved in development-related decision-making.

FURTHER READING

1 Macdonald, M. *What's The Difference: A Comparison of EA in Industrial and Developing Countries; Environmental Assessment and Development*, ed. R. Goodland and V. Edmundson, A World Bank IAIA Symposium (1994), Washington DC, pp 29–34.
2 Reynolds, P. J. "Canada's Environmental Assessment Procedure for a Water-Related Development", in *Environmental Impact Assessment for Developing Countries*, ed. A. K. Biswas and S. B. C. Agarwala, Butterworth-Heinemann, Oxford, 1992.

4

EIA methods

4.1 Introduction

EIA methods are usually taken to include the means of gathering and analysing data, the sequence of steps in preparing a report, and the procedure (who does what and when). The essential ingredients of the EIA process, such as scoping, IEE, and detailed EIA, are universally agreed upon, but EIA techniques vary widely.

Considering the complexity of the interacting systems that constitute the environment, and the infinite variety of possible impacting actions, it seems unlikely that a single method would be able to meet all the above criteria. The general applicability of all methods also has to be balanced against the administrative and economic constraints within which they are employed.

There is no single approved method for an EIA study. Therefore, what is important is the ability to think in a systematic way:

- to understand the interactions of the environment and technological change;
- to meet, in a practical way, the needs of the development manager; and
- to follow the fundamental process of preparing an EIA.

A distinction between EIA methods and tools must be carefully noted. The four fundamental methods which are commonly used as methods for conducting an EIA are checklists, matrices, networks, and overlays. Tools for EIA support the application of the above basic methods. Some of the commonly used tools are prediction models, geographical information systems, and expert systems. These tools can be used for purposes other than EIA.

Generally, more than one method and tool are used, depending on the tier of the EIA process, to accomplish the best results. Recommendations for the use of methods and tools are made in the form of a comprehensive flow chart (Fig. 4.1).

4.2 Checklists

Checklists serve as reminder of all possible relationships and impacts, out of which a set tailored for the specific assignment may be chosen.

It is always possible that an important local factor may be left out of the generic checklists that appear in EIA manuals. The guidelines from the ADB (various years) and the sourcebook developed by the World Bank are good examples because they stimulate investigation.

Checklists are designed to establish whether a proposed project is likely to have negative impacts on the environment. For such projects, all possible negative impacts must be assessed in detail in relation to the project's positive impacts. This is accomplished in the next steps of the EIA.

The checklists help people in key positions to become more aware of what they should be looking for when assessing a proposed project. They may also help to develop a higher degree of awareness of the environmental aspects of a project.

Checklists can be classified into descriptive and weight-scaling categories.

4.2.1 Descriptive checklists

The purpose of a descriptive checklist is to provide a list of important issues for the purpose of identification and scoping.

One of the simplest forms of the checklists is the one with project-specific questions. Box 4.1 shows an example of a checklist developed by the Norwegian Agency for Development Cooperation (NORAD) in assessing industrial projects. One must be careful of the questionnaire-type checklists where the answers can be "yes" or "no". These discourage thinking and may provide a false sense of assessment. If questions are asked, they should be phrased such as "to what extent?", "under what conditions?" and "in what ways?" rather than simply "does A result in

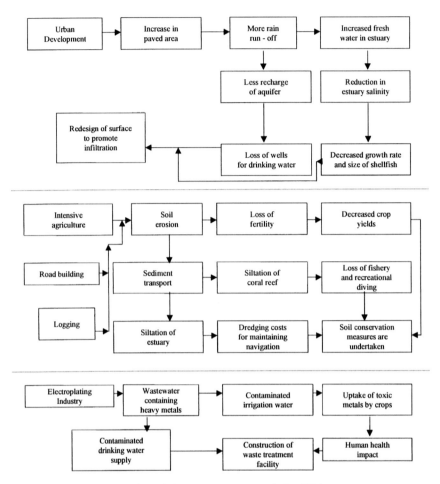

Figure 4.1 Three examples of the systems approach for EIA
Source: How to Assess Environmental Impacts on Tropical Islands and Coastal Areas. A Training Manual prepared for the South Pacific Regional Environment Programme by R. A. Carpenter, J. E. Maragos. Published by Environment and Policy Institute, East-West Center, Hawaii, 1989.

B?". However, the questionnaire-based checklists can serve as a good starting point for the purpose of project screening.

Checklists can be also developed based on issues. The issues can be later graded to identify those of significance based on the project and environment features, i.e., relevance. Issues of high significance can be later decomposed into responsible "activities" and "components of concern" to develop mitigation, protection, and monitoring measures in the succeeding levels of an EIA. Box 4.2 shows an illustration of an issue-

Box 4.1 Application of checklist for initial screening of industrial projects
(NORAD)

Environmental impacts often tend to appear in the form of chains of cause
and effect. If the first link in the chain is revealed, the subsequent impacts
will also be uncovered. In order to reduce the number of questions in each
checklist, the questions are most often related to the first link in the chain.

Industrial project

This will include all industrial projects involving a sizeable consumption of
natural resources and/or increasing pollution. Thermal power plants are
also included in this category. The project should be submitted to a more
detailed assessment if it fulfils one or more of the criteria set out below, or if
insufficient information is available to answer "no" with a reasonable
degree of certainty.
  Will the project:
1 Lead to substantial pollution of water, air, or soil?
2 Create waste disposal problems?
3 Affect areas which support animal and plant life worthy of protection or
  affect an especially vulnerable ecosystem?
4 Affect areas with historic remains or landscape elements which are of
  importance to the population?
5 Create a risk of accidents which may have serious consequences for the
  local population and the natural environment?
6 Change the way of life of the local population in such a way that it leads
  to considerably increased pressure on the natural resource base?
7 Lead to major conflicts with regard to existing land use and ownership of
  land?
8 Obstruct, or lead to considerable changes in the local population's
  exploitation or use of natural resources other than those directly affected
  by the project?

based checklist developed for projects on power development. The issue-
based checklists thus assist in the exercise of scoping and IEE.

Descriptive checklists can also be exhaustive to capture the impacts
during the various stages of the project and to provide a format for the
assessor to identify obvious mitigations. Here, the checklist can be used
for the purpose of scoping and IEE. Box 4.3 presents an example of a
detailed checklist developed by the ADB for fisheries and aquaculture
projects.

4.2.2 Weighted-scale checklists

Weighted-scale checklists are used to:
• recognize the relative differences between the importance of environmental issues;

Box 4.2 Environmentally significant issues for a power development project

- Expropriation of land which negatively affects aquatic habitat for biota, aquaculture, fishing, recreation, domestic/industrial water use, irrigation, recreation, water transportation.
- Construction activities of facilities and transmission corridors which negatively affect aquatic habitat, water quality, aquaculture, domestic/industrial water use, recreation due to chemical contamination, shoreline changes (e.g., riparian vegetation removal, retaining walls, diking), and sedimentation.
- Effects of discharge of SO_2 NO_x, TSP (total suspended particles) on air quality.
- Noise and flying rock from blasting and drilling operations.
- Increased ship traffic for coal transport.
- Effects of noise from boiler operation, gas turbines, and cooling towers on livestock.
- Social problems associated with integration of migrant construction workers with local community.
- Use of herbicides for maintenance of transmission corridors can negatively affect surface and groundwater quality.
- Disruption of crop farming by construction of transmission lines.
- Effects of SO_2 emissions on crop farming.
- Loss of forest area due to construction of transmission lines.
- Illegal logging from access roads for power developments.
- Effects of transmission line networks on animal and plant diversity.
- Effects of thermal discharge on aquatic ecosystem.
- Disposal and indiscriminate dumping of construction waste materials.
- Effects of channel dredging for ship traffic on aquatic habitat.
- Effects of earthworks on dust production.
- Emergency and disaster response (e.g., forest fire, earthquake) at power plants.
- Dams and impoundments in rivers cause major changes to riverine ecosystems, which can significantly affect water quality, habitat for aquatic biota, aquatic resources harvesting (e.g., fishing, aquaculture), recreation, domestic/industrial water use, water transportation, local water table levels and groundwater flow.
- Regulated flows and lake (impoundment) levels which affect habitat for aquatic and terrestrial biota, fishing, navigation, recreation, domestic/industrial water use.
- Impounded water provides habitat for vectors that carry disease.
- Effects of cooling water withdrawal (entrainment and impingement) for power plants on aquatic life.
- Effects of fuel storage on dust and safety of employees and local community.
- Risk of spills or accidents associated with fuel transport.
- Fate and effects of leachates of disposed sludge in landfills.
- Effects of groundwater and surface water consumption (pumping) on water supply and local ecosystems.
- Treatment and disposal of sewage generated at the power plant site.

Box 4.3 Checklist for environmental effects commonly associated with projects in fisheries and aquaculture

Fisheries projects (capture of species) and aquaculture projects for growing selected species often involve the entire gamut of potential adverse environmental impacts, including impacts on natural resources, economic development values, and quality-of-life values.

A Environmental problems related to site selection (which might be avoided or minimized by better site selection)

1 Conflicts with other site (waterway) uses. Such other uses may be the use of the same water area for tourism/recreation and navigation, and for creating more agricultural land by filling the area.
2 Hazards of serious pollution. Sites should preferably be upstream of pollution-emitting facilities (such as oil refineries). Single slug discharges can raise havoc with entire fishery/aquaculture (F/A) operations. If pollution hazards do exist, the F/A plan should ensure careful emissions control.
3 Remoteness from market requires freezer storage.
4 For aquaculture, steady availability of freshwater supply. Need to ensure year-round availability of supply which is basic for project economics. For dam/reservoir releases, this may conflict with other water use allocations in drought periods. If water is drawn from irrigation canals, canal O&M plan must enable steady delivery of water (not complete shutdown of delivery when cleaning/repairing canals).
5 For aquaculture, costs for importing needed foods.
6 Water quality and quantity. Water quality (WQ) suited to the project's needs is basic for F/A operations. This includes, for fisheries, impacts on WQ likely to result from pollution inflows, changes in local hydrology from probable upstream dams or other river development, and possible seawater influx during storms.
7 Hurricane and typhoon hazards. Facility design must consider these hazards (for example, the aquaculture facilities in Laguna Lake near Manila are designed to minimize this problem).
8 Labour supply problem including skilled labour needs.
9 Local soil properties. For aquaculture projects, the local soils may not be suitable for furnishing structural stability for berms made from the soil, and may be excessively permeable, and moreover some soils can adversely affect water quality. See item (6).
10 Resettlement.
11 Availability of species juvenile stock.
12 Peripheral development hazard. This concerns the effects of F/A waterbody region, including destruction of mangroves on which the project may be critically dependent for food.
13 Site filling hazards. This is the hazard when accelerating erosion in the upstream watershed reduces the volume of the water body used for the F/A operations.
14 Security from poachers. Poaching, either by outsiders or by insiders, can ruin the project economics. In some cases, it may be desirable to organize the overall operations into a series of sections of a size suited to operation and control by a single family management.

Box 4.3 (cont.)

B   Environmental hazards relating to inadequate design

1 Item (A) (1) to (12). Design omissions on items (A) (1) to (12) involve the same problems as noted under (A). Design expertise is needed to minimize/offset unavoidable adverse effects due to project location.

2 Unrealistic O&M assumptions. Such unrealistic assumptions on the available quality of O&M can greatly undermine and negate the project economics and result in serious adverse environmental impacts in a variety of ways, including many of those described in (A).

3 Inattention to special construction requirements. Customary types of plans and specifications must be modified to provide for incorporation of the environmental protection parameter into the plans/specifications and for construction stage environmental monitoring. It may involve periodic checks on the actual environmental impact of the project following completion of construction vis-à-vis those projected at the time of project appraisal.

4 Salability of product. For both F/A projects, an important criterion for economic viability is the presence of a suitable market for the product and the capture or raising of species which will be favoured by the intended customers.

5 Middlemen problems. One of the socio-economic problems commonly involved in protecting F/A is the advent, during the operations phase, of immigrants who take over the middleman's role, buying the fish from the fisherman for re-sale. Without any control, this practice can reduce the fisherman's earnings to unfair and unacceptably low levels.

6 Dredging and filling. These activities must be carefully planned so as not to destroy precious ecology.

7 Disease hazards. Planning of an aquaculture venture must give attention to fishery disease hazards, which can drastically reduce yields. The selection of species has to be appropriate from the point of view of previous aquaculture disease hazards in the area and the availability of feasible control methods.

8 Socio-economics. In addition to item (5), it is necessary to favour local population labour needs, especially those resettled by the project, and families of fishermen in the vicinity whose livelihoods will be impaired by the project, rather than imported labour (to become permanent new residents).

9 Downstream water quality. Discharges from aquaculture projects (especially those with high rates of productivity employing special aeration and feeding techniques) may need to be treated (by ponding) to prevent downstream WQ and beneficial uses.

10 New species hazards. Care must be exercised in introducing new species for aquaculture, i.e., to assess the impacts on existing fishery species distribution in the area and region.

11 Permit system. A competent management system should be established to manage the new F/A to ensure the proper selection of fishing rights by fisherman, financial assistance to enable them to get started, for preventing over fishing and illegal fishing methods, for assistance in controlling middlemen (item [5]), and assistance in marketing based on the use of an appropriate fee system for recovering costs.

Box 4.3 (cont.)

12 Fishing village sanitation. Proper planning and administration (see item [11]) and guidance in the establishment/growth of fishing villages in the project vicinity should be provided to ensure that these do not turn into "sanitation messes" that pollute the F/A waterbody and threaten public health.

C Environmental hazards related to construction stage

1 For F/A projects, common construction hazards for the environment include: (1) dredging/filling of ecologically sensitive areas; (2) discharge of silt which diffuses and permeates sensitive areas and/or recreation beaches in the vicinity; and (3) interference with navigation (including fishermen's travel) including silt deposition into navigation channels.

D Environmental problems relating to operations stage

1 O&M capabilities. A common problem in many developing countries is the failure to furnish the O&M specified in the design, even when the design specifications are realistic, appropriate, and affordable.
2 Monitoring. Another common problem is the failure to implement continuing periodic post-construction environmental monitoring as specified in the project feasibility and/or EIA. Thus, inadequacies in design assumptions and/or O&M may not be detected. Such feedback is essential for delineating and implementing corrective measures needed for acceptable environmental protection.

E Critical environmental review criteria

These are criteria of special interest to an environmentalist which should be applied to all major infrastructure or regional development planning projects.
1 Will the project cause unwarranted losses in precious/irreplaceable natural or other resources?
2 Will the project make an unwarranted accelerated use of scarce resources in favour of short-term rather than long-term economic needs?
3 Will the project result in unwarranted hazards to endangered species?
4 Will the project tend to intensify undesirable migration from rural to urban sectors to an unwarranted degree?
5 Will the project adversely depreciate the national energy/foreign exchange situation to an unwarranted degree? Will there be intensification of national socio-economic imbalances due to increase in affluent/poor income gap?

Source: Asian Development Bank

- allow for scoring and aggregation of impacts arising from the issues on the environmental components; and
- permit a quantitative comparison between alternatives.

The use of weighted-scale checklists thus encompasses IEE. One such weighted-scale checklist referred to in the literature is the Environmental Evaluation System (EES) (developed by the Battelle Columbus Laboratories, USA). EES was developed in 1973 to address water resource development projects. Because environmental properties are not commonly measured in similar units, it is difficult to evaluate the net environmental effects of a project and to make trade-offs in selecting among alternatives. EES attempts to solve this problem by transforming all parameters into similar units.

EES provides for environmental impact evaluation in four major categories: ecology, environmental pollution, esthetics, and human interest. These four categories are further broken down into 18 environmental components and finally into 78 environmental parameters. For each parameter, a value function is developed using a Delphi technique which would translate the sensitivity or scale of the parameter into equivalent environmental impact units (EIUs). To allow a correct aggregation of EIUs across the components and categories, each parameter is set an importance known as a parameter importance unit (PIU). PIUs thus provide weights for the purpose of aggregation. Results of using the EES include a total weighted score in EIU with and without the proposed project; the difference between the two scores is one measure of environmental impact.

The EES technique consists of three steps. Step 1 involves transforming parameter estimates into EIUs. In the evaluation system, environmental quality is defined in the following fashion. It is a value between 0 and 1, where 0 denotes extremely bad and 1 denotes very good quality. The transformation of a parameter estimate into environmental quality is achieved through the use of a value function relating the various levels of parameter estimates to the appropriate levels of environmental quality.

Step 2 consists of the weighing of parameters. Each parameter used in the EES represents only a part of the total environment. It is therefore important to view these parts together as part of the environmental system. To reflect the relative importance of the EES parameters, a total of 1000 points or PIU are distributed among the parameters. Sociopsychological scaling techniques and the Delphi procedure were used to quantify the value judgments. The process consisted of ranked pairwise comparisons and controlled feedback.

In step 3 EES is used to evaluate the expected future condition of environmental quality without the project, and with the project. The former evaluation is an expression of the modified current condition of the environment, whereas the latter is an expected (predicted) condition of the environment with the proposed development. A difference in EIUs between these two conditions constitutes either an adverse (loss in EIU) or a beneficial (gain in EIU) impact.

4.2.3 Advantages of the checklist method

- Checklists provide all possible relationships and impacts, out of which a set tailored for the specific assignment may be chosen.
- Checklists help people in responsible positions to become more aware of what they should be looking for when assessing a proposed project.
- Checklists may also help to produce a higher degree of awareness of the environmental aspects of a project.
- Quantification of impacts is possible using the weighted-scale method.

4.2.4 Limitations of the checklist method

- Descriptive checklists may be exhaustive, including the impacts during the various stages of the project. However, no quantitative information is provided regarding magnitude and degree of impact.
- Another important drawback of this method is the way it attempts to compartmentalize the environment. Environmental systems comprise a complex web of interrelated parts, often incorporating feedback loops. This fact is not included in the weighted checklists. This method should be therefore used with some caution. Its quantitative features may be used to distinguish between alternatives and so should be used only when a comparision needs a quantitative resolution.
- The main drawback of the checklist method is the inability to relate individual activities to environmental components affected by these activities.

4.3 Matrix

Matrices relate activities to environmental components so that the box at each intersection can be used to indicate a possible impact. The term "matrix" does not have any mathematical implication, but is merely a style of presentation.

The matrix can be used to identify impacts by systematically checking each development activity against each environmental component. If it was thought that a particular development activity was to affect an environmental component, a mark is placed in the cell at the intersection of the activity and the environmental component. A matrix analysis can systematically identify potentially important effects demanding more careful attention or analysis or focus attention on important possible effects that might otherwise be overlooked. Matrix is thus an extension of the basic checklist.

There are three types of commonly used matrices:
• descriptive matrices;
• symbolic and presentation matrices;
• scaled/weighted or numeric matrices.

4.3.1 Descriptive matrix

In descriptive matrices, short written descriptions are used. For each phase of a project, that is, site selection, construction, operation, and closure (if applicable), the various impacts associated with each activity are defined and short descriptions are provided. There is no scaling or quantification of these impacts. Table 4.1 presents a structure of the descriptive matrix for a quarry.

4.3.2 Symbolized matrix

A most noteworthy matrix presentation essentially improves the communication between the impact analysts, decision makers, and the public. In the symbolized matrices, symbols are used to capture the understanding of the impacts.

Environmental impacts may be described by words such as "important" or "significant". These subjective, qualitative words are difficult to deal with because their interpretation depend on cultural values and specific circumstances. Even when quantitative data are available, they must be gauged against some standard and often there is none or at least none widely accepted. There are, however, some useful guides for ranking impacts or assessing impact assessment.

There are several factors that must be taken into account when assessing the significance of an environmental impact arising from a project. The factors are interrelated and must not be considered in isolation. For a particular impact some factors may carry more weight than others, but it is the combination of all the factors that determines significance.

An example is to use abbreviations and scales, e.g., S for short term and L for long term or 10 to denote a very high order of the impact and 1 to denote almost negligible impact, etc. In this way, a symbolized matrix becomes a combination of descriptive and numeric scales. There are, however, some useful guides for the grading or classification of impacts. These are listed below:
• Sign of the impact
  Positive or negative. This is unfortunately not that simple.

Table 4.1 Environmental matrix for a quarry

Phase	Development action	Social	Physical	Biological
Planning	Consents, district plan, EIS timetable	Law, regulation, public participation, employment, land values, alternative sites, justification, risks and anxieties, cultural/historical	Location of access road	Water table effects on adjacent land
Engineering design	Design of quarrying plan, resolve environmental factors, evaluate options	Landscape effects	Design of quarry, restoration plan	Design of drainage system, including sediment traps to protect water quality in the river
Construction	Access road, drainage system, site crushing plant, energy supply, traffic discharge, stormwaters, silt, sewage, site staff facilities	Cultural/historical, safety, noise, vibrations, effect on farm animals	Disposal of stripping, stability, nuisance, landform noise, blasting, drilling	Sedimentation, surface water pollution
Operation	Stripping overburden, drilling, blasting, excavation, crushing, loading, traffic, review and adjust environmental measures	Landscape, farm animals, noise/vibration/dust, emissions, safety/risk, staff facilities, working environment	Landscape effect	Progressive restoration plan, sedimentation, surface water pollution
Termination	Remove plant, check stability, replace topsoil, plant ground cover, maintenance	Safety, landscape restoration		Maintain and monitor sediment traps

- Magnitude
  This is defined as the probable severity of each potential impact. Will the impact be irreversible? If reversible, what will be the rate of recovery or adaptability of an impact area? Will the activity preclude the use of the impacted area for other purposes? The answer to these questions may be difficult and may have to be speculated on a subjective basis. The size often depends on the source release, mitigation measures adopted, if any, and the assimilative capacity of the receiving environment, etc.
- Type of change: reversible or irreversible
  Irreversibilities always command attention because they signal a loss of future options. Species extinction, severe soil erosion, and habitat destruction are examples of irreversible changes. Pollution of groundwater is often irreversible because of its slow movement. Urbanization of agricultural land is virtually impossible to undo once the land use trend has begun.
- Prevalence
  This is defined as the likely eventual extent of the impact as, for example, the cumulative effect(s) of a number of stream crossings. Each one taken separately might represent a localized impact of small importance and magnitude but a number of such crossings could result in a widespread effect. Coupled with the determination of cumulative effects is the remoteness of an effect from the activity causing it. The deterioration of fish production resulting from access roads could affect subsistence fishing in an area many miles away, and for months or years after the project activity has ceased.
- Duration and frequency
  The significance of duration and frequency is reflected in the following questions. Will the activity be long term, short term, or sporadic? If the activity is intermittent, will it allow for recovery during inactive periods?
- Risk
  This is defined as the probability of serious environmental effects. To accurately assess the risk, both the project activity and the area of the environment affected must be well known and understood.
- Importance
  This is defined as the value that is attached to an environmental component in its present state. For example, a local community may value a short stretch of river for bathing or a small swamp for hunting. Alternatively, the impacted component may be of regional, provincial or even national importance.
- Mitigatability
  Are solutions to problems available? Existing technology may provide a solution to a siting problem expected during construction of

an access road, or to bank erosion resulting from a new stream configuration.

- Understanding

   For example, if an access road is to cross a stream and the assessor does not know the extent of use of that stream (for fish spawning, fish migration, subsistence fishing, river transport, etc.), then the impact would be classed as unknown. Similarly, the nature of the river crossing (ford, bridge, ferry, or causeway) may not yet have been planned and so the significance of the environmental impact of that crossing is therefore unknown.

The assessment of significance is best done by holding at least two group discussion meetings involving interdisciplinary expertise.

The most frequently used presentation of a comparison of alternatives is a matrix, in which +, 0 and – show how each alternative affects the different environmental aspects. This can be a useful way to provide a quick overview of the differences between the alternatives.

- the impacts of each alternative are evaluated against a reference (usually the existing situation); or
- for each alternative, it is shown how it contributes to the environmental objectives; or
- the impacts of each alternative are compared with the preferred alternative.

+ + and – – give extra possibilities for differentiation.

In each case it is important that the significance of the symbols is properly defined. If necessary, a reference should guide the reader to more ample information (Table 4.2).

Table 4.2 Example of plus/minus matrix on the theme "Why does the proposed activity improve the soil condition?"

	Existing situation	Proposed activity	Process alternative	Environmentally most friendly
Air	0	–	–	0
Soil	0	+	+	+
Surface water	0	–	0	0
Waste	0	+	+	+
Noise	0	–	–	–
Safety	0	(–)	(–)	(–)
Nature	0	0	0	0
Energy	0	–	0	+
Costs	0	–	–	–

Legend: – deterioration compared to the existing situation; + improvement; 0 no difference; (–) insignificant deterioration.

Table 4.3 Numeric matrix lending a quick but factual overview

	Lead concentration in air ($\mu g/m^3$)	NO$_x$ emission ($\mu g/m^3$)	Noise level at periphery area (dB(A))	Hazardous waste produced tons/year
Alternative 1	0.8	35	55	2674
Alternative 2	0.7	20	50	2350
Background level existing situation	1.0	80	43	–
Predicted background level 2005	1.2	110	45	–
Environmental standard	1.5	100	55	–

4.3.3 Numeric and scaled matrices

4.3.3.1 Simple numeric matrix

Simple numeric matrices are useful to derive facts to assist in showing the degree of impact or help in making a comparision. Table 4.3 presents a simple numeric matrix used for assessing the alternatives at an IEE level.

Numeric, ordinal, and interval scaled evaluations are given by numerical scores. Leopold *et al.* (1971) use a scale of 1 to 10 to score two impact attributes – significance and importance. Fischer and Davies use one score on a scale of −5 to +5 to indicate both positive and negative degrees of impact. An interscaled impact matrix has been attempted by Ross (discussed under mathematical matrices).

The second option is to lay down separate matrices describing each impact characteristic. For example, one can make a matrix presentation to show only the size attribute impacts, while another shows the nature of the impact, etc. It is also possible to use some order of shading or colour coding to draw attention to some of the critical cells. Against the apparent disadvantage of handling more matrices, the advantage of improved communication, as well as improved focus, lies in such separate presentations. We can call this approach a thematic matrix approach.

To get a quick overview of the results of an EIA, a comparison of alternatives can be presented as a graph, a map, a diagram, or some other kind of picture. Colours or shades of grey can enhance the presentation (Table 4.4).

The advantage of using colours is that they can be combined in a matrix with factual information. Shades of green can show the positive effects, and shades of red, the negative. This gives an indication of which environmental compartments can be expected to contain problems and which alternatives are most promising.

Table 4.4 Matrix using colours

Objectives	Indicator	Route 1	Route 2	Route 3
Limitation of car kilometres	Amount of car kilometres	293.700	297.700	293.700
Limit expansion of infrastructure	Kilometres new motorway	7	10	7
Nature conservation	Dissection of ecological zones	yes	no	Mitigation partly possible

4.3.3.2 Scaled matrices

Weighted-scale matrices typically use a scale of 1 to 10 to score two impact attributes, significance and importance. One of the most popular scaled matrices is the "Leopold matrix" named after Dr Luna Leopold of the US Geological Survey who developed it in the early 1970s. All development activities are listed across the top of the matrix and all environmental components that might be impacted are listed down the side. A Leopold matrix attempts to assign numerical ratings of magnitude and importance so that the completed matrices for alternative sites or technologies could each be added and compared. In the original Leopold matrix, scores from a 1–10 scale can be assigned to describe the importance and magnitude of individual impacts. Importance refers to the significance of an impact and the magnitude of its scale and extent. Leopold-type matrices are easy to use and are perhaps the most widely employed and successful of all EIA methods. Figure 4.2 shows a portion of a Leopold matrix, as used for the comparision of alternatives.

Another approach is the environmental impact matrix, with and without mitigation (from Biswas and Agarwal, 1992). This is a conventional technique for summarizing environmental impacts utilizing the matrix method. Initially, the predicted impacts are converted into an ordinal scale (ranking) of impact severity, as in the following example.

Severity	Impact score
No impact	0
Negligible	1
Minor (slight or short term)	2
Moderate	3
Major (irreversible or long term)	4
Severe (permanent)	5

A positive sign denotes a beneficial impact, while a negative sign denotes an adverse impact.

Evaluation criteria	Alternative quarry locations				
	Fraser's Quarry	Marsden Site	Penrose Quarry	Timms Hill	Garner's Quarry
Practical factors					
Accessibility	■	●	◆	◆	◆
Capacity	■	◆	◆	◆	■
Services	◆	■	◆	◆	◆
Ownership	■	■	■	●	■
Security	◆	■	◆	■	■
Current availability	◆	◆	◆	■	■
Economic factors					
Need for transfer station	Yes	Yes	No	No	No
Existing infrastructure	◆	■	●	◆	◆
Road condition	❖	●	●	■	■
Cover material	■	■	■	■	■
Operating cost	□	■	□	□	□
Environmental					
Adequate separation	◆	◆	●	■	◆
Hydrology	■	■	■	◆	■
Topography	◆	◆	■	◆	■
Visibility	◆	◆	■	◆	◆
Conservation value	◆	■	◆	◆	◆
Traffic route	◆	■	◆	■	◆

◆ Site satisfies criterion; ● Unfavourable; ■ Partial satisfaction; □ Information unavailable; ❖ Not relevant.

Source: Module on Selected Topics in Environmental Management. UNESCO Series of Learning Materials in Engineering Sciences, UNESCO, 1993.

Figure 4.2 Site comparison matrix for a quarry

A significant value (weighting) is attached to each environmental component (independent of the predicted levels of impact) based upon some expert or consensual (Delphi) system. Individual impact scores can then be calculated as the product of impact severity and significance. These may be summed by row and/or column to gauge the net impact of the project on a particular environmental component or, conversely, the net effect of a single project activity on the environment as a whole.

In this way, project alternatives can be systematically compared, and possible mitigation measures can be explored. In addition, this method can draw attention to the most significant impacts in the matrix, as revealed by individual cell scores. This procedure can also be used to identify negative impacts on environmental components that surpass a critical threshold. Such instances will have to be addressed through mitigation or project alternatives (Tables 4.5 and 4.6)

Table 4.5 Environmental impact matrix without mitigation

Environmental parameters	Importance value	Impacting actions											Impact score
		Premining phase				Operational phase							
		A	B	C	D	E	F	G	H	I	J	K	
Air quality	100	−1	−1			−2		−2			−1		−700
Water resources	75		−1				−1			−1			−225
Water quality	100						−2	−1		−1			−500
Noise and vibration	75	−1	−1	−1	+1	−1		−1			−1		−450
Land use	150	−3	−1		+1	−2		−1					−900
Forests and vegetation	150	−4			+1	−2		−1					−450
Wildlife	50	−2			+1	−1					−1		−150
Human settlements	75	−1	+1		+1				+1				+75
Health	100				+1	−3						+1	−100
Infrastructures and support services	50									+2	+1	+2	+250
Employment	50	+1	+1			+2				+1			+250
Places of tourist or archaeological importance	20												0
Total	1000	−1350	−275	−75	+525	−1000	−275	−525	+75	−25	−175	+200	−2900

+ sign shows beneficial impact; − sign shows adverse impact.

A, land acquisition and transformation; B, civil works construction; C, erection of mechanical and mining equipment; D, green belt formation; E, mining operations including CHP; F, disposal of liquid effluent; G, disposal of solid wastes on land for reclamation; H, housing provision; I, provision of water, sewage, electricity, and other civic amenities; J, transportation; K, medical facilities.

Table 4.6 Environmental impact matrix without mitigation

Environmental parameters	Importance value	Impacting actions												Impact score
		Premining phase					Operational phase							
		A	B	C	D	E	F	G	H	I	J	K	L	
Air quality	100	−1	−1		+1	−1		−1			−1		+1	−300
Water resources	75		−1				−1			−1				−225
Water quality	100						−1	−1					+1	−100
Noise and vibration	75	−1	−1	−1	+1	−1		−1			−1			−375
Land use	150	−3	−1		+1	−1		+1					+2	−150
Forests and vegetation	150	−4			+1								+4	+150
Wildlife	50	−2			+1	−1					−1		+1	−100
Human settlements	75	−1	+1		+1	−1			+1					+75
Health	100											+1		+100
Infrastructures and support services	50									+2	+1	+2		+250
Employment	50	+1	+1			+2				+1				+250
Places of tourist or archaeological importance	25				+1	−1								0
Total	1000	−1350	−275	−75	+625	−375	−175	−125	+75	+75	−175	+200	+1150	−425

+ sign shows beneficial impact; − sign shows adverse impact.
A, land acquisition and transformation; B, civil works construction; C, erection of mechanical and mining equipment; D, green belt formation; E, mining operations including CHP; F, disposal of liquid effluent; G, disposal of solid wastes on land for reclamation; H, housing provision; I, provision of water, sewage, electricity, and other civic amenities; J, transportation; K, medical facilities; L, land reclamation.

4.3.4 The component interaction matrix

The component interaction matrix (CIM) developed by Ross was first used in an EIA of five alternative sites for the transshipment of lumber on the Nanaimo estuary, British Columbia. The uniqueness of the area under consideration prompted an investigation of secondary impacts in an attempt to present the full implications of the project proposals.

In a CIM, the environment is represented by a list of environmental components, arranged along both horizontal and vertical axes. Direct dependencies between the components are identified and marked as "1" in the appropriate cells. Interdependencies up to the nth order (i.e., all higher order dependencies) can be determined by the use of a matrix powering procedure.

The Canadian CIM above used 21 environmental components, and 120 first-order dependencies were identified. Matrix manipulation (powering) was performed until fifth-order dependencies had been discovered. From the information revealed by the powering process, a minimum link matrix was derived. All cells of the original CIM were used to contain integer values denoting the length (in terms of intervening nodes) of the shortest linkages connecting the two components. A disruption matrix was also formulated in which the impacts of each project alternative on all primary dependencies were scored on an ordinal scale from 0 to 3.

Provided that the initial identification of dependencies is explicit, the values (derived by mathematical procedures) in the minimum link matrix are substantive. The processes of matrix multiplication are not complicated, but they are tedious for large matrices and would normally require the use of a computer. It is unfortunate that, while the minimum link matrix can indicate the existence and length of a linkage between any two components, the structure of these linkages is not exposed.

The results of the component interaction analysis were not readily incorporated into the overall assessment of the transshipment project. In fact, the ad hoc assessment report of the five Nanaimo Port site proposals made little use of the results displayed in the component interaction, minimum link, and disruption matrices.

The CIM has been reviewed by Clark *et al.* (1981) and Bisset, but has not received much positive comment. The minimum link matrix is useful as a means of communicating the complex structure of the environmental systems likely to be affected by a project.

4.3.5 Advantages of the matrix approach

- A matrix presentation has a better structure framework than the checklist approach. In fact, it makes a summarized analytical presentation of the project and environment-related checklists.

- Matrix structure allows for speculation of impact characteristics, albeit in a subjective way. This provides a gradation in the impacts, thereby providing a focus for further studies, verification, or discussions. It also helps in making priorities on some mitigation measures which are estimated to alleviate the impacts speculated.
- It presents an easily understood summary of a large number of primary impacts.
- It is a generalized but well defined approach, forcing a comprehensive consideration of environmental components and primary impacts.
- It is an easily performed process which can specify the overall character of a project early in the design phase.
- In an extended form, the method can include information about many impact attributes, and clarify the assumptions supporting the assessments.
- Matrices have low resource requirements.

4.3.6 Limitations of the matrix approach

Despite the elegance of matrix presentation, there are certain limitations which need to be addressed.
- Unless weight-scaled impact scores are used, the comparison of many project alternatives is difficult.
- Scaling the multitude of scores contained in a matrix is also not a tractable proposition, as the ability to independently replicate the method is undermined by a dependence on highly subjective judgments.
- The impact characterization step of the matrix involves subjective prediction as well as assessment.
- There is little opportunity for quantification. However, it is possible to accommodate further detailing in the matrix presentation if prediction/evaluation techniques are separately used.
- While developing matrix structure, it becomes apparent that higher order impacts are not accounted for using this approach.

For example, impacts propagate from one component to another and are not necessarily linked directly with the project activities. In the case of a thermal power plant, waste emissions alter the air quality and the altered air quality in turn affects crops, public health, or materials. A water resources project upstream of a river mouth entering the sea, alters the fresh river flow into the sea and this in turn changes the saline zone of the river mouth. This change in the saline zone influences the marine life feeding near the saline wedge, which influences the income of fishermen as well as the marine ecosystem in general. Both these examples question our rudimentary understanding of impacts. This implies that impacts on the nth environmental component can be due to simultaneous and/or successive changes in the other interlinked components.

There is a lot be learned from this improved understanding of impacts.

- In the case of component–component or secondary impacts, the project activity specificity ends. In other words, if a particular project activity alters a particular component, then, regardless of the project activity, this changed component would affect the linked component. For example, if the temperature of the water of the river is raised above a certain threshold (by any activity) then the fish life in the river would be affected.
- Impacts have non-linear relationships and due to the participation of more than one component in some cases, there is the possibility of a delay in their realization, especially in terms of time. Again, delayed impacts do not mean that the "size" of the impact is attenuated. It is possible that the size can be bigger, especially if there are processes such as "biomagnification" or if the receiving environment is fragile (e.g., mangrove ecosystems).
- The matrix style needs to be expanded to allow for component–component interactions. This is technically possible by writing a matrix adjacent to another and so on but it can become rather clumsy if there are multi-component (or multi-order) impacts. One may need here a presentation style which allows one to depict the interconnections in a causal style. Network presentation, discussed later, is perhaps a better choice.
- Writing a single matrix for infrastructure or spatial projects becomes rather difficult. For a thermal power plant, for instance, the impact of waste emissions on air quality depends on whether the region under consideration is mostly downwind or not. If a region (or portion of the neighbouring environment) is beyond a hill, then the waste emissions from the power plant almost get screened. Similar arguments would hold for describing the impacts upstream or downstream of a water resources reservoir. In other words, the impact association attempted in the matrix style assumes homogeneity or isotropy in the region, which is not the case in most situations. This may call for writing more than one (maybe five or six) matrix presentations for a project, describing specific situations happening in the spatial elements. This leads once again to technical as well as communication difficulties. Use of geographical information systems (GIS) coupled with impact assessments methodology becomes an attractive alternative.

4.4 Networks

Investigation of higher order linkages in two dimensions can be carried out by using directional diagrams called networks. Networks, although widely discussed in the EIA literature, have not been used as extensively as matrices and simple checklists. Networks were essentially developed to explicitly consider the secondary, tertiary, and higher order impacts that can arise from an initial impact. Here, any effect on the biophysical and socio-economic environments that arises from a cause directly related to the project activities is termed a first-order or primary impact. The secondary impacts are those affecting the biophysical and socio-economic environments which arise from an action, but which are not initiated directly by that action. Presentation matrices can only clearly show the primary or first-order impacts within any particular activity–component framework.

Figure 4.3 symbolically traces the secondary impacts which could arise from the dredging and filling of an estuarine mud-flat (supposing that the proposed project was the construction of a marina). The top row of rectangles shows a set of environmental components linked by various dependencies (i.e., second row of boxes). The way in which the primary impact of dredging and filling the mud-flats affects all the components is shown as a progression of causes and effects (viz. in rows three and four). Note that the commercial facilities component of the socio-economic system has a fourth-order dependency on salt marsh plants. Similarly, the action of dredging and filling the mud-flats has a fifth-order impact upon commercial facilities.

Various authors have used different terms to describe secondary impacts, but most are compatible with the above definition. Jain and Urban (1975), however, use the term "higher order impacts" to mean secondary impacts as given above, while reserving the terms "indirect" or "secondary" to cover impacts resulting from an induced action.

Box 4.4 presents a checklist of second-order impacts arising out of the use of pesticides in an irrigation project.

The network technique developed by Sorensen is probably the best-known approach for investigating higher order impacts. The objective of the network approach is to display, in an easily understood format, the intermediate links between a project and its ultimate impacts. This type of network includes the identification of probable importance of temporal effects as well as a list of data requirements. Complexity increases as higher order impacts are considered, and, as a result, the Sorensen network is restricted to third and lower order impacts. Figure 4.4 shows a portion of a network devised by Sorensen to display the possible consequences of various forms of land use for a section of Californian coastline. Three options for residential development are related to four primary impacts, and cause–effect linkages are developed for each identified primary impact. The diagram also takes notice of feasible mitigatory measures. This type of network includes the identification of probable importance of temporal effects as well as a list of data requirements.

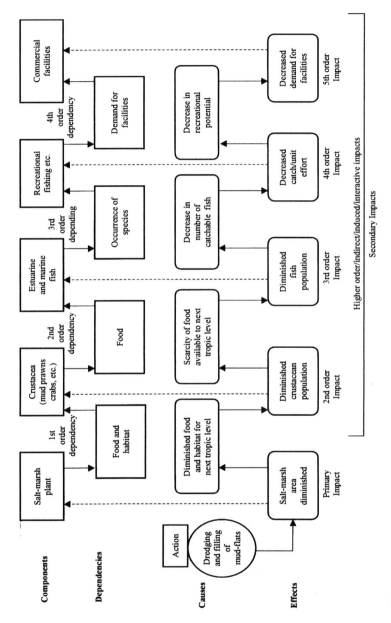

Figure 4.3 Symbolic representation of the secondary impacts which could arise from the dredging and filling of on estuarine mud-flat. The relationship between environmental components, their interdependencies, and the causes and effects of secondary impacts are illustrated
Source: J. B. Shopley, M. Sowman, R. J. Fuggle, Environmental Managment. 31, pp. 197–213, 1990.

93

Box 4.4 Example of secondary order impacts: Use of pesticides in irrigation projects

- Use of pesticides/insecticides/herbicides etc., in excessive quantities and the persistent nature of pesticides can contaminate the soil.
- Pesticide-contaminated soil contaminates the groundwater through leaching.
- Contaminated groundwater affects human health through ingestion.
- Contaminated soil reduces crop yield.
- Contaminated soil pollutes surface water through run off from the soil.
- Contaminated surface water affects aquatic biota through toxic contamination.
- Contaminated surface water decreases yield of fish.
- Use of pesticides/insecticides/herbicides, etc., often kill the natural predators. These predators eat the pests and hence are useful in maintaining the crop yield. Thus killing of natural predators by pesticides increases the population of pests and thus reduces yields.
- Use of pesticides/insecticides/herbicides etc., affects crops through deposition.

Methods are available for translating networks into mathematical models. These methods structure the relationships implied in qualitative simulations. Two common quantitative simulation models are GSIM and KSIM. In GSIM the verbal expression of relationships is made explicit at the simplest level: "if A increases then B will decrease (or increase or be unaffected)". In KSIM models the relative magnitude of the relationship must be specified: "if A doubles then B will decrease by 25%". The KSIM model at an extreme level approaches quantitative simulation modelling.

4.4.1 Advantages of the network method

- Presentation matrices can only clearly show the primary or first-order impacts within any particular activity–component framework. It is possible, however, to investigate higher order linkages in two dimensions by using networks.
- It is possible to translate networks into mathematical models for a more quantitative judgement. The network method structures the relationships implied in qualitative simulations.

4.4.2 Limitations of the network method

- One of the main limitations of the network method is that since impacts are not scored in any quantitative way, the comparison of project alternatives is not readily achieved.
- Spatial representation of impacts is not possible.

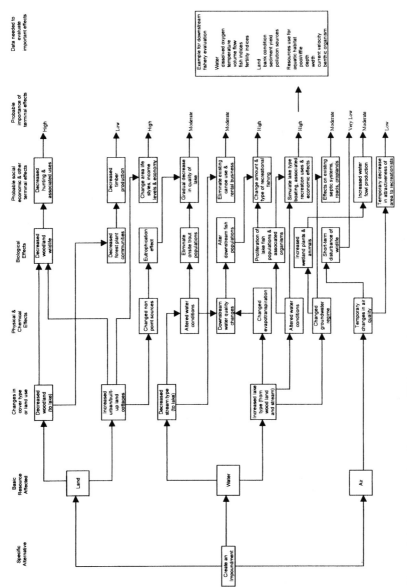

Figure 4.4 An example of a network diagram for analysing probable environmental impacts
Source: Guidelines for Environmental Impact Assessment in Development Assistance, FINNIDA, 1989.

4.5 Overlays

The overlay approach to impact assessment involves the use of a series of transparencies to identify, predict, assign relative significance to, and communicate impacts in a geographical reference frame larger in scale than a localized action would require. The approach has been employed for selecting highway corridors, for evaluating development options in coastal areas, and in numerous other applications.

The McHarg overlay is based on a set of transparent maps, each of which represents the spatial variation of an environmental parameter (e.g., susceptibility to erosion or recreational value). The maps are shaded to show three degrees of parameter compatibility with the proposed project. A composite picture of the overall social cost of affecting any particular area is approximated by superimposing all the transparent maps. Any number of project alternatives can be located on the final map to investigate the degree of associated impacts. The validity of the analysis is related to the type and number of parameters chosen. For a readable composite map, the number of parameters in a transparency overlay is limited to about 10 (Munn, 1979). Parameter maps present data in a summarized and easily interpreted form, but are unable to reflect the possibility of secondary impacts. They also rely heavily on cartographic skills and their effectiveness depends to a large degree on cartographic execution.

This method is easily adaptable for use with a computer programmed to perform the tasks of aggregating the predicted impacts for each geographical subdivision and of searching for the areas least affected. Automated procedures are also available for selecting sequences of unit areas for routing highways, pipelines, and other corridors. The computer method is more flexible, and has an advantage whenever the reviewer suggests that the system of weights be changed.

The overlay approach can accommodate both qualitative and quantitative data. The weakness of the overlay approach is that it is only moderately comprehensive, because there is no mechanism that requires consideration of all potential impacts. When using overlays, the burden of ensuring comprehensiveness is largely on the analyst. Also, the approach is selective because there is a limit to the number of transparencies that can be viewed together. Finally, extreme impacts with small probabilities of occurrence are not considered. However, a skilled assessor may make indications in a footnote or on a supplementary map.

FURTHER READING

A. K. Biswas and S. B. C. Agarwala, *Environmental Impact Assessment for Developing Countries*, Butterworth-Heinemann, Oxford, 1992.

B. C. Clark, K. Chapman, R. Bisset, P. Wathern and M. Barrett, *A Manual for the Assessment of Major Development Proposals*, HMSO, London, 1981.

R. K. Jain and L. V. Urban, *A Review and Analysis of Environmental Impact Assessment Methodologies*, Technical Report E-69, Construction Engineering Research Laboratory, Champaign, June 1975.

L. B. Leopold *et al.*, *A Procedure for Evaluating Environmental Impact*, US Geological Survey Circular 645, Highway Research Board, Washington DC, 1971.

R. E. Munn, ed., *Environmental Impact Assessment*, SCOPE 5, Wiley, Chichester, 1979.

5

EIA tools

5.1 Impact prediction

The essence of EIA is predicting future environmental conditions, either with the proposed development or without. A comparison of the two predicted situations is also often made with the present. Prediction is the process of determining the nature and extent of the environmental changes that will result from a proposed activity. From an examination of the methods available for predicting different effects, the following main "types" of methods could be identified: physical models, experimental methods, and mathematical models.

Physical models, illustrative or working scale models constructed to represent the environment, may include visual representations of the environment by picture, photograph, film, or three-dimensional model and working models of the environment using, for example, wind tunnels or wave chambers.

Experimental methods, practical field or laboratory work, include field experiments, in which tests are carried out at the proposed site, and laboratory experiments, in which tests are carried out in the laboratory in conditions simulating the environment.

Mathematical models, in which the relationship between the cause and effect is represented by one or more mathematical relationships, may be either empirical (black box) models, where the relationships between inputs and outputs are established from statistical analysis of observations in the environment, or "internally descriptive", where the mathematical relationships within the model are based on an explicit representation of the mechanisms of the processes occurring within the environment. These latter models range from simple formulations, which can be applied manually, to complex dynamic models, which require computer application.

Evidence from case studies suggests that the methods most often used in the Environmental Protection Agency (EPA) are the simpler methods, for example:

- steady-state, single source, Gaussian plume dispersion models for air quality;
- simple run-off and leachate models based on catchment area and rainfall;
- simple dilution and steady-state dispersion models for water quality;
- simple inventory approaches for both direct and higher-order effects on receptors (e.g., man, plants, habitats, etc.).

These methods can usually be applied manually or graphically, or using simple computer programs. The predictions obtained using these methods are usually very approximate, although the quality of results will depend on the particular problem and circumstances for which the method is used.

Environmental Resources Limited, UK, commissioned a study to examine the predictive methods used in EIA. The study covered 140 EIAs and environmental planning studies. There were 910 predictions of 36 different types of impact processes or effects. Mathematical, physical, or experimental modelling methods were used in 25% of these examples; in a further 15%, simple methods such as inventories of the factor affected (e.g., numbers of people or properties, area of habitat, etc.) were used to describe effects. In the remaining cases, other approaches not involving the use of formal methods were adopted.

Some of the reasons for the lack of application of more complex prediction models in EIA are related to their time and resource requirements for data input, calibration, and application, and the diminishing returns achieved in terms of the quality of result relative to their resource requirements, compared with simpler forms of predictive methods.

Types of methods less frequently used in EIA include:

- working physical models of atmospheric, aquatic, and acoustic effects (wind tunnels, hydraulic models, etc.);
- field and laboratory experiments (tracer experiments, bioassays, etc.);
- site-specific mathematical models and dynamic mathematical models.

These types of methods take into account more of the specific characteristics of the particular activity and environment, and make fewer generalizing assumptions. They may also take into account complex sources. As a result they have greater input and resource requirements for calibration and application (unless an existing model is available for use in the study area). As a general rule, they provide more detailed information about effects, but not necessarily more accurate information.

5.1.1 Application of methods to different levels of prediction

In the case studies, it is often observed that different levels of predictive methods are generally used for different purposes in EIA.

The simplest methods are used for: (i) initial screening and comparison of "clear-cut" alternatives (for example, at the scoping stage) where only approximate predictions are required; (ii) assessment of project alternatives at the early stages of development when little information is available about the activity; (iii) assessment of policy and planning activities, where little information is available about the specific receiving environment; and (iv) long-term predictions based on simple relationships, allowing for the lack of information about future circumstances.

Intermediate methods are used for more detailed predictions, usually at the stages of siting and alternative design decisions, and for identification of appropriate mitigating measures.

The more complex methods are used for activities which have the potential for major and irreversible effects on the environment where very detailed information may be required about the nature and magnitude of these effects.

Approaches other than "formal methods" are often used in EIA for predictive purposes.

5.1.2 Informal modelling

In some circumstances, it is either impossible or impracticable to model environmental systems in a formal way using mathematical, physical, or experimental simulations of the real world. This may be because no methods are available to adequately describe the system, or because the methods that are available require more resources for their application than are justified by the requirements of the particular application. In these circumstances, an alternative is to use a less formal approach based on the advice of experts and on experience drawn from historical and scientific evidence.

An ad hoc model can be constructed and used to predict effects. This model may involve some explicit mathematical relationships but it may also involve conceptual relationships which can only be described verbally. These qualitative word models may be based either on concrete evidence or on an intuitive understanding of how the environment will respond to particular influences.

When an expert predict effects, they are asked to provide an estimate of the likely size of an effect, based on their knowledge and experience. In coming to a conclusion, the expert may draw on observations made at other activity locations, or may use formal methods implicitly in the assessment.

In some cases the expert may be able explicitly to describe the theoretical base for the conclusions; in other cases they may use empirical observations from other circumstances where the mechanism by which the effect occurs is not explicitly understood.

5.1.2.1 Approaches to informal modelling

The "one man prediction" can be considered as the most informal method of qualitative simulation; a single expert gives their view of the likely effect. From this starting point an increasing formality can be imposed by:

- requiring the "one man" to justify the opinion by verbal and or mathematical description of the relationships has used, and/or to support the findings by reference to historical and scientific evidence;
- asking "more than one man", i.e., a group of experts, for their individual opinions and taking some view of their overall conclusions;
- asking a group of experts for their opinion of the likely effect;
- asking the experts to get together in some formal structure for consensus production (e.g., Delhi) and agree on their opinion of the likely effect.

Prediction by analogy is where an effect is predicted by direct extrapolation from a similar activity already operating at another site. The observations from the existing site may be corrected to allow for the different conditions at the site of the proposed activity. In this area, there is an overlap with formal techniques, so empirical models may be developed from an analysis of results from comparable locations.

If the proposed development activity is an addition to an existing situation, a correlation of impact may lead to a prediction. For example, when a resort doubles the number of guest rooms, it will also double the sewage output. The impact on water quality, however, may be much greater if the sewage treatment system is already near its maximum capacity. Trends and correlations may or may not be linear and continuous; thus, extrapolation must be done with care and understanding.

Interpolation may be used to estimate the impact of a new development where the impacts of both larger and smaller similar developments are known. The result is usually more accurate than extrapolation if the assumptions of a linear correlation are true. The analogy between an existing development and a new project allows prediction of impacts depending on the extent of similarity of the sites in both cases. Prediction methods anchored in actual experience are always preferred to estimates with no basis of direct observation.

Comparison with standards is where an effect is predicted to be acceptable by direct evaluation against predetermined standards or norms. This approach is most often used for higher order effects on receptors where environmental standards have been laid down for their protection. For example, the health effects of air pollutants are assessed by comparing air quality with standards for protection of public health.

These informal approaches to prediction are often used together with formal methods in order to qualify and interpret the results.

5.1.3 Physical models

In physical models the environment is simulated at a reduced scale. Physical models can be either two or three dimensional. Illustrative models simply present a visual image of the environment before and/or after implementation of the activity by sketches, photographs, cinefilms, or 3D models. They can be used to illustrate the effect of activities on the visual environment.

In working physical models the processes which occur in the environment are simulated at a reduced scale. When the proposed activity is simulated in the model (e.g., the release of a substance or a change in morphology) the resulting changes can be observed and measured in the model. Working physical models are used to predict air, water, and noise effects, either by direct simulation or by analogy. Direct simulation modelling is carried out in wind tunnels, wave chambers, and similar facilities. In analogy models, the environmental medium or the source is simulated using another medium (e.g., water to simulate water flows).

For a model to correctly represent all the phenomena and physical processes occurring in the environment, different conditions must be met with regard to scale. Usually it is not possible to satisfy all these conditions at the same time. As a result, most models are a compromise in which mistakes arising from scaling are minimized. In some circumstances it may be necessary to construct more than one model to overcome different scaling problems.

Most modelling exercises are carried out in ready-built facilities which are adapted to suit the particular requirements of a prediction. Such facilities are available at both public and private research organizations. However, in some circumstances special facilities must be constructed.

5.1.4 Mathematical models

In a mathematical model the behaviour of an environmental system is represented by mathematical expressions of the relationships between

Box 5.1 Simple mathematical model

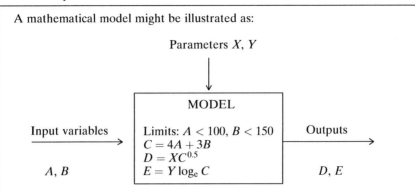

A mathematical model might be illustrated as:

Parameters X, Y

MODEL

Input variables → Limits: $A < 100$, $B < 150$ Outputs →
$C = 4A + 3B$
$D = XC^{0.5}$
A, B $E = Y \log_e C$ D, E

Simple representation of a mathematical model

The model consists of two rules imposing limits on variables A and B, and three equations. There are two kinds of inputs: A and B are external inputs to a system, while X and Y are parameters, which are actually internal to the system, but which can be changed to calibrate the model to fit observed data.

C is an intermediate variable, which is not outputted. D and E are the outputs of interest to a user. The model could be implemented easily as a computer program, making it easy to process many inputs A and B, or to vary the parameters to tune the model.

Suppose that measurements have been made for a particular event. A is 70, B is 100, and D has been recorded as 25 and E as 11. To match these values with the above model, we need to vary X and Y. This is easy as these parameters are simple multipliers and the required values can be found by algebra. These are $X = 1.038$ and $Y = 1.729$. In more complex models, parameters are fitted by trial and error or using an optimization technique.

variables. In general the output variable (x) is a function of one or more input variables $(A, B, C, \ldots)$:

$$X = f(A, B, C, \ldots)$$

A model is a representation of the significant attributes of a real proto-type, but is simpler and is easier to build, change, or operate.

The number of different variables in a model and the nature of the relationships between them are determined by the complexity of the system. The aim in mathematical modelling is to minimize the number of variables and keep the relationships as simple as possible, while retaining a sufficiently accurate and workable representation of the environment system.

When the structure and processes of ecosystems are understood, models such as Box 5.1 can be used to describe systems such as those below.

- The universal soil loss equation predicts erosion rates from knowledge about rainfall, slope, soil structure, vegetative cover, and management practices.
- The water budget is essentially a materials-balance equation involving rainfall, evapotranspiration, runoff, infiltration, and storage in a watershed or other hydrologic system.
- The salt budget accounts for all sources of salt, movement by solution, deposition (precipitation), uptake by plants, and export by leaching.
- Population dynamics predict the rise and fall of biological organisms and communities from knowledge of lifecycles, predator–prey relationships, food webs, and other factors affecting the lives of various species.

An example of a mathematical model is a simple form of the Gaussian plume dispersion equation for predicting air quality around a point source of emission:

$$c = \frac{Q\exp[-1/h^2]}{\mu\sigma_y\sigma_z 2\sigma^2}$$

where c = ground level concentration ($\mu g/m^3$) at a distance of x meters in the wind direction; Q = rate of emission ($\mu g/s$); h = height of emission (= stack height + plume rise) (m); and σ_y and σ_z = lateral and vertical dispersion coefficients calculated for the required value of x from standard empirical formulae appropriate to the emission height, the roughness of the surrounding surface, and the atmospheric stability.

The exact shape of the relationship in a model is defined by establishing the model parameters, which may vary according to the circumstances in which the model is applied; for example, the dispersion coefficients in the example above must be defined according to the conditions of atmospheric stability, the surface roughness of the surrounding area, and the emission height. Various standard empirical formulae for these coefficients have been established by different workers for different types of emission and different meteorological and topographical conditions.

5.1.5 Modelling procedure

Modelling procedure has to be carried out in a systematic way to get an optimum allocation of limited resources to relevant activities. The primary focus is to define the problem, bound by the constituents of space, time, and subsystems. Once the problem is defined, a suitable model has to be selected or developed to fit the situation. Before this decision can be made, a thorough study of the available data, resources, and an assessment of the required level of detail should be conducted. This will help to choose the correct model, whether simple or complex.

Calibration should be carried out after analysing the data. This can be done by reconciliation of the values predicted by the model and the actual observed values. Various curve fitting and optimization methods can be used to aid the calibration procedure.

After the calibration is carried out, it is important to validate the model, preferably against a series of measures from a period with changed conditions. For this second step, a set of available data can be used. If significant discrepancies exist, the general model formulation should be reviewed and the calibration and validation cycle repeated.

After the calibration, the model is ready for application. First, the model is applied to the existing conditions without the project. Next, proposed project parameters are added and the model is run again to predict the quality of environment after the establishment of the project. The difference between the two predictions comprises the environmental impact of the proposed project.

Sensitivity analysis is the integral and important component of the entire model study. This enables the modeller to evaluate the relative importance of the basic parameters and input data in the model study.

5.1.6 Sensitivity analysis

Any analysis of an environmental model, a cost/benefit study, or other investigation, will involve a number of input factors which have different degrees of uncertainty. These will influence the outcomes of the study to varying extents. The process can be considered as an input/output process, as shown earlier in Box 5.1. Usually we select the inputs as "most likely" values. The relative response of outputs to changes in inputs, is their sensitivity.

As an example, consider the model shown in Box 5.1. The factors in the analysis can be seen as inputs (A, B), and the outcomes as outputs (D, E). If the parameters were set at $X = 1.1$ and $Y = 1.9$, and the most likely inputs were $A = 75$ and $B = 102$, the outputs will be $D = 27.1$ and $E = 12.2$.

Now suppose that input A is considered to be accurate to $\pm 40\%$ and input B to be accurate to $\pm 25\%$. The limits for A might therefore be from 45 to 105, and B from 76.5 to 127.5. Taking the highest and lowest sets of values, we can repeat the calculations. The low values of A and B lead to outputs of $D = 22.3$ (-18%) and $E = 11.4$ (-7%). The high values of inputs (with A truncated from 105 to 100) will give $D = 30.8$ $(+14\%)$ and $E = 12.7$ $(+4\%)$. The percentage figures show that the outputs are relatively insensitive to the 25% changes in inputs; this is due to the square root and log functions in the equations for D and E. Other relationships might amplify changes in inputs, and give sensitive responses.

Sensitivity analysis is a powerful, yet simple, technique for determining the effects of individual factors and their variations on the overall results of an analysis. By changing the value of an input variable in an equation, the response of a system to new external influences can be tested.

Taking the plume dispersion equation above, the concentration of an air pollutant can be calculated (i) at different distances from the source by changing x (and therefore changing y and z), (ii) resulting from different chimney heights can be calculated by changing h, and (iii) for different emission rates by changing Q.

5.1.7 Probabilistic modelling

The model in Box 5.1 can be used with probabilistic inputs A and B, resulting in probabilistic outputs D and E. For example, the "most likely" values of A and B were taken as 75 and 102. These might be considered to be normally distributed, with A having a distribution which is $N(75, 15)$, this notation indicating that it has a mean of 75 and a standard distribution of 15. Likewise, B might be $N(102, 25)$.

Unfortunately, the "analytical" equations given above cannot be applied to the model in Box 5.1, as it is non-linear, with limits, $A \leq 100$ and $B \leq 150$ truncating inputs, and square root and log transformations in the equations defining D and E. However, we can allow for probabilities by a process known as Monte Carlo analysis (Box 5.2). This uses random number generation to produce sets of values from the input probability distributions.

Each set of possible inputs is used to calculate a set of outputs. This may be repeated hundreds or thousands of times using a computer. The many outputs can then be treated as a statistical sample, and analysed to find means, standard deviations, and confidence limits. To illustrate this, suppose that we use random number generators to generate ten sets of possible inputs, A and B. These produce the ten sets of outputs D and E, from which means and standard deviations can be calculated (Table 5.1). This method effectively generates many possible outputs and then analyses these statistically. It can cope with limits on variables and with non-linear relationships.

Even when inputs are not normally distributed, it is possible to calculate the distribution of outputs for linear processes. Knowing the standard deviations of outputs provides considerably more information than just knowing the mean. It enables analysts to define confidence limits and gives a much better idea of the consequences of failure.

5.1.8 Points to be considered when selecting a prediction model

Many models used at varying levels of sophistication depend on the quality of information required to select suitable methods. With an

Box 5.2 Modified mathematical model

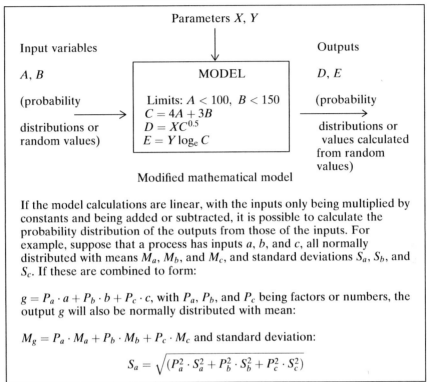

Parameters X, Y

Input variables

A, B

(probability

distributions or
random values)

MODEL

Limits: $A < 100$, $B < 150$
$C = 4A + 3B$
$D = XC^{0.5}$
$E = Y \log_e C$

Outputs

D, E

(probability

distributions or
values calculated
from random
values)

Modified mathematical model

If the model calculations are linear, with the inputs only being multiplied by constants and being added or subtracted, it is possible to calculate the probability distribution of the outputs from those of the inputs. For example, suppose that a process has inputs a, b, and c, all normally distributed with means M_a, M_b, and M_c, and standard deviations S_a, S_b, and S_c. If these are combined to form:

$g = P_a \cdot a + P_b \cdot b + P_c \cdot c$, with P_a, P_b, and P_c being factors or numbers, the output g will also be normally distributed with mean:

$M_g = P_a \cdot M_a + P_b \cdot M_b + P_c \cdot M_c$ and standard deviation:

$$S_a = \sqrt{(P_a^2 \cdot S_a^2 + P_b^2 \cdot S_b^2 + P_c^2 \cdot S_c^2)}$$

Table 5.1 Generation of random numbers for calculating means and standard deviations

Set No.	Input A	Input B	Output D	Output E
1	82	79	26.1	12.0
2	62	107	26.1	12.1
3	74	93	26.4	12.1
4	70	95	26.1	12.0
5	79	101	27.4	12.2
6	67	121	27.6	12.1
7	65	117	27.2	12.2
8	70	92	25.9	12.0
9	88	105	28.4	12.4
10	73	85	25	12.0
	Mean		26.7	12.1
	Standard deviation		0.90	0.13

increase in the sophistication, the complexity of model also increases. This leads to an increasing number of uncertain parameters. The error in estimating parameters is carried over through the model, thus producing a less accurate model.

Where limited resources are available, decisions have to be made about information needs for different effects and therefore about the allocation of these resources between the different effects. If specially designed methods are already available this will help to reduce the use of resources.

5.1.9 Difficulties in prediction

When a system is complex and continuous changes are occurring, prediction becomes difficult. Time and money are often the main constraints. Sometimes, predictions which provide information for decision makers may be complicated and not clear cut. There are often a range of methods that may be used to predict a particular change and these may vary depending on the complexity of the change.

5.1.10 Auditing of EIAs

Put simply, EIA is intended to analyse and evaluate the environmental impacts of a proposal and to recommend on their management – what is likely to happen and what can be done about it. The purpose of auditing is to provide feedback into this process and to find out whether EIA is an effective tool in environmental management. Does putting a proposal through EIA result in environmentally better decisions being made? Related questions are:

- Are the significant impacts of the project correctly identified?
- Are technically appropriate mitigating actions identified?
- Are these actions then recommended?
- Are mitigating measures implemented even if they are recommended?

Tomlinson and Atkinson have recently put forward a series of definitions for seven types of EIA audit, with the aim of developing a standardized vocabulary for the subject. The following audit types are the main ones, focusing on post-project evaluation.

- Implementation audit. Checks on the proponent's compliance with mitigation and other imposed conditions, and is used mainly on a practical level as a "policing" operation.
- Project impact audit. Analyses the environmental impacts that have occurred as a result of project implementation. In addition, it provides useful feedback for other similar projects through identifying relevant areas of concern, and can identify areas where knowledge is deficient.

- Predictive techniques audit. Compares predicted impacts with actual consequences, and so provides a means of comparing the accuracy and utility of different methods of predicting environmental impacts.
- EIA procedures audit. Utilizes as many of the other audit types as necessary (including audits relevant to pre-project appraisal) to provide a review of EIA procedures at the macro level.

Generally, predictive techniques audit is the audit most extensively discussed in the overall EIA audit framework.

5.1.10.1 Auditing prediction in EIAs

Bisset examined 791 impact predictions from four projects in the UK, and found that only 77 of these predictions could be audited, and that 57 were probably accurate.

Henderson considered 122 predictions from two projects in Canada. Of these, 42 could not be audited because of lack of monitoring data, and 10 either because they were too vague or because of modifications to the project. Out of the 70 predictions audited, 54 were substantially correct, 13 partly correct or uncertain, and 3 were definitely wrong.

The fifth and most extensive environmental impact audit was performed by Culhane, who examined 239 impact predictions from 29 EIAs, intended to form a representative cross-section of EIAs prepared in the USA between 1974 and 1978. The projects were concerned principally with agriculture, forestry, infrastructure, waste management, and uranium processing. Culhane found that most of the impact predictions in these EIAs were very imprecise, with less than 25% being quantified. Few predictions were clearly wrong, but less than 30% were "unqualifiedly close to forecasts".

More recently, 181 different predictions in EIAs were audited by Buckley in Australia as a nationwide exercise. The study showed that the average accuracy of quantified, critical, testable predictions in environmental impact statements in Australia to date is around 40–50%, and that predictions where actual impacts proved more severe than expected were on average 33% more than those where they proved as much or less severe (estimated to be around 54%). Table 5.2 shows some highlights of Buckely's study.

5.1.10.2 Problems in conducting predictive techniques audit

Predictions can be inauditable for a variety of reasons. If any events or conditions which were assumed to apply in the formulation of the prediction do not in fact occur, the prediction is inauditable.

There are several categories of accuracy. Baily and Hobbs have found it useful to include a category "mostly accurate". This category allows one to assess the overall success of a complex prediction, and it

Table 5.2 Selected outcomes of prediction auditing from Australia

Component/ parameter	Type of development	Predicted impact	Actual impact	Accuracy/ precision
Ambient air quality: SO_2	Power station	Annual mean $[SO_2] <$ 60 mg m^{-3}	<5 mg m^{-3}	Correct: 8%, better
		24-hr mean $[SO_2] <$ 260 mg m^{-3}	<40 mg m^{-3}	Correct: 15%, better
	Power station	Max. annual mean −1.3 mg m^{-3}	Max. annual mean −2 mg m^{-3}	Incorrect: 65%, worse
	Power station	Max. annual mean = 5.0 mg m^{-3}	Max. annual mean = 12.4 mg m^{-3}	Incorrect: 40%, worse
	Power station	Mean annual mean within 20 km = 0.65 mg m^{-3}	Mean annual mean within 11.5 km = 0.25 mg m^{-3}	Incorrect: 38%, better
	Power station	Mean annual mean within 20 km = 1.3 mg m^{-3}	Mean annual mean up to = 6.33 mg m^{-3}	Incorrect: 20%, worse
	Power station	Max. 3-minute mean = 930 mg m^{-3}	Max. 3-minute mean = 1524 mg m^{-3}	Incorrect: 61%, worse
	Power station	Max. 3-minute mean = 430 mg m^{-3}	Max. 3-minute mean = 679 mg m^{-3}	Incorrect: 63%, worse
Ambient air quality: NO_x	Power station	$[NO_x] - 0.7 \times$ $[SO_2]$	$0.85 \times$	Incorrect: 82%, worse

also allows one to deal with situations in which non-compliance, design changes, or imprecisely worded predictions affect the auditibility of the prediction to a degree such that strict "accuracy" is not appropriate, but the prediction is still relevant enough to be auditable in practice.

Some observations on the difficulty in the auditability of the EIA follow.

• EIA documents often contain few testable predictions: instead, they simply identify issues of concern. Predictions made often refer to relatively minor impacts, with major impacts being referred to only in qualitative terms.

• Environmental parameters which are monitored often do not correspond with those for which predictions were made.

• Monitoring techniques often do not enable predictions to be tested: for example, the predictions may have been made for one point, but monitoring data collected from another, or predictions (particularly in relation to pollutant concentrations) may have been made for one time period, but monitoring data collected or expressed for a different period (e.g., hourly, weekly, or annual averages instead of 3-minute, daily, or monthly).

- Monitoring data are often inadequate for statistically valid testing of predictions: for example, they may contain too few samples, too many missing data points, inadequate controls, inadequate information on other possible factors which may influence parameters monitored, etc. In general, environmental monitoring programmes are aimed at monitoring compliance with standards rather than testing impact predictions.
- Development projects are almost always modified, sometimes substantially, between the conceptual or design stage, as used for EIA, and the actual operation.
- Most monitoring data are collected and provided by the operating corporations concerned, which may possibly provide only data favourable to themselves.

In view of the above points, it may be realized that the instances of "auditable" prediction cases in developing countries such as India may be much less than the number of predictions made. The EIA reports submitted and the post-project monitoring reports forwarded later by the project developers as such did not provide sufficient basis to quantify the precision of predictions.

5.1.11 Precision in prediction and decision resolution

Much recent research has focused on auditing the accuracy of predictions, although the term "predictive techniques audit" is not generally used. These studies tend to focus on the scientific and technical aspects. The main issue identified by most research workers is the degree of precision possible in assessing and predicting environmental parameters, most researchers concluding that improving prediction accuracy is at the heart of successful EIA.

Several research workers have concluded that predictions need to be written in a manner that facilitates auditing, and should therefore be presented as falsifiable hypotheses. In addition, they should present information on: (i) the variable subject to an impact; (ii) the magnitude, extent, and time scale of the impact; (iii) the probability of its occurring and its significance; and (iv) the confidence to be placed in the prediction.

There is also a general belief (and India is no exception) that prediction and assessment in EIA is acceptable or improved only when it is presented in a quantitative manner. This has increased the application of mathematical models (notably air quality or dispersion models, followed by water quality models with an emerging interest in consequence modelling for risk assessment) as well as increasing the utilization of assessment schemes on the basis of scoring (or rating) and ranking.

Application of mathematical models sometimes requires non-routine data. If it is not generally available, then assumptions have to be made. Typical assumptions in the case of air dispersion models refer to atmospheric stabilities for which data is not available on a routine basis. Emission data supplied by the project proponent is treated as accurate.

The models themselves have problems of incompleteness and it is not correct to attach a significant amount of certainty to the model's estimate. For example, well-constructed dispersion models with good a database are noted to have a variance of the order of 60%. Most of the water quality models applied consider the presence of complete mixing of pollutants near the discharge point in the x, y, and z directions. The consequence models generally used treat a chemical plume as having a density comparable to air with no reactions and heat exchange, which is not the case in reality.

The common mathematical models used in EIA enable calculations up to ambient concentrations and not directly to the estimation of impacts, for which one needs to take the opinion of experts, use guidelines (standards), or apply valuation models. Further, models are not available for a variety of other issues like socio-economic and health impacts. Despite these limitations, it is noticed that the EIA documents sometimes include a dominating section on the use of a mathematical model and the review members spend more time in checking the equations, coefficients, etc., of the model applied. Intensive debates are not uncommon, for example whether the 8 hourly sulphur dioxide concentration at 3 km downwind (where there is a sanctuary) is 50 $\mu g/m^3$ or 70 $\mu g/m^3$ (60 being the standard value) when it is possible that the model estimate can be anywhere between 5 and 100 $\mu g/m^3$! Mature application of mathematical models is rarely seen.

It should be remembered, however, that precision is preferable, but striving for precision could result in a prediction defined too narrowly to be of practical use. Also, it is often unreasonable to expect a high degree of accuracy from predictions. Added to this doubt is the question of how accurate the prediction needs to be on an operational level: if underlying processes are sufficiently understood, then the appropriate management response may still be evoked by an impact even if it is not precisely predicted.

It is suggested that trying to make predictions rigorously testable in a context where decision-making is done at a practical level is, in most cases, not appropriate. Obviously, precision is preferable when it is possible and appropriate. However, the philosophy of "better qualitative and useful than quantitative and wrong" may be more appropriate in most cases in developing contries.

What this statement means in terms of auditing is that the totally pragmatic evaluation of a prediction would become "Did it result in appropriate management action being taken?" compared with the totally scientific evaluation of "Did it correctly describe the type, magnitude, extent, and duration of the impact?" The focus should be to try and incorporate aspects of both these approaches in an auditing programme. In other words, we should be concerned with whether the EIA procedural framework results in good management, as well as showing how well the individual steps in the process perform. At a practical level, individual steps can be no more effective than the whole of the process. What point is there in correctly predicting 99% of impacts if none of them gets managed properly?

5.2 Geographical information system

Geographical information system (GIS) is a computer-based system incorporating the collection, storage, retrieval, transformation, manipulation, and display of spatial data. It can be used as an EIA tool for the effective identification and evaluation of impacts.

A GIS database is divided into geographic units or cells. The data associated with each cell can be based on political, geographic, geological, or biological characteristics or a combination of any of these. Environmental and social statistics can then be organized as attributes or tables within each cell. With GIS, data are readily displayed and interpreted in a conventional map format. Both the proposed development project and existing environmental characteristics can be displayed as an overlay or attribute on the map, allowing easy visual interpretation of the impact potential. Data can often be directly imported into a GIS database from other spatial display programs (such as computer-aided drafting systems), other GIS programs, and spreadsheet or database files. The GIS database can in turn be exported to other spatial, spreadsheet, or database files.

5.2.1 Data overlay and analysis

One of the early methods of environmental planning (McHarg, 1969) used an overlay approach, where environmental (including socio-economic and cultural) data were graphically displayed on mylar sheets that could be assembled in various combinations to determine areas of environmental constraint. Areas of constraint were determined by visual interpretation of the varying degrees of darkness as the mylar sheets marked with constraints were overlain. The extent of the constraints in any given area was measured and calculated manually. GIS improves on this system in several ways. The attribute layers are stored electronically rather than on mylar sheets. Different layers can be electronically combined, removed, or ignored at any time. Constraint areas and degrees of multiple constraint can be calculated by computer. Constraints can also be assigned numerical weights that can be added mathematically. Analysis results can be displayed numerically in tables or graphically with colours or shades being assigned to depict areas where limits would preclude specific types of development.

5.2.2 Site impact prediction

Impact can be predicted by overlaying various development scenarios. Areas can be calculated for each ecosystem or land use type affected by construction or other development activities. Aerial, linear, or point impacts can be calculated. For example, an area affected by a construction project could be identified within an ecological database and the GIS program could then calculate the size of each resource within that area.

5.2.3 Wider area impact prediction

The use of buffers in GIS allows the calculation of impacts in an area of influence, reflecting the distance the impacts spread into the surrounding environment. For example, large game hunting in certain areas may quickly affect animal populations within a kilometer of any new access road. By placing a 1-km-wide buffer on either side of the access road, one can calculate the area in which big game animals will be at risk. Many species, such as bald eagles or spotted owls, are susceptible to impacts from significant human activities within their nesting areas. By putting appropriate buffer circles around the known nesting habitats, one can depict the area of constraints or impact potential. Sociologically, buffers can be used to identify the extent of impacts from noise or air pollution or the property value effects of development proposals.

5.2.4 Corridor analysis

Corridor analysis has become an important developing planning concept, including such areas as the Niagara Escarpment or Oak Ridges Morain of Southern Ontario's highly developed Golden Horsehoe area in Canada. GIS has been used to determine both the location and area of existing natural corridors needing protection and the potential for linking these

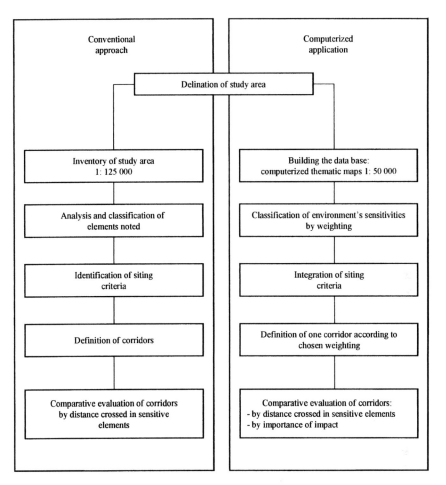

Figure 5.1 Environmental assessment method for transmission lines and substations
Source: Environmental Assessment Method for Transmission Lines and Substations, Hydro-Quebec, Canada, 1992.

corridors further and extending their natural value. This is very important in a highly developed area because many species that require large areas of continuous natural habitat or migration routes depend on such corridor linkages. A typical case is illustrated in Figure 5.1.

5.2.5 Cumulative effects assessment and EA audits

The ability to store environmental and developmental data electronically also facilities cumulative effects assessment (CEA) and EA audits. Once the GIS data layers are recorded and stored they are available for the analysis of future projects and can be easily updated. Each new development proposal can be overlain with previous and other foreseeable proposals to allow the evaluation of the cumulative effects. If these data files are stored in a central location, the costly redundancy of having to recollect the same environmental and developmental information for different projects is avoided. For example, the US Fish and Wildlife Service has made thousands of GIS files available for wetlands throughout the USA, free over the Internet.

5.2.6 Trend analysis

GIS can be used to make long-term impact predictions more reliable. Impacts can be predicted in a real time environment. Data can be continuously updated. GIS can serve as a valuable tool in the development of impact assessments because of its broad applicability and its flexibility. These characteristics are reflected in its ability to:
• store large multidisciplinary data sets;
• identify complex interrelationships between environmental characteristics;
• evaluate change over time;
• be systematically updated and used for more than one project;
• serve as a data set for a variety of mathematical models;
• store and manipulate three-dimensional in addition to two-dimensional files;
• serve the interest of general public, as well as the technical analyst;
• store large multidisciplinary data sets.
  For more information on GIS applications, see Boxes 5.3 and 5.4.

5.2.7 Predicting impacts in a real time environment

GIS techniques have been recently applied in several large forest management areas. In one area (approximately 1.4 million hectares), forest management and habitat models were combined with social, economic, natural, and cultural data to evaluate impacts and recommend optimal forest management approaches over the 100 year forest cycle. Initially, geographic cells were created, based on areas with similar forest vegetation (species, age, size), climate, and soils. In each cell, all available and relevant data on natural, social, economic, and cultural resources of the area were recorded on the attribute tables. Based on the average harvest requirement of the forest industry, the forest management model was run in the GIS. This allowed prediction, on a cell-by-cell basis, of the harvesting areas and road network required to meet annual industrial

Box 5.3 GIS applications by ACA, IIASA

An example of application of integrated environmental information systems with various technologies combined include MEXSES, an expert system for environmental impact assessment that includes both GIS and dynamic simulation models (Fedra and Winkelbauer, 1991). The inference engine processes the rules to assess environmental impacts and can use more rules to infer facts. It can, if appropriate, get data from the GIS (example would be soils and slopes, vegetation, land use, etc., for a given project location), derive them from a simulation model, or ask the user. Where the information required comes from is more or less transparent for the user, and the strategy (i.e., which source of information to try first) is controlled by the knowledge base of the system and can be modified dynamically, based on context and state of the system.

REPLACE is another spatial expert system for site suitability analysis. Implemented in PROLOG and with a graphical user interface, it matches the spatial requirements of "activities" such as industrial plants or hospitals with spatial properties such as physiography infrastructure, or environmental constraints. By sharing data with a number of related simulation and optimization models as well as statistical and geographical databases, it is an integrated component of a modular regional information and decision support system.

XENVIS is a national level environmental information system implemented for the Netherlands, that incorporates a GIS, a water quality model for simulation of spills of toxins into the Rhine, a transportation risk analysis model, and an interface to a fault tree-based risk assessment system for process industries. Model output, including risk contour plots based on plant safety characteristics, weather data, and population distribution, is displayed over an interactively constructed map. Designed for risk analysis and risk communication, the system also includes a noise analysis module for railways and a number of interrelated databases, implemented in a hypertext structure, covering topics such as hazardous installations or chemicals.

harvest plans. The model was also used to project the subsequent growth of the forest. Thus, calculations could be made on the size and distribution of every forest, type of species, age, and size for any future time. These calculations were used in parallel with habitat suitability index (HSI) models to predict the effect on a variety of representative wildlife spieces from the area.

GIS modelling also predicted potential features and times when the reforestation rate might not meet the forest-harvesting requirements. Thus, plans could be made for how to handle such situations, in light of the ultimate goal of sustainability. Overall impacts on the environmental resources in the area also could be evaluated over the life cycle of the forest. Alternative developmental scenarios could be applied over the life cycle of harvesting and reforestation. The results could be used to help optimize forest management decisions from both industrial and environ-

Box 5.4 Computerization OPTRAC: GIS route optimization method

Objectives

Hydro-Quebec's preliminary project studies for lines had two principal goals. The first is to determine the optimum location from the environmental point of view. This will be the transmission line route that has the least impact on the environment, taking into account technical and economic aspects. It is found by successive reductions of the potentially usable territory and tends to become evident in two phases. In the first phase, the line corridor with the least impact within a study zone is defined. Then, in the second, the route with the least impact within that corridor is determined.

The second goal of Hydro-Quebec's preliminary project studies is to assess a project's environmental impacts, so that they can be reduced. This is done by defining, locating, and assessing the significance of a project's impacts, and then identifying and describing measures which would allow their reduction. Finally, the negative and positive impacts persisting after the application of any mitigation measures are compared and evaluated.

Results

GIS modelling represents a major advance in this environmental assessment method. It is now possible to use formal analysis procedures instead of what were more qualitative methods whether applied by experts or the general public. The OPTRAC process exploits this development. It makes it possible to formalize the analysis of values and suspected impacts. It also allows rigorous definition of the optimal route of a given ranking of elements, using a formal optimization algorithm. This computerized approach also makes it possible to find and analyse alternatives resulting from a different ranking of elements of different impact considerations. The use of OPTRAC will inevitably bring important changes to the course of preliminary design studies because it will be possible to propose concrete solutions from the outset of a project.

mental perspectives. This approach can be closer to the goal of planning for long-term sustainable development, something we all discuss but seldom know how to attain.

5.2.8 Continuous updating

GIS allows for continuous updating of information. For example, a forest fire can consume large areas. The GIS database can be easily adjusted and analysis models recalibrated to accommodate such environmental catastrophes. As a part of the forest management EA described above (Section 5.2.7), a GIS system and training were provided so the forest industry can now continuously monitor, update, and manage its resources for the future. Continuous storage and updating of the database will also facilitate future EA and environmental planning within the study area.

5.2.9 Multi attribute tradeoff system (MATS)

Another type of impact model that works well in GIS is the US Department of Interior's multi attribute tradeoff system (MATS). This model provides a basis for weighing alternatives, utilizing a large number of environmental, social, cultural, and economic factors. One can allow MATS to use a large variety of geographic cells on a simultaneous basis, each with different environmental sensitivities. Thus, alternatives can be quickly evaluated and compared, the relative importance of impact factors identified, and overall project development planning optimized.

5.2.10 Habitat analysis

HSIs model the potential for vegetation, fish, or wildlife species to live in an area. In impact assessments, they represent a better long-term evaluator of the overall project impacts than site surveys, which are only representative of a short-term population estimate. A variety of HSI models have been made available through the US Fish and Wildlife Service.

Since the value of a habitat depends on soils, geology, vegetation, climate, and geographic location, habitat value can vary substantially from place to place within the area affected by a proposed development. Within such an area, one could have hundreds or thousands of different habitat types. In GIS, each type can be identified within the database and separate HSI modelling conducted. By running the models with and without a proposed development, the impacts are identified. The speed of the computed database and model analysis allows different scenarios to be compared quickly. The GIS can also be used to evaluate impacts over the long term when habitat would have evolved naturally.

5.2.11 Aesthetic analysis

Three-dimensional GIS models can be used to interpret viewscapes and aesthetic impacts. In one of our organization's case studies, topographic, physiographic, and vegetation layers were used to create a three-dimensional image of a road corridor. Viewscapes were then developed for different corridors and used in an initial selection of potential parking and picnic areas. In a second case study, topographic and forest layers in the GIS were used to analyse the visual impacts of a proposed art gallery expansion along the edge of a deep river valley. In a third case, three-dimensional GIS was used to evaluate the aesthetic impact of timber harvesting on nearby picnic areas in the state of Washington. To mitigate impacts, the harvest plans were modified significantly.

5.2.12 Public consultation

Finally, the visual display capability of GIS lends itself for explaining development plans or alternatives to the public. Local public interest and understanding can be raised by using both drawing and aerial phototype files that show the relationship between the proposed project and individual properties, neighbourhoods, local landmarks, community services, and other features.

5.2.13 Advantages of the GIS method

- Potential for storing and accessing very large data set.
- Consolidates data from various sources for geographic analysis.
- Effectively performs multiple map overlays, incorporating logical and mathematical manipulations.
- Generates descriptive statistics regarding the distribution of spatial phenomena.
- Allows a number of different scenarios to be investigated quickly and effectively by varying input parameters for successive analysis runs.
- Can generate maps for output to hard copy as well as displaying map information on the computer screen.

5.2.14 Limitations of the GIS method

- Expensive and requires highly trained personnel.
- Not specifically structured for EIA.
- Digital data costly and difficult to acquire.

5.3 Expert systems for EIA

Expert systems, an emerging technology in information processing and decision support, are becoming increasingly useful tools in numerous areas, including EIA. Expert systems are man/machine systems that perform problem-solving tasks in a specific domain. Here, traditional numerical data processing is supplemented by symbolic elements, rules, and heuristics, in the various forms of knowledge representation to deduce conclusions from stored and supplied information.

Clearly, a model that "knows" about the limits of its applicability, what kind of input data it needs, how to estimate its parameters from easily available information, how to format its inputs, runs itself, and interprets its output, will require not only less computer expertise from its user, but it will also assist the user with domain expertise in the application area.

5.3.1 Artificial intelligence and expert systems

In discussing a domain as loosely defined as expert systems, it may be useful to present a few definitions selected from the literature. Equally instructive are the essentially graphic definitions that are available.

Expert systems, or knowledge-based systems, are a loosely defined class of computer software within the more general area of artificial intelligence (AI), that go beyond the traditional procedural, algorithmic, numerical, and mathematical representations or models. They contain largely empirical knowledge, for example, in the form of rules of heuristics, and inference mechanisms for utilizing this form of information to derive results by logical operations. They are fashioned along the lines of how an expert would go about solving a problem, and are designed to provide expert advice. Like any other model, they are sometimes extreme simplifications and caricatures of the real thing, that is, the human expert.

5.3.2 Basic concepts behind expert systems

What makes expert systems different from ordinary models and computer programs? Rather than trying to define differences in any formal way, it may help to introduce and discuss some of the basic concepts and approaches used in expert systems.

Expert systems are alternatively referred to as knowledge-based systems. Knowledge representation, therefore, is one of the fundamental concepts and building blocks in expert systems.

Knowledge is represented in various forms and formats, following different paradigms. The more commonly used forms include rules, attribute-value lists, frames of schemata, and semantic networks.

Probably the most widely used format, and also the most directly understandable form, of knowledge representations are rules, also referred to as productions or productions rules, or situation–action pairs. They are close to natural language in their structure, and they are familiar to programmers used to classical procedural languages such as FORTRAN or C. IF ... THEN ... ELSE is easy enough to understand. Examples of rules would be:

RULE 1010320 # encroachment corridor by forest type
```
IF          landuse              == forest
AND         forest_value         == high
AND         [vegetation          == rain_forest
            OR vegetation        == dense_forest]
AND         wildlife             == abundant
THEN        encroachment-corridor == very_large
ENDRULE
```

Another example is,

RULE 1010532 # USLE soil_erodibility
```
IF          [soil_type == very_fine_sandy_loam
            OR soil_type == silt_loam]
AND         soil_organic_content < high
THEN        soil_erodibility == high
ENDRULE
```

Obviously, the terms used in rules can be more or less cryptic and require proper definition and interpretation in the system:

RULE 1010201   # degradation by watershed class
                # and land requirements
```
IF          project_country      == Thailand
AND         [watershed_class     == WSC1
            OR watershed_class   == WSC2]
THEN        impact = major
ENDRULE
```

Many expert systems are described in the literature. The number of operational systems in everyday use for practical purposes, however, seems to be rather small, in particular when looking at an area such as EIA.

There are only a few purely knowledge-based systems that do not contain a substantial conventional component. Some of the operation and control systems, in particular in the wastewater treatment area, seem to fit into this category. Further, a large number of systems are being developed for hazardous waste site assessments and related topics, such as permitting or water site management, e.g., WA/WPM Generator; RPI Site Assessments; GEOTOX; DEMOTOX; or SEPIC. Reviews of these systems can be found in Ortolano and Steineman (1987).

However, it is important to realize that expert systems are certainly no substitute for many time-tested methods and models, but should be seen as complementary techniques which can improve many of these models. Obvious applications related to numerical models are in data pre-processing, parameter estimation, the control of the user interface, and the interpretation of results. There are certainly enough techniques in numerical modelling that open attractive opportunities for all techniques.

FURTHER READING

F. L. Fedra, L. Winkelbauer and V. R. Pantula, *Expert Systems for Environmental Screening. An Application to the Lower Mekong Basin*, Report No. RR-91-19, International Institute for Applied Systems Analysis, Luxemburg, 1991.

I. McHarg, *Design with Nature*, Natural History Press, Garden City, NY, 1969.

L. Ortolano and A. C. Steineman, "New Expert Systems in Environmental Engineering", Journal of Computing in Civil Engineering, Vol. 1, No. 4, 1987, pp 298–302.

6

Environmental management measures and monitoring

6.1 Introduction

The major objective and benefit of utilizing EIAs in project planning is to prevent avoidable losses of environmental resources and values. This is done through the development of a judicious and appropriate environmental management plan (EMP). Environmental management includes protection, mitigation, and enhancement measures as well as monitoring.

In the process of planning, it is essential for every project to formulate an EMP to ensure that resources are used with maximum efficiency, and that each of the adverse impacts identified and evaluated as "significant" be prevented, attenuated, or, when required, compensated. Possible mitigation measures include:

- changing project sites, routes, production technology, raw materials, disposal methods, engineering designs, safety requirements;
- introducing pollution controls, recycling and conservation of resources, waste treatment, monitoring, phased implementation, landscaping, inclusion of a plan for developing a green belt in an industrial plant site development, personnel training, special social services or community awareness and education;
- devising compensatory measures for restoration of damaged resources, monetary compensations for affected persons, offsite programmes to enhance some other aspects of the environment or quality of life for the community.

Monitoring is required to evaluate the success or failure (and consequent benefits and losses) of environmental management measures and subsequently to reorient the EMP. Regardless of the quality of an EIA and consequent environmental management measures, they are of limited value unless implemented. As experience has increased in using EIA process for environmental planning, the need and justification for continuous monitoring in order to establish meaningful databases has become obvious.

6.2 Environmental management plan (EMP)

Usually EMPs are evolved following the processes of scoping, IEE, and/ or detailed EIA, and consist of identification, prediction, and assessments.

- Identification of mitigation as well as enhancement measures based on the speculation of the issues emerging out of the implementation of the project (as well as associated sub-projects). For example, if air pollution due to particulate emissions is considered critical to the environment, measures such as electrostatic precipitator (ESP), fabric filter, Venturi scrubber, etc., may be identified as candidate mitigation measures.
- Detailing the possible mitigations/enhancement measures such that a cost-effective selection is made while ensuring that the objectives, legal regulations, etc., are satisfactory met. If the former example is extended, this would mean identification of the technology, that is ESP, filter, or scrubber, based on cost effectiveness. If a filter is found to be the appropriate or the cost-effective option, its minimum particulate removal efficiency should be considered.
- Implement the identified mitigation in terms of physical as well as human resource-based requirements. In the case of a fabric filter, the developer would need to estimate the location as well as the area required by the filter house, show the same in the factory map or layout, account for the power requirements in the overall energy requirements, explore the possibility of recovery of any valuable fractions from the filtered material, and provide for the disposal of the waste either on-site or off-site. The issue here is not really the technical design (i.e., what type of filter material or what would be the critical pressure drop) but to carry out an exercise of "accounting for the mitigation measure" in the overall resource requirements to ensure implementability. Additional considerations would include, hiring the required manpower who could operate the filter to the required efficiency to ensure a proper treatment/handling/disposal of any waste.
- Develop appropriate monitoring mechanism and in-plant institutional/

reporting systems which would provide a regular and continuous assessment of the functioning of the mitigation system. In the case of the "filter", this step would involve setting up a system for monitoring of particulates at the inlets and outlets at specified intervals (e.g., once in 24 hours) as well as specifying inspection visits to the disposal sites of the waste, if any.

EMP can thus include several technological and managerial interventions such as:

- recycling and conservation of resources;
- pollution control measures;
- phased implementation;
- monitoring;
- personnel training;
- landscaping (e.g., inclusion of a plan for developing a green belt around industry);
- devising compensatory measures for restoration of damaged resources;
- monetary compensations for affected persons;
- off-site programmes to enhance some other aspects of the environment or quality of life for the community.

As stated in the description of EMP, the starting point of establishing an EMP is always a list of critical issues and associated list of mitigation measures. Once such an identification is done, then steps detailing the mitigation measures with the required monitoring, and human resources needs, etc., can be identified.

Some of the relevant issues for which mitigation measures are generally required in industrial projects are compiled in detail below. In addition to this, certain project issues and the relevant mitigation measures for the fertilizer industry, oil and gas pipelines, water resources projects, and infrastructure projects (ports and harbours), are also given.

6.2.1 Issues and mitigation measures

In this section, the following approach has been adopted to assist in the development of an EMP. (i) Identification of environmentally significant issues at each stage of an industrial project, and (ii) recommendation of suitable mitigation measures for each issue identified in the previous step. This information may be used as a starting point for developing a comprehensive EMP.

Environmental issues for various industrial projects at the various stages would be very similar for all types of projects. For each issue the relevant mitigation measures are also recommended.

The environmentally significant issues and suitable mitigation measures may be identified at the following stages:

- project siting;
- site preparation and construction of the facility;
- operation of the plant;
- project closure.

6.2.1.1 Project siting

During project siting, it should be ensured that alternative sites be selected in the event of the project being located in any of the following areas:

- ecologically sensitive habitats such as mangroves, estuaries, wetlands, coral reefs, etc.;
- watercourses, causing their eventual degradation;
- areas where meteorological and topographic conditions are conducive to temperature inversions and air pollution episodes;
- areas with significant environmental problems (air, water, and noise pollution);
- areas with proximity to human settlements, resulting in impacts on human health.

Siting should ideally be done in an area with proximity to raw materials, local workforce, and transportation facilities. Sites selected should fulfil the following conditions:

- plot size should be sufficient for landfill or disposal on-site, or should be close to suitable disposal site(s);
- should be convenient for public/private contractors to collect solid wastes for disposal;
- plot should be situated on a watercourse having maximum water dilution and absorbing capacity;
- situated in an area where wastewater can be reused, with minimal treatment, for agricultural or industrial purposes;
- situated within an area that is able to accept plant wastes in their sewage treatment system.

When possible, the project should be located in industrial zones where there is provision of adequate water supply, sewerage, and wastewater treatment facilities. Industries with gaseous emissions should be located at high elevations in an area not subject to temperature inversions, and where the prevailing winds are towards relatively unpopulated areas. Transport sector studies should be prepared and safe transport routes selected to reduce likely impacts from spillage. Contingency measures for spillages should be drafted.

6.2.1.2 Plant construction and operation

The subsequent stages of construction and operation will now be examined for potential issues, and relevant mitigation measures for each issue

will be listed. These stages will be examined for significant issues related to:
- air pollution;
- water pollution;
- noise pollution;
- solid and hazardous waste pollution;
- socio-economic status;
- hazards;
- associated impacts (urbanization, transportation, and resource depletion).

In the following text, for each issue (I) the recommended mitigation measure(s) (M) is listed. For example, for the first issue under "Air pollution," AI1 is used while the recommended mitigation measure is AM1.

(i) Air pollution during site preparation and construction

AI1
Air pollution due to dust and particulates caused by:
- land clearing, grading, levelling, surface excavation;
- surfacing and paving;
- construction traffic;
- construction of the plant buildings and roads;
- quarrying and mining (where applicable);
- blasting and drilling (for mining activities);
- storage of raw materials/waste in piles.

AM1
The recommended mitigation measures are:
- proper blasting practices (such as controlled blasting) to minimize air-borne particulates;
- watering of haulage roads;
- application of sealants and dust suppressants;
- limiting earth movement and soil exposure to the dry season;
- balance cut with fill;
- resurface and revegetate exposed surfaces.

(ii) Air pollution during plant operation
The environmentally significant issues emerging during plant operation are largely governed by the type of industry, the raw materials used, and the type of process adopted.

AI2
Air pollution due to dust and emissions such as SO_x, NO_x, hydrocarbons, and particulate matter caused by:

- gaseous emissions from processes, energy production;
- possible accidents, hazards, and process malfunctions;
- plant operations such as crushing, material handling;
- kilns, clinker coolers in case of cement industry;
- transportation of raw materials, products, etc.

Air pollution is also caused due to some specific emissions, such as hydrogen sulphide from petroleum refinery process gas, carbon monoxide from catalyst regenerators, and process emissions of fluorine in the fertilizer industry.

AM2

Some basic housekeeping measures recommended for mitigating the above issues for all types of industries are:

- classify emission sources according to their geographical location to ensure dispersal of pollutants over the airshed;
- reduce discharges of fumes through use of fume collection systems and suction hoods at the point of emission and enclosed structures and buildings;
- prevent dust and particulates by using control systems such as mechanical dust collectors, electrostatic precipitators, filters, or high energy scrubbers, by conducting dust-generating operations in enclosed structures and buildings, by covering dry material during transportation, by installing wet-spray to minimize dust generation, and by installing hydrocarbon vapour control at all fuel transfer points.

Specific control measures that may be adopted for each type of air pollutant are listed below.

1 Suspended particulate matter (SPM): (i) control of SPM using electrostatic precipitators, bag filters, or cyclones at the point of emission; (ii) in coal mining, SPM levels can be reduced by conducting coal beneficiation; and (iii) mitigation of SPM in the ambient environment can also be done by developing a green belt.

2 Oxides of sulphur (SO_x) levels in emissions may be controlled by flue gas desulphurization and the double contact double absorption process.

3 Oxides of nitrogen (NO_x) can be controlled by modification of combustion and use of catalytic converters.

4 Fluorine can be controlled by scrubbing the reactor vapour and evaporator vapour during fertilizer manufacture.

5 Carbon monoxide (CO) emissions may be controlled by stripping, recycling, and reusing the gas released from coke production and fuel burning. Other control measures include use of a CO boiler, combustion of CO, use of ESP or multiple cyclones.

6 Hydrocarbons (HC): for control of HC released from solvents and amines (especially in petrochemical industry) closed circuit recovery units may be provided. Source control measures that may be adopted to reduce

HC and odours are vapour recovery systems, pressure tanks, floating-roof tanks, and vapour incineration.

7 Hydrogen sulphide (H_2S) control is possible through ethanolamine absorption and by sulphur recovery.

8 Mercaptans can be controlled by steam scrubbing, neutralization, incineration, and conversion to disulphides.

9 Ammonia (NH_3) emissions may be controlled through conversion to ammonium sulphate, oxidation of the gas, or by gas incineration.

(iii) Noise pollution during site preparation and construction

NI1
Noise pollution and vibrations due to construction, drilling, and quarrying activities.

NM1
Blasting and drilling procedures used should give rise to minimal vibrations to nearby residences and structures, and monitoring instruments should be installed at sensitive locations.

(iv) Noise pollution during plant operation

NI2
Noise pollution due to process and traffic noise.

NM2
During mining, blasting procedures used should have minimal vibrations to nearby structures, and monitoring instruments should be installed at sensitive locations. In the case of process noise, the impact should be reduced by enclosing and insulating noise-emitting processes or equipment in buildings or by use of other noise abatement procedures. Traffic noise should be minimal, especially during night hours, to avoid disturbance to the local residents.

(v) Water pollution

The efficient use of water can reduce the impact of over-extraction for other users. This might involve the re-use and recycling of wastewaters after treatment. Further efficiency can be achieved through maintaining high procedural standards and good housekeeping, for example, ensuring that pipe faults and leakages are detected and rectified rapidly.

Storage facilities and waste disposal areas need to be prevented from causing accidental release, or being affected by rainfall that may result in contaminated runoff and leaching. For spillage and other accidents, mitigation equipment will be required to combat the risk of industrial hazards, both within the plant (operations and storage) and in the transport of raw materials and wastes.

On-site and off-site solid waste disposal areas should be prevented from contaminating the surrounding soil. Lined disposal facilities will need to be secured and monitoring systems established to watch landfill sites for leakages. Landfill sites should be sited away from towns as they present a potential health hazard and unpleasant odours. Some wastes may be incinerated, but this operation needs to be carefully controlled.

(vi) Surface water pollution during site preparation and construction

WI1
Water pollution in the form of suspended matter caused by the run-off from the clearing and construction activity during the erection of a facility.

WM1
- Control required of stormwater run-off and prompt revegetation on disturbed areas.
- Disturbance of streams, drainage, ponds, and wetlands to be avoided.
- Where disturbance cannot be avoided, sediment control structures and practices to be used.
- Sedimentation basins should be provided.
- Receiving surfaces should be lined with stones or concrete.

WI2
Resuspension of toxic sediments during construction of offshore pipelines.

WM2
- Alternative location for laying pipeline to be selected.
- Alternative pipeline construction techniques to minimize resuspension of sediments (e.g., laying pipeline versus burying pipeline) during construction of pipelines.
- The pipeline should be laid at a period of minimal circulation.
- Erosion, run-off, and sedimentation from construction of pipeline, grading for access roads and substation facilities.

WI3
Impacts from selection of right of way.

WM3
- Right of way (ROW) to be selected so as to avoid impacts to water bodies and hilly areas.

- Sediment traps or screens to be installed to control run-off and sedimentation.
- Soils to be stabilized mechanically or chemically to reduce erosion potential.

WI4

Adverse effect on the flora and fauna in the area due to dredging and any other disturbance of the area for site preparation and during construction of the facility.

WM4

- Select water intake in an area that avoids significant impact.
- Install screens to eliminate entrainment and impingement.
- Select alternate site or site layout to avoid loss of wetland.
- Re-establishment of habitat in some other area.
- Prohibit or restrict disturbance of significant habitat wetlands.
- Require prompt reclamation to forage and habitat favourable to local wildlife.
- Require prompt reclamation of disturbed areas and revegetation with native species.
- Minimize surface area of tailings and leach ponds, and require that they be promptly drained or closed when not in use.
- Net covering, fencing, or scaring may be required at active ponds.

(vii) Surface water pollution during plant operation

WI5

Surface water pollution due to discharge of liquid effluents, process spills, process cooling water, surface run-off from raw material and/or waste piles, excess heat from process, cleaning and maintenance of machines, buildings, etc., transportation by water, solid waste disposal, and settlements accompanying the project.

There is also the potential for increased surface water degradation by pipeline transport of products or new materials.

WM5

Treatment of process effluents, mine drainage, sanitary/domestic and stormwater run-off to meet water quality standards before discharge. Some examples of treatment options are:

- reduction of suspended solids (e.g., by sedimentation, flocculation, and filtration through use of filtration systems, settlement lagoons, and clarifiers);
- removal of oil and grease (e.g., by skimming, filtration, ultrafiltration, and flotation);

- neutralization;
- reduction of toxic chemicals such as chromium, copper, nickel, and zinc (e.g., by chemical precipitation, filtration, and ion exchange);
- reduction of chemical oxygen demand (COD) by appropriate methods of chemical, physical, and/or biological treatment;
- land application of process wastewaters;
- biological treatment (nitrification/denitrification).
  Sediment control structures/practices should be used:
- water quality standards should be established for all wastewater discharges – laboratory analysis of effluent should include total dissolved solids (TDS), total suspended solids (TSS), alkalinity, potassium, sulphates, biological oxygen demand (BOD), COD, heavy metals (process specific), nitrogen, phosphorus, pH, and temperature;
- prompt clean-up of any spills (oils, lubricants, and cleaning solvents);
- storage areas should be lined;
- rainfall allowed to percolate through piles and run-off in uncontrolled facilities should be minimized;
- stormwater should be collected and monitored before discharge;
- secure storage facilities and on-site/off-site waste disposal site should be used to prevent accidental release of chemicals and protect against rainfall that may result in contaminated run-off and leaching;
- thermal pollution due to power plants, etc., should be controlled by use of alternative heat dissipating design, installation of mechanical diffusers, cooling water on-site in holding ponds, and exploring opportunities to use waste heat.

WI6
Eutrophication of natural water systems.

WM6
Directions for use should be provided to minimize nitrate and phosphate pollution potential.

(viii) Water pollution – groundwater

WI7
Contamination of groundwater due to leaching from tailing ponds in mining areas, waste disposal sites, run-off from storage piles leading to percolation to groundwater.

WM7
Groundwater contamination maybe minimized or prevented wherever possible by using secure lined disposal facilities and establishing

monitoring systems for leakages and using a leachate collection system and an on-site chemical treatment before discharge.

In the case of mining projects, special care should be taken to prevent groundwater contamination by avoiding or minimizing penetration of aquifers below the strata being mined and by properly casing or sealing drill holes outside or below the mine area.

(ix) Solid wastes

SWI1
Solid waste disposal may result in soil and surface and groundwater contamination due to:
• disposal of industrial solid or liquid wastes;
• burning of industrial wastes;
• mining of minerals;
• rubble from demolition, overburden from mining, slag from smelting operations, tailings from mineral ore concentration;
• sludge disposal.

SWM1
• Site selection for solid waste disposal, for example, ash disposal by land filling, mounding, and in secure lined ash ponds.
• Source reduction, source segregation, by-product utilization, appropriate planning, and management of disposal sites such as lining of sites with a collection system for run-off water and leachate.

(x) Hazardous wastes during site preparation and construction

HWI1
The site may have been used as a hazardous waste disposal or storage site which can lead to contamination of groundwater and soil as well as being harmful to labourers working on the site.

HWM1
Due diligence and assessment of the site must be done prior to site selection.

(xi) Hazard identification – on-site/off-site
Many industrial facilities include operations with inherent hazards which require careful management. Industrial hazards are minimized and managed through the use of engineering controls, administrative controls, personnel protection, occupational health and safety training, health and safety planning, and medical monitoring.

(xii) Hazard identification during site preparation and construction

HI1
Hazards to employees and residents in the surrounding areas may originate from accidents, hazardous material transport, and storage.

HM1
Facilities with a risk of structural collapse, rupture, fire, or explosion will need to be located in geotechnically stable locations (e.g., minimal risk of seismic activity or subsidence). Based on the nature of the potential hazard (e.g., fireball, toxic gas release, spill), facilities will need to have an appropriately sized buffer zone. Within an installation with industrial hazards, unit operations will need to be laid out so that incompatible substances are not located within proximity of each other (e.g., substances which would react upon mixing to generate heat, fire, gas, explosion, or violent polymerization). Also, incompatible operations are not to be located within proximity of each other (e.g., welding operations are not to be located near storage of ignitable materials).

HI2
Contaminated dust raised, especially during site preparation, in areas where hazardous material has been stored in the past, may cause serious health problems.

HM2
Dust control measures during construction include spraying water (or water with a wetting agent) at the source of dust dispersion, to minimize the generation of dust.

(xiii) Hazard identification during plant operation

HI3
Fires, explosions, emission of toxic and hazardous gases, vapours, dust, emission of toxic liquids, radiation, and various combination of these effects.

HM3
- Provision of bunkers or blast walls.
- Firewalls/fireproofing of structures.
- Provision of safety buffer zones around the plant boundary.
- Storage and handling of substances should be according to the manufacturer's recommendation.

- Special precautions should be taken against theft and fires and during destruction.

  The following general rules should be applied:
- lighting in the storage area should be natural or by permissible lights;
- lamps should be vapour proof and the switch should be outside the building;
- only tools of wood or other non-metallic materials should be used;
- cases of explosive should not be piled in stacks more than 2 m high;
- cases of explosives should be stored topside up, so that cartridges are lying flat.

In the case of fire hazards due to flammable materials the following are the recommended mitigation measures:

- store in places that are cool enough to prevent accidental ignition in the event that vapours of the flammable materials mix with the air;
- provide adequate ventilation in the storage space, so that leaked vapours from containers are diluted enough to prevent a spark from igniting them;
- locate the storage area well away from areas of fire hazard (for example, where torch-cutting of metals is to be performed);
- keep powerful oxidizing agents apart from materials that are susceptible to spontaneous heating (explosive or materials that react with air or moisture to evolve heat);
- provide fire-fighting equipment;
- prevent smoking or use of bare filament heaters;
- the storage area must be electrically grounded and equipped with automatic smoke or fire detection equipment.

The following control measures should be adopted during pressurized storage of flammable fluids:

- tanks should be stored upright and chained or otherwise securely attached to some substantial support to minimize the chance of falling over and breaking or straining the valve or other part of the tank;
- tank storage area should be kept cool, out of direct rays of the Sun, and away from hot pipes;
- provide means (e.g., sprinkler) of keeping the tanks cool in case of external or internal fire;
- take care to avoid damaging tanks in handling;
- valves must be operated carefully and kept in good condition;
- do not hammer valve cocks;
- discourage tampering with tanks in any way;
- hazardous gases should be stored as a refrigerated liquid rather than under pressure;
- shutdown and secondary containment should be improved, which will reduce the amount escaping from containment or from site;

- automatic shutdown will reduce the amount of material escaping from containment;
- water curtains may be provided for restricting gas release;
- dikes (or bunds) will restrict liquid release.

HI4
- Occupational health effects on workers due to escaping dust, materials handling, noise, or other process operations.
- Accidents occur at a higher than normal frequency because of level of skill or labour.

HM4
- Provision of escape routes for employees.
- Implementation of emergency procedure on-site and off-site.
- Provision of public address systems and public education.
- Planning and training for evacuation.
- Facility should implement a safety and health programme designed to identify, evaluate, monitor, and control health hazards as well as provide safety training especially to the unskilled labour.
- Periodic training and continual safety reminders to all operating staff;
- Periodic drills in emergency procedures.
- All visitors should be briefed on potential hazards and the necessary safety precautions.
- It is to be ensured that appropriate safety and rescue equipment is available and employees trained in its use.

HI5
Accidents due to pipelines transporting hazardous material.

HM5
- Locations of buried pipelines in high-use areas should be clearly marked.
- Emergency evacuation plans and procedures should be developed.
- Pipelines should be monitored for leaks.
- Alarms should be installed to notify the public of accidents.
- Spill containment techniques should be utilized.
- Clean up and restore affected areas.

HI6
Transit patterns disrupted, noise and congestion created, and pedestrian hazards aggravated by heavy trucks transporting raw materials to/from the facility.

HM6

- Site selection can mitigate some of these problems.
- Special transportation sector studies should be prepared during project feasibility to select best routes to reduce impacts.
- Transporter regulation and development of emergency contingency plans to minimize risk of accidents.

Some general techniques that should be adopted to minimize hazard related accidents are discussed below.

- Within processing operations, substitute a hazardous material with a nonhazardous material. Change the form of the material (e.g., to a gas or a liquid) if the resulting form would be less hazardous (e.g., store toxic gases in a suitable solvent form).
- Minimize the quantities of hazardous materials used by recovering and recycling them within the process operation. Reduce the inventory of hazardous materials in storage. Use more efficient processing techniques.
- Ventilation, collection, and filtration are effective for dust control. Dusty operations should be isolated and/or contained to the largest extent possible, especially when the dusts could lead to lung diseases, most prevalent at mines, brickyards, glass making plants, and sand-blasting operations. Occupational asthma is caused by a broad array of chemicals and natural substances, including isocyanates, acid anhydrides, danders, grain dust, cotton dust, and wood dust.
- Limitation of personnel to those specifically trained in the work conditions in a potentially hazardous area, including use of personnel identification, double locks, security services, and barriers.
- Complete hazard labelling of all switches, valves, containers, and unit operations. In addition to identifying specific hazardous substances by name, also identify the type of hazard (e.g., toxic, reactive, ignitable, explosive).
- Provision of air temperature control may be needed at certain operations in order to avoid heat stress or cold stress. A particularly hot or cold operation may need to be segregated from the others in order to minimize the number of personnel exposed.
- Monitoring of the environment in the immediate vicinity of potential hazards, as well as at the fence-line of the installation, provides an early warning of a hazard occurring. For example, air quality monitoring for volatile organics, oxygen levels, combustible gas levels, and/or specific air constituents, could be conducted on a regular basis using portable equipment or a continuous basis with stationary equipment. Smoke detectors, heat monitors, radiation detectors, as appropriate to the type of installation, are used to signal that a hazard is occurring.
- Provide manual and automatic systems for shut-down of electrical

systems and/or process operations, so that the release of hazardous material is minimized.

(xiv) Socio-economic issues during site preparation and construction

SEI1
Land use pattern in the surrounding areas changes significantly, that is, project-induced changes such as urbanization and the creation of new settlements. There is then an effect on the social and economic fabric of the region due to dislocation of population from the project site, migrant labour, stress on the local infrastructure, effects on public health, and effects on local lifestyle and values.

SEM1
* Select alternative site or alter site layout to avoid displacement.
* Proper provision for rehabilitation or resettlement action plan, and adhere to state/central governmental policies for compensation. In areas where tribal and indigenous people are affected, it is advisable to prepare an indigenous people development plan wherein the compensation packages are clearly worked out.
* Involve affected parties in the resettlement planning and programme.
* Construct socially and culturally acceptable settlements/infrastructure development.
* Find suitable employment opportunities in or around the project site.
* Provide an infrastructure plan and financial support for increased demands.
* Construct utility facilities such as hospitals, post offices, shopping centres, etc., to reduce demands or improve existing facilities to meet the increasing demands.
* Phase construction activities to control traffic.
* Construct alternative traffic routes.

(xv) Socio-economic issues during plant operation

SEI2
The socio-economic effects due to the implementation of the project may be beneficial as well as detrimental to the social structure in the project area. The effects may be as follows:
* employment opportunities created;
* migrant population may lead to stress on social services;
* effect on public health due to plant operation;
* stress on water supply, power, and associated utilities;
* land values affected;
* population structure and dynamics affected.

SEM2
- Develop plans to educate workers on sensitive values and patterns.
- Provide behavioural/psychological readjustment programmes.
- Select alternative site or site layout.
- Construct visual buffers (e.g., green belt).
- Develop and implement "change find" procedures to recover, relocate, or restore structure.
- Proper planning of employment opportunities.
- Training of local people.

A socio-economic study of potentially affected communities to identify possible impacts on service, infrastructure, dislocations, and conflicts is required pre-development. These impacts can be addressed by:
- community assistance grants, loans, prepayment of taxes;
- phasing mineral development;
- constructing needed community facilities.

Cooperative and open working relations should be established early with local communities and maintained throughout the life of the project. Project workers should be encouraged to participate in community affairs. All employees should be briefed to ensure awareness of and sensitivity to the local cultures, traditions, and lifestyles. It should be ensured that native leaders are aware of the projected activities, are assisted in identifying impacts that may be of particular concern to them, and have a voice in appropriate mitigation measures. Mitigation may include isolating the work force from the native community.

SEI3
Changes in air and water quality and noise levels may result in adverse effects on public health.

SEM3
- Provision of healthcare facilities.
- Control of emissions and green belt planning.
- Proper planning for impending rise in townships and utility services.
- Facility should implement a safety and health programme designed to identify, evaluate, monitor, and control safety and health hazards at a specific level of detail, provide safety training, and propose procedures for employee protection.

(xvi) Associated impacts
Apart from the direct impacts on the environment due to the project activities, a number of associated impacts arising from these direct impacts are also observed. These associated impacts also need to be considered while developing an EMP as they may have long-term impli-

cations on the resources in the project area. The issues arising out of these impacts may be categorized as associated urbanization, transportation, and infrastructure and resource depletion related issues.

(xvii) Associated urbanization

AUI1
As a result of the industrial project employment opportunities get created, leading to immigration, the migrant population may lead to stress on social services, and land value is affected.

AUM1
• Proper planning for impending rise in townships is required.
• Proper planning of employment opportunities.
• Training of local people.
• Careful planning of industrial and urban boom.

(xviii) Transportation

TI1
An increase in traffic due to need for transport of raw materials, products, by-products, wastes, etc., will result in stress on the existing roadways, railways, or waterways where applicable. During plant operation there will be an increase in commuter traffic to the project site.

TM1
• Design roads for adequate capacity and visibility.
• Conduct specific studies to develop a transport sector development plan, depending on the need for the mode of transport.
• Ensure that roads are properly signed, vehicles are well maintained, and drivers are trained and safety conscious.
• Provide buses or require that commuting workers car-pool.
• Develop a plan for provision of fuelling stations.

(xix) Infrastructure related and resource depletion issues

II1
Stress on water supply, power, and associated utilities. Raw material exploitation may cause depletion of the resource. This is specially relevant in the case of non-renewable resources such as minerals and fossil fuels. Depletion may also be a risk to renewable resources, such as water and forest resources, if they are overexploited and not used on a sustainable basis.

IM1

- In the case of extractive mining, plan for resource usage to fit availability and impose restrictions on the manner of mining.
- Coordinate with the responsible agency to examine site reclamation options once the facility is decommissioned.
- Operate metals-processing operations at hours when other power-consuming industries are not operating.
- Increase power generation capabilities.
- Mitigation measures based on identified resource conflicts may include avoidance, timing of operations, recovering and archiving cultural and historic resources, and segregation and stockpiling for use in reclamation (soils).

6.2.2 Illustrations of guidelines for mitigation measures for specific projects

Guidelines for mitigation measures that may be adopted to alleviate the adverse impacts due to the fertilizer industry, oil and gas pipelines, water resource projects, and ports and harbours are given in Tables 6.1, 6.2, 6.3, and 6.4.

6.2.2.1 Fertilizer industry

The main positive socio-economic impact due to the fertilizer industry is that it is critical to achieving the level of agricultural production needed to feed the rapidly growing world population. However, negative environmental impacts from fertilizer production can be severe (Table 6.1, pages 143–146). Wastewaters, which may be highly acidic or alkaline depending on the type of plant, and may contain ammonium compounds, metals, urea, and elevated levels of BOD, are the major problem.

6.2.2.2 Oil and gas pipelines

Having discussed the industrial sector, it appears relevant at this point to also examine the impacts due to oil and gas pipeline projects since they serve as feedstock for a number of industries such as power plants as well as raw material for industries such as fertilizers, petrochemicals, etc.

Oil and gas pipelines may be viewed as contributing to environmental quality by making cleaner fuels more available (e.g., low sulphur gas as opposed to high sulphur coal) for energy production and/or industrial purposes. However, the magnitude of their negative impacts, especially on the ecological environment, is profound. The significant potential negative impacts due to these projects are given in Table 6.2 (pages 147 and 148), together with various appropriate mitigation measures.

Table 6.1 Potential impacts and mitigation measures for fertilizer industries

Environmental parameters	Impacts	Mitigation measures
Physical resources (a) air quality		
SPM (dust)	• Human health, respiratory diseases, emphysema, cardiovascular diseases, asthma • Decrease in plant respiration, change in foliage pattern	• Cyclones, bag filters • Green belt
SO_x	• Increased mortality, morbidity, bronchitis, and other respiratory diseases • Chronic plant injury • Corrosion of material	• Various tail gas cleaning processes • Dilution through stack
NO_x	• Lung diseases, chronic nephritis • Factor in causing smog • Material damage	• Scrubbing processes such as extended absorption using nitric acid, selective catalytic reduction using ammonia • Dilution through stack
Specific gases: fluorine, ammonia	• Can cause metabolic disorders and mortality in plants • Increase in levels causes irritation to eyes, nose, throat, damage to respiratory system, rapid asphyxia	• Reactor vapour scrubbing and evaporator vapour scrubbing • Scrubbing and recycling the resulting ammonium nitrate solution; condensation to liquid form using coolers and chillers
Physical resources (b) water quality		
Surface water quality	• Affects aquatic plant and animal life, causes eutrophication	• Take appropriate steps to reduce input of pollutants to the water system
BOD	• Affects aquatic species	• Construct wastewater treatment plants and ensure they function efficiently
COD	• Increase in levels	
Dissolved solids	• Increase in levels	

Table 6.1 (cont.)

Environmental parameters	Impacts	Mitigation measures
Suspended solids	• Along with ammonia causes algal blooms which increases cost of water treatment	
Phosphorus	• Causes dental and skeletal fluorosis, affects hatching of eggs in fish	
Fluorides	• Toxic to fish and aquatic life, causes fish kills	
NH_3, N, etc.	• Eutrophication	
Groundwater quality	• Percolation of pollutants from soil and surface water bodies may contaminate groundwater	• Use of liners in landfill sites and proper disposal of solid wastes, especially sludge
Physical resources (c) land quality		
Soil	• Weak acid from sulphuric acid plant causes acidification of soils • Nitric acid formed due to NO_x in the atmosphere causes acidification	• For mitigation of impacts reduce the discharge of pollutants into water
Land use	• Change in land use • Loss of agricultural land	• Proper siting of project • Control of land use activities
Ecological resources		
Vegetation (flora)	• Destruction due to construction activities	• Degradation of forests should be as little as possible
Aquatic life	• Condensates from ammonia and urea plants can have a toxic effect • Purge water from the phosphate industry can be detrimental to fish	• For mitigation of impacts reduce the emission of pollutants into water
Terrestrial wildlife	• Destruction of habitat has adverse effects	• The destruction of the natural habit of endangered/other species should be as less as possible

Table 6.1 (cont.)

Environmental parameters	Impacts	Mitigation measures
Quality of life values		
• Socio-economic	• Human population displacement • Change in socio-economic structure • Induced secondary development including demands on infrastructure	• Selecte alternative site or site layout to avoid displacement • Find suitable employment opportunities in or around project site • Provide infrastructure plan • Construct facilities to meet demands
Cultural	• Changes in demographic patterns and social and cultural values and patterns	• Develop plans to educate workers on sensitive values and patterns
Aesthetics/historical/ archaeological/ tourism	• Visual impact/ modification of historically or archaeologically important structures	• Select alternative site or site layout • Construct visual buffers (e.g., green belt)
Public health	• All the pollutants affect human health directly or indirectly	• Provision of health-care facilities for workers; proper safety measures and safety equipment for workers; control of emissions; green belt planning
Human use values		
Public utility services	• Consumption by the new industries causes pressure on resources	
Water	• Increased demand for water	• Recycling of hydroflurosilicic acid in the plant; process condensates; turbine condensates in the ammonia and urea plants can be used as boiler feed water after proper treatment; cooling tower blowdown in the sulphuric acid plant can be recycled again as make up water after proper treatment

Table 6.1 (cont.)

Environmental parameters	Impacts	Mitigation measures
Energy	• Consumption by the new industries causes pressure on energy resources	• Efficient waste heat recovery system in the sulphuric acid plant; catalyst developments; improved heat recovery integration; purge gas recovery unit; process evaluation based on optimization of operating parameters, etc., in case of ammonia plants
Accommodation	• Crowding due to arrival of more people	• Provision of proper housing facilities for the newly arrived people as well as local displaced people
Employment	• Increase in employment • Unemployment of local unskilled displaced people possible	• Proper planning of employment opportunities • Training of local people

6.2.2.3 Water resource projects

The above cases have been illustrations of industrial projects. Another major sector where developmental projects have a profound impact on the environment are water resources development projects. This may include construction of dams and reservoirs to meet the demands of irrigation and/or power. Table 6.3 (pages 149–156) lists the major potential negative impacts due to these projects and appropriate mitigation measures to minimize them.

6.2.2.4 Infrastructure projects

Another large scale and primarily irreversible impact on the environment is due to infrastructure projects such as construction of roads, transportation, urban infrastructure, and construction of ports and harbours. Although they have far reaching benefits in terms of improving the standard of living for the population, they also exert a number of adverse impacts on the environment. Table 6.4 (pages 157–160) examines the potential negative impacts of construction of ports and harbours, together with the relevant mitigation measures that may need to be adopted.

Table 6.2 Mitigation measures for oil and gas pipelines

Potential negative impacts	Mitigating measures
Direct	
Resuspension of toxic sediments from construction of offshore pipelines	• Select alternative location for laying pipeline • Use alternative pipeline construction techniques to minimize resuspension of sediments (e.g., laying pipeline versus burying pipeline) • Lay pipeline at a period of minimal circulation
Interference with fishing activities from offshore and nearshore pipelines	• Select pipeline route away from known fishing areas • Mark on a map the location of offshore pipelines • Bury pipeline that must be located in critical fishing areas
Habitat and organism loss along offshore and upland pipeline ROWs and pumping and compressor station sites, and increased access to wildlands	• Select ROW to avoid important natural resource areas • Utilize appropriate clearing techniques (e.g., hand clearing versus mechanized clearing) along upland ROWs to maintain native vegetation near pipeline. • Replant disturbed sites • Use alternative construction techniques
Erosion, run-off, and sedimentation from construction of pipeline, grading for access roads and substation facilities	• Select ROW to avoid impacts to water bodies and hilly areas • Install sediment traps or screens to control run-off and sedimentation. • Use alternative pipeline laying techniques that minimize impacts • Stabilize soils mechanically or chemically to reduce erosion potential
Alteration of hydrological patterns	• Select ROW to avoid wetlands and flood plains • Minimize use of fill • Design drainage to avoid affecting nearby lands
Evasion of exotic species and habitat fragmentation	• Select corridors and ROW to avoid important wildlands and sensitive habitats • Maintain native ground cover (vegetation) above pipeline • Make provisions to avoid interfering with natural fire regimes

Table 6.2 (cont.)

Potential negative impacts	Mitigating measures
Loss of land use due to placement of upland pipeline and substations	• Select ROW to avoid important social (including agricultural) and cultural land uses • Design construction to reduce ROW requirements • Minimize off-site land use impacts during construction • For buried pipelines, restore disturbed land along ROW
Creation of barriers for human and wildlife movement	• Select ROW to avoid travel routes and wildlife corridors • Elevate or bury pipeline to allow for movement
Increased traffic due to construction	• Phase construction activities to control traffic • Construct alternative traffic routes
Chemical contamination from wastes and accidental oil spills	• Develop waste and spill prevention and clean-up plans
Hazards from gas pipeline leakage or rupture	• Clearly mark locations of buried pipelines in high-use areas • Develop emergency evacuation plans and procedures • Monitor for leaks • Install alarms to notify the public of accidents • Utilize spill containment techniques • Clean up and restore affected areas
Indirect Induced secondary development during construction in the surrounding area	• Develop comprehensive plan for location of secondary development • Construct facilities and provide financial support to existing infrastructure
Increased access to wildlands	• Develop protection and management plans for these areas • Construction barriers (e.g., fences) to prohibit access to sensitive wildlands

Table 6.3 Potential impacts and mitigation measures of water resources development projects

Environmental parameters	Impacts	Mitigation measures
Physical resources		
Air quality	• Air quality is affected due to exhaust gas, dust, noise, and vibration in the construction phase • Overall a minor consideration for water resources projects	• Frequently sprinkling water on fresh construction spoils • Maintaining green belt • Providing masks to people working in dusty environment
Water quality		
Surface water quality	• Development of new industries and population concentration due to urbanization leads to increased wastes and hence deterioration of river water quality • Deforestation leads to erosion which in turn causes increased sediment load and hence high turbidity in the river • Intensification of agriculture due to increased demands for food leads to leaching of fertilizers which affect surface water quality	• Catchment area treatment to reduce sediment load • Adequate treatment of effluents to attain the standards prescribed in appropriate International Standard (IS) and consideration of assimilative capacities of receiving water bodies • Proper control of discharges from non-point sources • Efficient application of pesticides, fertilizers, and other agrochemicals to reduce their losses due to leaching • Proper treatment of domestic and industrial wastes to reduce the concentration of nutrients reaching water bodies especially quiescent ones • Efficient application of fertilizers to the crops so that the amount leached is kept to a minimum • Soil conservation measures to be adopted

Table 6.3 (cont.)

Environmental parameters	Impacts	Mitigation measures
Groundwater quality	• Percolation of pollutants such as pesticides and wastes from soil and surface water bodies may contaminate groundwater	• Prevention with use of liners • Use of leachate collection system • On-site chemical treatment before discharge
Land quality		
Soil	• Deforestation due to new development such as industries and population growth and increased flood and drought leads to erosion of soil • Fertilizer and pesticide residue may lead to a change in the physico-chemical properties of the soil and increased salinity of soil	• Education of relevant people to develop widespread understanding of the problems that are likely to arise and the methods of sound land use • Actions by individuals through local mechanisms with the help of the governments • Efforts to relieve economic and social maladjustments in the use of land and which impede conservation
Land use	• Change in land use patterns • Loss of agricultural land	• Proper siting of the project is very important
Other specific physical resources		
Water hydrology	• Change in surface and ground water hydrology (existing flow patterns) due to construction of the water resources project • Increased sedimentation in the river or other water body	• Adequate site investigation and appropriate site design and siting is necessary • Use of sedimentation models will help estimate the change in hydrologic regime

Table 6.3 (cont.)

Environmental parameters	Impacts	Mitigation measures
Drainage	• Change in the natural drainage pattern occurs due to erosion of soil and changes in level of the groundwater table • Components such as deep percolation from reservoir and canal irrigated areas and seepage loss from main canals, branch canals, and tributaries lead to a change in groundwater recharge	• Reservoir operations should be such that two or three spills of reasonable discharge are allowed in the river on a regular basis • Minimum flow in the river should not be less than the average 10 days minimum flow of the river in its natural state • Priorities and requirements downstream should be taken care of
Meteorology	• The reservoir causes higher relative humidity due to increased evaporation from the reservoir and the newly irrigated area • There can also be moderating effect on extreme temperatures if reservoir is very big	• Proper siting • Regular monitoring
Seismicity	• Construction of the water resources project involving drilling, blasting, and quarrying may affect the seismicity of the area, especially if there are already existing major faults nearby	• The prediction of seismicity can be done with the help of equations • The design should ensure that the hydraulic structures area is safe against the largest expected earthquake • For large reservoirs of depth >100 m or/land volume 10^9 m^3 detailed investigations of nearby faults must carried out • A more detailed description of seismic consideration is given in the *EA Sourcebook* (see Further Reading)

Table 6.3 (cont.)

Environmental parameters	Impacts	Mitigation measures
Water resources	• Impact on rainfall, run-off, and groundwater levels • Increase in live storage capacity and hence utilizable water	• The live storage capacity can be determined by matching demand and water availability patterns • This matching is possible by using mass curve technique, sequential peak algorithm or through stochastic simulation • Utilizable water should be worked out in relation to the ratio of live storage capacity to average annual yield • For maintaining live storage capacity on a long-term basis, appropriate sediment control measures in the catchment area should receive priority attention • Sediment deposition in a reservoir can be controlled to a certain extent by designing and operating outlets in the dam in such manner as to point selective withdrawals of water having a higher sediment content • The effective method of silt control is by releasing water through a series of outlets at various elevations

Table 6.3 (cont.)

Environmental parameters	Impacts	Mitigation measures
Ecological resources		
Vegetation (flora)	• Air pollution during construction leads to damage to plant life • Development of new industries and urbanization leads to deforestation and loss of valuable species	• The total forest area lost by siting of the dam, reservoir, canals, and other structures can be estimated by superimposing the project layout maps on the land use maps • The loss of forest in terms of its biomass can be estimated on the basis of forest productivity • The total area of forest loss due to reservoir, dam, canals, and other items have to be afforested as a compensatory measure
Aquatic life	• Population concentration leads to increased wastes in the river, nutrient uptake, and light interruption and hence reduced primary productivity of useful planktons • Increased nutrient load leads to reduced fish yield • Deforestation leads to high turbidity of river water and hence low primary productivity and low fish yield	• From baseline data it is possible to identify the migrating fish species as well as their migration routes upstream and downstream • The change in fish species due to change in hydraulic regime of the river can be predicted by observing other similar project areas
Terrestrial wildlife	• Displacement and reduction in species of wildlife due to habitat encroachment • Danger of extinction of endangered and endemic species	• Proper site selection and rehabilitation measures by the creation of alternative habitats

Table 6.3 (cont.)

Environmental parameters	Impacts	Mitigation measures
Ecological cycles	• Danger of extinction of unique or rare species	• If the area to be affected contains any unique or rare species, an alternative site has to be considered for the project site or suitable measures should be taken to rehabilitate the species
Quality of life values		
Socio-economic	• Human population displacement • Change in socio-economic structure, standard of living, income distribution, etc. • Induced secondary development including demands on infrastructure	• The rehabilitation plan should consider socio-economic aspects as well as quality of life and the requirements of society • In this regard various state governments have formulated policies which could be followed
Cultural	• Changes in demographic patterns and social and cultural values	• Develop plans to educate workers on sensitive values and patterns
Aesthetics/historical/ archaeological/ tourism	• Visual impact on historical, archaeological, and cultural resources and on landscapes • Modification of historically or archaeologically important structures • Decline of tourism due to deterioration of aesthetic value due to pollution	• Rehabilitation of monuments likely to be affected by the project should be undertaken if possible • Sites chosen for total rehabilitation should be similar to the earlier one in terms of access and environmental setting

Table 6.3 (cont.)

Environmental parameters	Impacts	Mitigation measures
Public health	• Alteration in vectors and risk of transmission of vector-borne diseases as a result of the project, arising mainly from urbanization and new bodies of water	• Three types of measures should be taken for public health: vector control, increase in awareness of public health, and engineering design and control • Vector control can be achieved through engineering, biological, chemical, and agrochemical measures • Engineering design and control measures include proper design and straight alignment of canals, lining of canals, provision of steep and regular banks for the reservoir, provision for clean drinking water, sanitary facilities, bridged crossings, adequate drainage measures, and maintenance of canals and drainage systems in order to prevent creation of better habitats for vectors
Other specific values		
• Population rehabilitation	• Displacement of local population occurs due to the project • Migration to project area leads to rise in population	• Population projection should take into account migration to project area because of enhanced agricultural and other economic activities • Proper steps for rehabilitation of displaced farmers, etc., should be undertaken

Table 6.3 (cont.)

Environmental parameters	Impacts	Mitigation measures
Human use values		
Public utility services Water supply and sanitation	• Existing sanitary and waste disposal practices could have linkages to qualities of surface water and groundwater	• The water requirement can be predicted on basis of crop, water, livestock, and human requirements after taking into account rainfall and evapo-transpiration
Accommodation	• Increased water requirement due to population growth and growth of industries • Increased demand for housing due to growth of population	• The domestic water demand for present and future can be worked out by data on population • The industrial water demand can be estimated on basis of survey • Provision of proper housing facilities for the newly arrived people as well as the local displaced people
Employment	• Increase in employment opportunities • Means of livelihood of farmers/regional tribes likely to be affected	• Proper planning of employment opportunities • Provision of employment to displaced farmers/regional tribes • Careful planning of industrial and urban boom
Other specific values Flood and droughts	• Increased flood and droughts due to deforestation and urbanization and hence problems in reservoir management	• Prediction by use of probabilistic models using data collected for previous years • Proper design of houses (stilts) for floods and efficient water supply via tankers, etc., in time of drought

Table 6.4 Information on impacts and mitigation measures for ports and harbours

Environmental parameters	Impacts	Mitigation measures
Physical resources (a) water quality		
SPM – Dust and coal dust	• Respiratory diseases, emphysema, asthma • Cardiovascular diseases • Decrease in plant respiration, change in foliage pattern • Damage to materials	• Good housekeeping, such as water spraying, shielding of dusty areas, cleaning of equipment, and maintaining proper operating methods • Use of coal dust suppression systems • Transport of coal in a slurry form • Agglomeration system whereby fines of coal are bound to the larger particles
SO_x, NO_x – Emissions from vehicles and burning of wastes	• Increased mortality, morbidity, irritation, bronchitis	• Avoid burning of waste material • Proper gaseous control equipment
Physical resources (b) water quality		
Surface water quality	Affected by: • dredging and reclamation • discharge of sanitary effluent	• Construction of breakwater and silt basin to minimize sediment release
Groundwater quality	Affected by • oil spills/leakages • soil run-off	• Avoid overspills from loading barges • Provide floating booms or skimmers to contain oil spills • Use of chemical dispersants to dissolve floating oil • Provide drainage control systems, ponding basins, storm drains
Physical resources (c) land quality		
Soil	• Soil erosion due to earth moving during construction activity	• Proper design and siting; avoid sensitive areas • Excavation of accumulated sand to mitigate adverse effects of erosion

Table 6.4 (cont.)

Environmental parameters	Impacts	Mitigation measures
Land use	• Change in land use, loss of agricultural land	• Resource management • Compensation to displace land owners • Displaced fishermen to be given financial assistance or alternative employment • Strict boundary regulations should be enforced to avoid illegal settlements and overspill of activities • The boundary should be securely fenced and regularly inspected
Other specific physical resources		
Water hydrology	• Change in the hydrological regime due to construction and operation of ports and harbours • High demand for raw and potable water	• Adequate site investigation and appropriate site design is necessary • Emphasis is to be placed on the need to establish objectives and formulate a methodology • Provision of an adequate water supply system including pier installation to supply freshwater to ships
Ecological resources		
Vegetation (flora)	• Degradation/depletion of forest, especially mangrove forests which may affect local fisheries	• Alternative site selection • Afforestation, social forestry • Green belt around the project as a buffer
Aquatic life	• Substantial loss of marine life • Habitat destruction and species loss	• Timing of activity so as to avoid spawning/migratory activity

Table 6.4 (cont.)

Environmental parameters	Impacts	Mitigation measures
Terrestrial wildlife	• Displacement of roosting/breeding/ feeding sites for the coastal birds • Depletion of food sources for the birds or oil coats on birds and fish due to oil discharges • Habitat encroachment and increased hunting	• Alternative site selection for preventive reasons • Re-establishment of habitat in some other area
Other specific ecological resources, e.g., coral reef	• Destruction of corals due to silting from the construction activities, disposal of dredging spoils, and structural damage from boats during collisions	• Avoid undue disturbance • Minimize sediment release from dredging and barge loading • Draft harbour regulations for piloting, anchorage, and ship movements
Quality of life values		
Socio-economic	• Human population displacement • Urbanization • Induced secondary development including demands on infrastructure	• Select alternative site or site layout to avoid displacement/relocation of displaced people • Land use planning • Provide infrastructure plan and financial support for increased demands • Construct facilities to reduce demands
Cultural	• Changes in demographic patterns and social and cultural values and patterns	• Develop plan to educate workers on sensitive values and patterns • Provide behavioural/ psychological readjust- ment programmes

Table 6.4 (cont.)

Environmental parameters	Impacts	Mitigation measures
Aesthetics/historical/ archaeological/ tourism	• Destruction of important archaeological/historical sites thereby affecting the cultural resources • Visual impacts due to accumulation of waste such as floatables, liquid/solid, and dredging wastes	• Prior archaeological survey/excavation • Proper design and siting to avoid any such problems • Disposal regulations • Normal standards of good design and maintenance should be adopted to avoid visual clutter
Human use values		
Public utility services	• Increase in demand for public utility services such as water supply, sanitation, power, surface transport, and post and telegraph	• Provision of adequate water distribution system • Provision of adequate collection, treatment, and disposal facilities for sanitary waste • Local police, fire, and medical facilities and other basic amenities of a township to be provided
Employment	• Increase in employment opportunities with onset of project and impending growth of industries, towns, and related support services	• Proper planning of employment opportunities • Generation of employment for local people

6.2.3 Development of a green belt as a mitigation measure

All the mitigation measures identified thus far have been impact specific. However, one mitigation measure that has a much broader definition, in as much as it can be used to alleviate a number of adverse impacts due to industries, is the development of a green belt around industrial facilities. In addition to pollution control measures, the negative impacts due to industrial development should be further attenuated by the development of green belt. Green belts not only absorb air and water pollutants but

Table 6.5 Width of green belt for various industries

Type	Industry	Examples	Area of works (ha)	Width of green belt
1	Heavy industry	Oil refineries, chemical works, metallurgical and seaport industries, nuclear reactors	>500	<2 km
2	Heavy industry	Machine manufacture, ship-building, big harbour industries, power stations	200–500	>1 km
3A	Medium-heavy industry with much air pollution	Manufacture of straw boards, artificial fibres, and ceramic products, cement works	100–200	500 m or more
3B	Medium-heavy industry with little air pollution	Manufacture of cars, foods, and textiles		200 m or more
4A	Light industry with some air pollution	Tanneries, textiles and food industries	50–100	50–100 m
4B	Light industry with some air pollution	Manufacture of electronic apparatus and domestic machines		
5	Service industry	Printing works, bakeries, laboratories	10–50	>100 m
6	Workshops, handicrafts, etc.	Fashion studios, photoprinting shops, potteries	1–10	>50 m

Adapted from *Manual on Urban Air Quality*, WHO Regional Publications, European Series No. 1, Copenhagen, 1976.

also help in arresting noise and soil erosion, and creating favourable aesthetic conditions.

Guidelines on the width of green belt for various industries are listed in Table 6.5. The selection of plant species for the green belt is an important feature. It should be based on considerations of soil and agro-climatic conditions, and the types of pollutants emitted by the industry. The guiding principles for selection and placement of plant species within the green belt are presented in Table 6.6.

Table 6.6 Guiding principles for green belt development

1 Selection of plant species
- Plant species should be fast growing, perennial, and evergreen with thick canopy cover, large leaf index, and resistant to specified pollutants.
- Plant species should preferably be indigenous so that the ecological balance in the region could be preserved.

2 Placement of plant species
- Trees growing up to 10 m or more should be placed in encircling rows around the installation along road sides.
- Shrubs should be grown amongst the trees to give coverage to the tree trunks normally devoid of foliage.
- Differential zones for shrubs and trees could also be defined based on wind speed and stability conditions.
- Sensitive species should be placed in patches along the entire green belt.

3 Maintenance of green belt
- Wastewater from the industry should preferably be recycled for maintaining the green belt.

6.3 Post-project monitoring, post-audit, and evaluation

Monitoring is required to evaluate the success or failure (and consequent benefits or losses) of environmental management measures and subsequently to reorient the management plan. It is essential that a good detailed monitoring programme be designed for appropriate projects (this design should be prepared as part of the EIA study and should be presented as a major component of the report including the detailed monitoring workplan, reporting procedure, and manpower and costs budgets) and that regular monitoring reports be submitted to environmental agencies. When these procedural needs are fulfilled, the EIA planning tool is put to use in a much more effective manner, and benefit analysis will be possible, which will determine how successful the EIA process is in preventing or minimizing environmental degradation.

The EIA procedures should include a formal requirement to review completed projects and judge the predictions and recommendations made against actual experience. The purposes of such an audit are to determine whether consequences were accurately predicted, to identify additional significant effects warranting corrective action, and to use the results to refine the impact predictions for future projects of the same type and magnitude.

Monitoring is essential for continuing EIA inputs to management (i.e., mid-course corrections, compliance with mitigation actions, and improvement of predictions). We have seen that predictive accuracy is limited because of the scarcity of information on impacts and natural

Table 6.7 Definitions of monitoring assessments procedures

Operations	Definition
Monitoring	Long-term, standardized measurement, observation, evaluation, and reporting of part of the environment in order to define status and trends
Survey	A finite duration, intensive programme to measure, evaluate, and report the quality of part of the environment for a specific purpose
Surveillance	Continuous, specific measurement, observation, and reporting for the purpose of environmental management and operational activities

variations in the environment. All development projects should be managed with the expectation of surprising outcomes and the necessity to adapt and change implementation actions if the goals are to be met. Monitoring provides an early warning that adverse impacts (predicted or not) are occurring.

Measures recommended to mitigate the impacts of development must be actually installed, operated, and maintained. Even so, their efficacy is often uncertain; thus, monitoring is necessary to see how well they work out and how cost-effective they are. As in the case of post-audit, compliance monitoring should be independent of the project operator, or at least the data should be verified by an independent group.

The overall evaluation of EIA in a particular government should be undertaken from time to time. All participants in the process should contribute constructive criticism and judgement as to how well EIA has helped achieve sustainable development.

The owners of the projects will be obliged to carry out the monitoring or surveillance programme, continuously or at defined intervals, and to report results to the regulatory body. If adverse effects beyond those anticipated in the original environmental impact assessments become apparent, remedial actions would have to be taken. In an extreme case, if suitable remedies cannot be found, closure of the project might be required.

The various procedures that may be adopted during monitoring, and the distinction between them, are shown in Table 6.7.

Monitoring may involve sampling of air, water, and soil, and the data collection programme should be planned to obtain the greatest value from the data, which is often expensive to collect and process. Care should be taken to classify and store data for easy retrieval, so that it can be useful as baseline or reference data for other assessments.

In the few retrospective studies made, the findings have been disconcerting. Forecasts are admittedly difficult, but they are often so imprecise and vague that their accuracy cannot really be ascertained. Many impacts are presented as unquantified assertions without any indication of their likelihood or significance. Not surprisingly, physiographic information is usually more complete and precise than biological impact prediction. Social considerations often occupy disproportionate space (in terms of what is actually known) in an EIA, but that is a reflection of the essential political use of these documents.

The post-audit can begin at once with existing EIAs on completed projects. It is a valuable training device and also helps to find empirical evidence for cause–effect relationships that will be useful in ongoing and future EIAs. Post-audit may be difficult in that the performers of past EIAs are being second guessed. Therefore, it should be carried out by a group independent of the environmental agencies, perhaps a panel drawn from the academic community.

The post-implementation monitoring of a project may involve audits which are somewhat different from the industrial audit. Three types of audit relevant to an EIA on a motorway project are listed here as an example:

- implementation audits, for determining whether the recommendations or requirements in an EIA were implemented;
- project impact audits, which determine the actual impacts of a project, independent of the predictions made, and
- predictive techniques audits, assessing the predictions made in the EIA report, and the methods of prediction used, by comparing actual outcome with the forecast ones (this would aid future studies).

FURTHER READING

EA Sourcebook, Vol 111, *Guidelines for EA of Energy and Industry Projects (Environment Department)*, World Bank, Technical Paper No. 154.
UNESCO series of learning materials in Engineering Sciences Module on Selected Topics in Environmental Management, UNESCO, 1993.

7

EIA communication

7.1 Introduction

Communication of EIA findings to policy and decision makers is difficult because they are often not technically trained. The task of communication is one of translation and interpretation from the language of the scientist into a clear and concise summary that matches the client's constraints and timetables. Another problem in using research results is the gap between the expectations of decision makers for certainty and the probabilistic realities of science. If a scientist reveals this uncertainty, the client may reject the findings as unhelpful, whereas disguising the uncertainty may cause the scientist to lose credibility when unpredictable results do occur.

Prediction should be straightforward, logical, and systematic regardless of the completeness or accuracy of the data available. All assumptions must be explicitly stated. The users of the assessment can follow the predictive method and, if they wish, substitute alternative assumptions where factual information is lacking.

A four-part format in reporting predictions is helpful in avoiding misunderstanding by the users about the uncertainty that inevitably accompanies EIA results.

First, the prediction should state what is known and with what confidence (a narrative statement of the statistical reliability). For example,

"With the chance of being wrong one time out of ten, we believe that the increase in turbidity will result in a 25 to 50% lower catch of fish."

Second, state what is not known and why. For example, "Tests have been run only on species A and B so we cannot be sure of the response of other organisms."

Third, explain what could be learned from further investigation if more time and money were available.

Fourth, indicate what should be known in order to proceed in a prudent manner, that is the risk of going ahead based on present knowledge as opposed to the risk of delaying the project.

To summarize, the EIA predictions should state what we do know, do not know, could know, and should know.

7.2 What is expected from the user of EIA findings?

The users of EIA findings and advice also should be urged to:
• understand the probabilistic nature of science and differences among sciences;
• accept uncertainty in environmental science and learn to live with it;
• manage adaptively and plan for surprise;
• avoid unnecessarily tight timetables;
• participate with scientists in the assessment process;
• find out the value and cost of better information and agree to pay and wait for it.

Since policy and decision makers have very little time to read, the title, abstract, and executive summary of the EIA should each repeat the key message for these individuals. Figure 7.1 shows, in a lighter vein, how the information from an EIA study can be communicated to decision makers.

7.3 Communication to the public

Effective public participation is critical in order to promote developmental projects successfully. Since the general public is the ultimate recipient of the economic benefits and environmental damage, every EIA should involve the public as part of the decision-making process of project development.

It must be remembered that there are many possible factors that can lead to miscommunication while disseminating information to the public. When communication events take place across socio-economic or multicultural levels, the possibility for mistakes increases significantly. Language translation mistakes are the most obvious cause. The ability of technical and scientific personnel to put information into an understand-

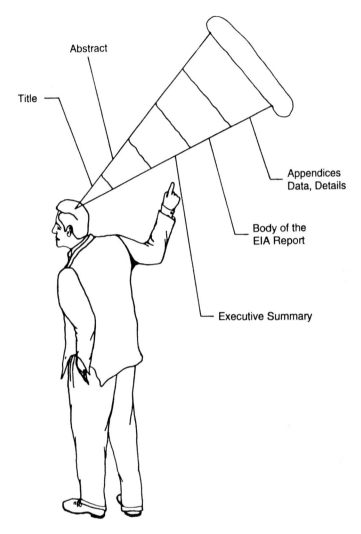

Environmental Management Centre

Figure 7.1 Getting the message of the EIA into the minds of decision makers

able context for non-technical or lay people is critical. Some of the points of miscommunication are illustrated by Figure 7.2.

Although the specific nature and degree of public participation can vary, it may be generally viewed as:

- access to information gathered during the assessment process;
- contribution of information to the assessment process;
- right to challenge decisions made during the assessment process.

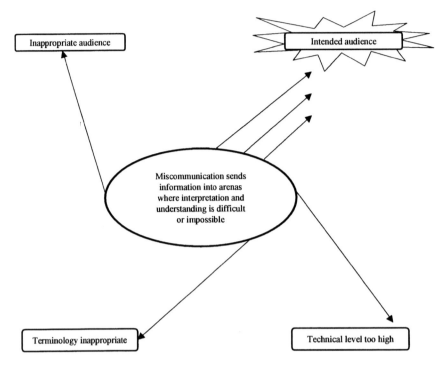

Figure 7.2 Illustrative points of miscommunication
Source: Environmental Risk Assessment for Sustainable Cities, Technical Publication Series [3] UNEP International Environment Technology Centre, Osaka/ Shiga, 1996.

Unfortunately, public involvement in an assessment project is generally not done in a very organized and effective manner, and not implemented as per policy statements. The assessment teams generally view the public as an adversary rather than as a partner in the assessment process. This seriously hampers the chances that the public may play a constructive role in the identification and evaluation of potential impacts.

Instead of concentrating on the risks and difficulties of including the public in the assessment process in a meaningful way, assessment teams must concentrate on the benefits that can be derived from enhanced and much expanded communication among team members and the public. Communication between the assessment team and the public is the key to public participation. The assessment teams should try to:
• communicate with the public as early as possible;
• communicate with as many people as possible;
• communicate in as many different ways as possible.

Although effective communication is an essential process in EIA, the

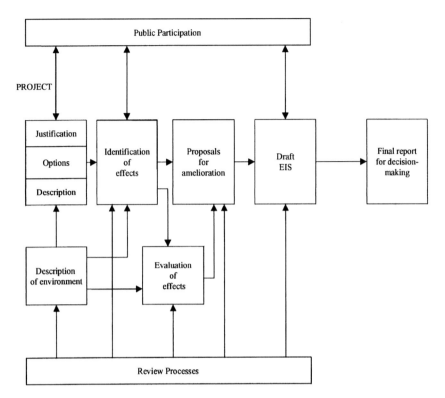

Figure 7.3 Public participation in environmental assessment processes
Source: Module on Selected Topics in Environmental Management, UNESCO
Series of Learning Materials in Engineering Sciences, UNESCO, 1993.

following points must be considered prior to devising a concrete strategy
for communication:

- commissioning and briefing an independent coordinator and expert
  study team (the disciplines that will be presented are decided after the
  'scoping' stage, but the team must always include a communications
  expert);
- identifying the key decision makers who will plan, finance, permit, and
  control the proposed project, so as to characterize the audience for the
  EIA;
- researching laws and regulations that will affect these decisions;
- making contact with each of the various decision makers;
- determining how and when the EIA's findings will be communicated.

Public participation may arise at any time during the EIA, construction,
operation, and maintenance phases, as discussed above. This is schematically represented in Figure 7.3.

7.3.1 Factors that may result in effective public participation

The process of communication that is devised, hopefully through wide consultation, will be inevitably project-specific because the sponsors, the people directly affected, the general public interest, and the project sponsors will be different for each project. There will not be one "public" so far as a specific project is concerned. There may, in fact, be several "publics". For example :
- the experts within the community, the scientific organizations, the expert government agencies, university departments, and expert professional groups;
- local authorities, citizen groups, and NGOs;
- the "stakeholders", that is, those with a direct interest in, or who are directly affected by, the project;
- societies, cultural groups, and individual citizens interested in, or affected by, the project;
- the general community.

Identifying "the public" in relation to a particular project, and perhaps consulting to establish the level of information and involvement they would like to have, will do a lot for the credibility and the ultimate success of the EIA. As well, it will help to ensure that knowledge of the intention to carry out an EIS is disseminated at a vital time, before it starts. One of the most certain routes to damaged credibility and unnecessary objections is the discovery by affected citizens that their opportunity for intervention has been preempted.

This can be expressed in the first of some general rules:
- ensuring that all the identified "publics" have been advised before the EIS starts about the project, its objectives, programmes, the proposed public involvement process, and the anticipated documentation;
- remembering that information most be communicated, not just provided. What language, format illustration, and media vehicle is appropriate to a particular public?

A stepwise list of factors to be considered to ensure effective communication during public participation follows.

7.3.1.1 Preplanning

Preplanning includes communication of the scope of the programme and the issues of concern to the public, for example:
- history of similar projects;
- socio-economic data;
- attitudes toward the resources under consideration;
- local groups interested or affected by the proposal.

7.3.1.2 Policy of the executing agency

Public attitudes about the executing agency can influence the acceptance of the proposed project. Care should be exercised in order to enhance public confidence. Policies concerning the time when the public will be involved and what decision-making power the public will have should be addressed and formalized.

7.3.1.3 Resources

A successful public participation programme needs time, money, and trained staff. However, this factor seems to be neglected by many executing agencies. Public opposition to projects can result in a much higher expenditure than that required to carry out a public campaigning programme.

7.3.1.4 Target groups

Identification of appropriate target groups is a critical element of successful public participation. These target groups include:
- related agencies responsible for approval of certain activities of the project;
- financing agency;
- public interest groups, for example, sociologists, environmentalists, technologists, etc.
- others, for example, teachers, religious leaders, etc.

7.3.1.5 Effective communication

Timely and accurate information in simple language should be used while transmitting information to target groups.

7.3.1.6 Techniques

The techniques employed in the public information process should focus on the identification and resolution of problems.

7.3.1.7 Responsiveness

The public should be made aware that their contribution will receive attention and that their ideas and concerns will be heard.

7.3.2 Overview of the roles of the public

Within the broad scope of assessment goals and objectives, the public can constructively participate in each of the following tasks:
- provide data and information that is essential for the assessment of impacts on the physical and social environment;

- help identify local citizens and groups with special expertise who might be used by the assessment team for specific tasks;
- identify local and regional issues that should be addressed in the assessment process;
- provide a historical perspective to current environmental conditions and trends in the local and regional area of the proposed development project;
- help generate field data;
- provide criteria for evaluating the significance of identified impacts;
- identify project alternatives;
- suggest and help organize forums and mechanisms for public participation in the assessment process;
- monitor the relevance and adequacy of the on-going assessment efforts;
- review interim assessment reports and findings for public readability and relevance to local issues and concerns;
- help analyse and evaluate direct, indirect, and cumulative impacts of project development;
- help define the scope of work and schedule for the overall assessment process;
- provide liaison between assessment team members and key organizations and other public groups and individuals;
- identify and evaluate potential mitigation measures that might be incorporated into project design and/or management.

Different groups and individuals in a local area may undertake one or several of these tasks, depending on individual interests, availability of time, knowledge, and experience. Therefore, the responsibility of the assessment team is to help diverse public groups and individuals to identify assessment functions that each may undertake successfully. This is possible only through effective communication, which should be one of the first tasks of the assessment teams.

7.3.3 Public participation techniques

A wide variety of techniques can be used to facilitate public participation in EIA. These techniques can be classified as media-based, research, political, structured group, large group, bureaucratic decentralization, and intervener techniques.

7.3.3.1 Media techniques

Participatory radio and television, newsletters, news releases, public service announcements, advertisements.

7.3.3.2 Research techniques

Sample polls, community profiles.

7.3.3.3 Political techniques

Citizen referendum lobbying, lobbying.

7.3.3.4 Structured group techniques

Nominal groups, Delphi techniques, workshops.

7.3.3.5 Large group meetings

Public hearings, public meetings.

7.3.3.6 Bureaucratic decentralization

Field office, information van.

7.3.3.7 Interveners

Citizen advisory committees, advocacy planning, ad hoc committees.

7.3.4 Implementing public participation

In selecting and implementing any technique for involving the public in the assessment process, adequate consideration should be given to the following questions:

- what specific assessment objectives can be achieved by the proposed team?
- what are the key criteria (e.g., physical settings, timing, nature of target group) for the successful utilization of the proposed technique?
- what follow-up actions and related budgetary, personnel, and information resources will be required if the proposed technique is implemented?
- how can the implementation of the proposed technique be monitored to ensure the timely correction of any counterproductive conditions and tendencies?
- how can local conditions (e.g., attitudes, previous experience with public participation measures) influence the successful utilization of the proposed technique?
- what criteria can be used to ensure the most appropriate assignment of team personnel with respect to the successful utilization of the proposed technique?

The appropriateness of any type of public participation programme, and the particular skills required for the successful implementation of

Table 7.1 Techniques for communicating with the public

Number of people reached	Ability to handle specific issues	Degree of two-way communication	Public communication techniques	Inform/ educate	Identify problems and values	Get ideas/solve problems	Get feedback	Evaluate	Resolve conflict/ obtain consensus
2	1	1	Public hearings	X	X		X		
2	1	2	Public meetings	X	X		X		
1	2	3	Informal small group meetings	X	X	X	X	X	X
2	1	2	General public information meetings	X					
1	2	2	Presentations to community organizations	X	X		X		
1	3	3	Information coordination seminars	X			X		
1	2	1	Operating field offices		X	X	X	X	
1	3	3	Local planning visits		X		X	X	
2	2	1	Information brochures and pamphlets	X					
1	3	3	Field trip and site visits	X	X				
3	1	2	Public displays	X		X	X		
2	1	2	Model demonstration projects	X		X	X	X	X
3	1	1	Material for mass media	X					
1	3	2	Response to public inquiries	X					
3	1	1	Press releases inviting comments	X		X			

Table 7.1 (cont.)

Public communication techniques	Number of people reached	Ability to handle specific issues	Degree of two-way communication	Inform/ educate	Identify problems and values	Get ideas/solve problems	Get feedback	Evaluate	Resolve conflict/ obtain consensus
Letter requests for comments	1	3	1			X	X		
Workshops	1	3	3		X	X	X	X	X
Advisory committees	1	3	3		X	X	X	X	
Task forces	1	3	3		X	X		X	
Employment of community residents	1	3	3		X	X			X
Community interest advocates	1	3	3			X		X	X
Ombudsman or representative	1	3	3		X	X	X	X	X
Public review of assessments decisions	2	3	1	X	X	X	X	X	X

1 = low; 2 = medium; 3 = high; X = capability.

that programme, are largely determined by local conditions, including local attitudes and concerns, as well as by the previous experience of citizens with public participation programmes. Thus, any recommendations for utilizing a particular technique to involve public groups and individuals in the assessment process must be made keeping in view the team's knowledge of these conditions. The main features of various techniques that may be used are shown in Table 7.1. In summary, the benefits of achieving effective communication and thereby ensuring a quality public involvement programme are immense. The greatest benefit will be trust and confidence. The conclusions, even if unpalatable, will be more likely to find acceptance if the "public" develops confidence in the work, the methods, and the objectivity and professionalism of the approach to the EIA study. In addition, a great deal of valuable information, particularly about local conditions, can be obtained and the people who actually live in an area often know it best.

FURTHER READING

How to Assess Environmental Impacts on Tropical Islands and Coastal Areas, eds. R. A. Carpenter and J. E. Maragos, prepared by Environment and Policy Institute East-West Center, October 1989.

8

Writing and reviewing an EIA report

8.1 Writing an EIA report

Report writing is an important part of any EIA study to enable communication of the findings of the study to a wide range of professionals, decision makers, administrators, and the general public. It is essential that the report be concise; the format and the presentation of the report may vary with EIA teams and practitioners.

8.1.1 Guidelines for preparing EIA reports

Each individual EIA report should ideally be tailored to fit the circumstances of the project. However, it is useful to follow certain general guidelines to fit together the essential components of the study so as to generate a coherent advisory report helpful to the decision makers as well as the general public. A brief description of the typical contents of each section of an EIA report is given below.

Chapter 1 Introduction

This chapter would be introductory in nature and should provide a background of the project. It presents a review of the existing situation and demonstrates the need for the proposed project. Details regarding the composition of the EIA study team, the budget adequacy (in professional person months), work plan, and the report organization should also form a part of this chapter.

Chapter 2 The site and surroundings

The site and surrounding areas should be described in this chapter, in accordance with the prevailing guidelines. Published literature and educational and government agencies can be the major source of information for this chapter. This information can be augmented by field studies. The chapter should include the following information.

- A description of the location and layout, including a vicinity map.
- Existing land use patterns should be described. Emphasis has to be on existing agriculture activities, presence of forest land, habitations, etc.
- Existing water use in the area is to be identified.
- Demographic profile which includes population density, population centres, and employment statistics.
- Soil profiles, including identification of soil types.
- Hydrology and water quality, which should include surface and groundwater resources, hydraulic, and water quality characteristics. Water quality parameters can be based on drinking water quality standards. Data on groundwater quality and the profile of the groundwater table, etc., should also be provided.
- Meteorology and air quality; meteorological data such as temperature, rainfall, relative humidity, wind speed and direction, and air quality data such as levels of nitrogen oxides, carbon monoxide, sulphur dioxide, hydrocarbons, etc.
- Ecology; ecological data will include a description of aquatic and terrestrial ecosystems in the area. Rare and endangered species, if any, will be identified.
- All the baseline information to be included in this chapter would be one year of monitoring data in the case of a detailed EIA.

Chapter 3 About the project

This chapter should describe the relevant systems of the proposed project. This should include the plant layout, inclusive of the drainage system, description of materials utilized and produced (mass balance), design criteria adopted, and the access ways to be used. Project information should be described in terms of the following activities, such as site preparation, construction, operation on site, transportation, welfare, and closure.

Amongst this classification, all major activities should be identified and shown in the form of a bar chart to convey the implementation as well as operation of the project. Any potential as well as non-routine or less frequent activities should also be paid attention to. Examples are the storage facilities, start-up, and shut down of the plant, etc.

Attributes of all the major activities should be described so as to appreciate their size and duration.

Chapter 4 Environmental effects of project operation

The anticipated impacts of the project operation on the environment should be described in this chapter. Impacts on air quality, water quality, agriculture, and aquatic and terrestrial ecosystems have to be stressed. A logical use of the information presented in Chapters 2 and 3 should form the crux of Chapter 4. EIA methods such as matrix and network, together with tools such as prediction models, may be useful at this stage. All direct and indirect (first order and higher order) impacts should be speculated at this stage. To assist in this exercise, tools of prediction modelling may also be used, if necessary.

Chapter 5 Evaluation and analysis of impact

The type of evaluation method or tool, for example, weighted/scaled matrix, network, GIS, index method, cost-benefit analysis, etc., used to quantitatively evaluate the impact due to the proposed action, should be highlighted in this part of the report. Expert systems may also be useful for this evaluation.

Chapter 6 Environmental management plan (EMP)

This chapter should describe in detail the implementation plan to be adopted by the proponent during plant operation for the mitigation, protection, or enhancement measures which are recommended in Chapter 5. The EMP documents should contain an implementation plan for each of the selective mitigative protection and enhancement measures. The chapter may be structured as follows:
- objective;
- work plan;
- implementation schedule;
- manpower requirements;
- budgetary provision for EMP.

This chapter is the most crucial and significant part of the entire EIA report. It is therefore essential that this chapter be presented with precision and clarity. It might be useful in this case to identify issues of significance due to the project and specify the corresponding mitigation measures. Representation of this in a tabular form may be useful.

Chapter 7 Environmental monitoring programmes

The proposed monitoring programmes to be implemented to monitor environmental impacts due to the operation of the project should be described in this chapter. The programmes should be initiated prior to the commencement of the construction activities. The following sections have to be discussed:
- surface water;
- groundwater;
- air quality;
- ecological – aquatic and terrestrial;
- socio-economic condition.

8.1.2 Comparison of guidelines of suggested/required components of an EIA report

Guidelines for writing an EIA report are established by most countries specifically for the EIA system followed in their country. However, what has been suggested in the preceding section is a generalized set of recommendations. In addition to various countries, aid agencies also have established guidelines for the EIA of projects supported by them. Table 8.1 presents a comparison of the recommended contents required for an EIA report.

8.2 Review of an EIA report

Review serves several purposes, each requiring somewhat different review skills. Technical accuracy and completeness are assumed by using independent experts who have no vested interest in promoting development or withholding project approval.

8.2.1 Purpose of the review

An EIA will usually contain a large amount of information about the form and consequences of a development. It is the purpose of a review to:

Table 8.1 Suggested/required components of an EIA report

Contents	Aid agency				
	World Bank	EBRD	IDB	AsDB	AfDB
Executive summary	Yes	Yes	Yes by project team	Yes	Yes
Policy, legal, institutional framework	Yes	Yes	Yes	Yes	Yes
Project description	Yes	Yes	Yes	Yes	Yes
Baseline data	Yes	Yes	Yes	Yes	Yes
Environmental impact analysis	Yes	Yes	Yes	Yes	Yes
Cost/benefit analysis	No	No	Yes (case-by-case)	Yes	No
Analysis of alternatives	Yes	Yes	Yes (when applicable)	Yes	Yes
Mitigation plan	Yes	Yes	Yes	Yes	No[a]
Institution building	Yes	Yes	Yes	Yes	No
Environmental monitoring plan	Yes	Yes	Yes	Yes	Yes
Consultation	Yes	Yes	Yes	Yes	Yes

[a] But discussion of mitigative measures adopted in project plan. EBRD, European Bank for Reconstruction and Development; IDB, Interamerican Development Bank; AsDB, Asian Development Bank; AfDB, African Development Bank.

- provide the reviewers with a framework within which to interpret this information;
- enable reviewers to assess the quality and completeness of the information relatively quickly;
- enable reviewers to make an overall judgement of the acceptability of the EIA as a planning document.

8.2.2 Information and expertise needed for review

Reviewing is normally done by planners and other interested parties who are familiar with the requirements of the regulations relating to environmental assessment and have at least a basic, non-specialist knowledge and understanding of impact assessment methodologies and current ideas on best practice in EIA.

8.2.3 Strategy of the review

Reviewers should not attempt to refute the findings presented in an EIA report or to supplant them with conclusions of their own. Reviewers should, rather, be alert to areas of weakness, omission, or even concealment in the report. These may most often occur when certain tasks are omitted, unsuitable or ad hoc methods are used, biased or inaccurate supporting data are introduced, often without references, or the rationale or justification for conclusions is not given.

It should be noted that, in order to promote objectivity in EIA report reviewing, it is recommended that each EIA report should initially be separately reviewed by two different reviewers who should then endeavour to reconcile any differences when finalizing their joint review.

The minimum information that an EIA report should contain, in any particular case, is usually specified in the regulations of the respective country. It is clearly an important consideration in deciding the suitability of the environmental impact statement as a planning document that these minimum data should be provided.

8.2.4 Approach

Most of the few pieces of literature which have addressed the problem of reviewing and evaluating environmental impact statements have attempted to increase the evaluator's depth of understanding of the subject matter associated with the problem area. The evaluator, familiar with the document, then presumably is better prepared to examine the statement and either agree or disagree with its contents as developed by the author. This section presents various approaches to systematic EIA review and suggests other examples related to the review procedure classifications previously identified.

8.2.4.1 Independent analysis

In order to conduct an independent analysis, the reviewer theoretically should have complete familiarity and knowledge of the proposed projects and alternatives. Utilizing this information, a "mini-EIA" could be developed and the resultant analysis compared with the document being reviewed. If a particular EIS methodology was utilized in the analysis, the reviewer could repeat the analysis, utilizing a different methodology, and compare results. Obviously, the majority of reviews and reviewers outside the proponent agency would not have this degree of familiarity with the project and its associated alternatives and impacts. At second best, the project purpose and discussion of alternatives and description of the affected environment must be sufficiently detailed in the EIA for the reviewer to evaluate the environmental consequences of the proposal.

During the independent analysis, the reviewer can utilize points which can be developed from the outline of the EIA report content described earlier. Other summaries can be developed utilizing general document review and technical review considerations. After the review has been completed, summaries may be reported. The responsible official and/or decision maker may then utilize these summaries in determining:

- changes or modifications needed in the EIA;
- decisions to release the document for public and inter-agency review;
- decisions to proceed with, modify, or halt the project and/or alternatives.

8.2.4.2 Predetermined evaluation criteria

Evaluation criteria for use by reviewers could take many forms. The form could range from a short, concise statement answering certain questions concerning the proposed activity, to a weighted checklist which portrays numerical values for different criteria which can be compared to index values. The contents of this analysis could be attached to the EIA and used in the decision-making process. Majority and minority opinion of the reviewers could also be included as another decision parameter to be considered by the responsible official.

A wide variation in mission and programmes is encountered between agencies and even within a single agency. This increases the difficulty in developing a single set of criteria that can be utilized to evaluate all federally related projects. The more specialized the agency activities, the more detailed the criteria that can be utilized, whereas the more variable the projects that can be encountered, the greater the generalization of the criteria. Generalized criteria, if properly selected, still have the capability of directing the statement review so that it is an effective tool for decision makers.

8.2.4.3 Ad hoc review

A third form of review will be discussed for those who may find themselves in the position of wanting to review an EIS but not wishing to employ the detailed, structured approaches suggested above. For those reviewers, the following sequence of activities is suggested.

1 Familiarize yourself with the prescribed outline and content of the respective agency implementing the EIA. This will provide you with an idea of the general sequences and format to be expected as you examine the body of the EIA.
2 Read the summary. This will provide an overview of the project, its alternatives, and the anticipated environmental consequences.
3 Examine the table of contents to determine the location of the various parts of the EIA. Depending on your familiarity with the project and/ or the affected environment, you may wish to go directly to a specific section of the document.
4 Study the content of the EIA, looking for those items specifically identified in Table 8.2.

Table 8.2 General document review criteria

Area of concern	Criteria
A Readability	• Write clearly • Removal all ambiguities • Avoid use of technical jargon; all technical terms should be clearly explained
B Consideration and focus	• Do not slant or misinterpret findings • Avoid use of value-imparting adjectives or phrases • Avoid confusion or mix-up among economic, environmental, and ecological impacts and productivity • Avoid unsubstantiated generalities • Avoid conflicting statements
C Presentation	• Use well-defined, acceptable qualitative terms • Quantify factors, effects, uses, and activities that are readily amenable to quantification
D Data	• Identify all sources • Use up-to-date data • Use field data collection programmes as necessary • Use technically approved data collection procedures • Give reasons for use of unofficial data
E Methods and procedures	• Use quantitative estimation procedures, techniques, and models for arrival at the best estimates • Identify and describe all procedures and models used • Identify sources of all judgements • Use procedures and models acceptable by professional standards
F Interpretation of findings	• Consider and discuss all impact areas before any are dismissed as not applicable • Analyse controversial issues, and discuss the implications of all results • Consider the implications for each area of a range of outcomes having significant uncertainty • Analyse each alternative in detail and give reasons for not selecting it • Scrutinize and justify all interpretations, procedures, and findings that must stand up under expert professional scrutiny

5 Focus on issues and concerns regarding administrative, general document, and technical review concerns previously identified.
6 Evaluate the EIA on the basis of your review.

The kinds of questions that may be asked by decision makers while reviewing an EIA report are given below.

1 To what extent are both the beneficial and adverse environmental effects clearly explained?
2 How are the risks of adverse consequences evaluated and what are they?
3 What is the scope of the EIA in terms of external factors and time-lag effects?
4 What (if any) are the impacts on environmentally sensitive areas, endangered species and their habitats, and recreational/aesthetic areas?
5 What alternatives are considered: no project? other sites? other technologies?
6 What lessons from previous similar projects are incorporated?
7 How do the environmental effects change the costs and benefits of the project?
8 What adverse effects are unavoidable?
9 What public participation and review of project plans or the EIA have occurred?
10 What mitigation measures are proposed, and who is responsible for implementing them?
11 What are the parameters to be monitored so that the state of the environment can be studied throughout the project?

8.2.5 Specific document review criteria

This is a list of hierarchically arranged topics for reviewing the quality of environmental statements. There are four areas for review.
(a) Description of the development, the local environment, and the baseline conditions.
(b) Identification and evaluation of key impacts.
(c) Alternatives and mitigation of impacts.
(d) Communication of results.

(a) Description of the development, the local environment, and the baseline conditions

Description of the development.
• The purpose(s) and objectives of the development should be explained.
• The design and size of the development should be described. Diagrams, plans, or maps will usually be necessary for this purpose.

- There should be some indication of the physical presence and appearance of the completed development within the receiving environment.
- Where appropriate, the nature of the production intended to be employed in the completed development should be described, as well as the expected rate of production.
- The nature and quantities of raw materials needed during both the construction and operational phases should be described.

Site description.
- The land area taken up by the development site should be defined and its location clearly shown on a map.
- The uses to which this land will be put should be described and the different land use areas demarcated.
- The estimated duration of the construction phase, operational phase, and, where appropriate, decommissioning phase should be given.
- The numbers of workers and/or visitors entering the development site during both construction and operation should be estimated. Their access to the site and likely means of transport should be given.
- The means of transporting raw materials and products to and from the site, and the approximate quantities, should be described.

Wastes.
- The types and quantities of waste matter, energy, and other residual materials, and the rate at which these will be produced, should be estimated.
- The ways in which it is proposed to handle and/or treat these wastes and residuals should be indicated, together with the routes by which they will eventually be disposed of to the environment.
- The methods by which the quantities of residuals and wastes were obtained should be indicated. If there is uncertainty this should be acknowledged and ranges of confidence limits given where possible.
(Wastes include all residual process materials, effluents, and emissions. Waste energy, waste heat, noise etc., should also be considered.)

Environment description.
- The environment expected to be affected by the development should be indicated with the aid of a suitable map of the area.
- The affected environment should be defined broadly enough to include any potentially significant effects occurring away from the immediate construction site. These may be caused by, for example, the dispersion of pollutants, infrastructural requirements of the project, traffic, etc.

Baseline conditions.
- The important components of the affected environments should be identified and described. The methods and investigations undertaken for this purpose should be disclosed and should be appropriate to the size and complexity of the assessment task. Uncertainty should be indicated.
- Existing data sources should have been searched and, where relevant, utilized. These should include local authority records and studies carried out by, or on behalf of, conservation agencies and/or special interest groups.
- Local land use plans and policies should be consulted and other data collected as necessary to assist in the determination of the "baseline" conditions, that is, the probable future state of the environment, in the absence of the project, taking into account natural fluctuations and human activities (often called the "do nothing" scenario).

(b) Identification and evaluation of key impacts

Definition of impacts.
- A description should be given of the direct effects and any indirect, secondary, cumulative, short-, medium-, and long-term, permanent and temporary, positive and negative effects of the project.
- The above types of effect should be investigated and described with particular regard to identifying effects on or affecting humans, flora and fauna, soil, water, air, climate, landscape, material assets, cultural heritage (including architectural and archaeological heritage), and the interactions between these.
- Consideration should not be limited to events which will occur under design operating conditions. Where appropriate, impacts which might arise from non-standard operating conditions, due to accidents, should also be described.
- The impacts should be determined as the deviation from baseline conditions, that is, the difference between the conditions which would obtain if the development were not to proceed and those predicted to prevail as a consequence of it.

Identification of impacts.
- Impacts should be identified using a systematic methodology such as project-specific checklists, matrices, panels of experts, consultations, etc. Supplementary methods (e.g., cause/effect of network analyses) may be needed to identify secondary impacts.
- A brief description of the impact identification methods should be given, as should the rationale for using them.

• Methods should be used which are capable of identifying all significant impacts.

Scoping.
• There should be a genuine attempt to contact the general public and special interest groups, clubs, societies, etc., to appraise them of the project and its implications.
• Arrangements should be made to collect the opinions and concerns of relevant public agencies, special interest groups, and the general public. Public meetings, seminars, discussions groups, etc., may be arranged to facilitate this.
• Key impacts should be identified and selected for more intense investigation. Impact areas not selected for thorough study should nevertheless be identified and the reasons they require less detailed investigation should be given.

Prediction of impact magnitude.
• The data used to estimate the magnitude of the main impacts should be sufficient for the task and should be clearly described or their sources be clearly identified. Any gaps in the required data should be indicated and the means used to deal with them in the assessment should be explained.
• The methods used to predict impact magnitude should be described and be appropriate to the size and importance of the projected impact.
• Where possible, predictions of impacts should be expressed in measurable quantities with ranges and/or confidence limits as appropriate. Qualitative descriptions, where these are used, should be as fully defined as possible (e.g., "insignificant means not perceptible from more than 100 m distance").

Assessment of impact significance.
• The significance to the affected community and to society in general should be described and clearly distinguished from impact magnitude. Where mitigating measures are proposed, the significance of any impact remaining after mitigation should also be described.
• The significance of an impact should be assessed, taking into account appropriate national and international quality standards where available. Account should also be taken of the magnitude, location, and duration of the impact in conjunction with national and local societal values.
• The choice of standards, assumptions, and value systems used to assess significance should be justified and any contrary opinions should be summarized.

(c) Alternatives and mitigation of impacts

Alternatives.

- Alternative sites should have been considered where these are practicable and available to the developer. The main environmental advantages and disadvantages of these should be discussed and the reasons for the final choice given.
- Where available, alternative processes, designs, and operating conditions should have been considered at an early stage of project planning and the environmental implications of these investigated and reported where the proposed project is likely to have significantly adverse environmental impacts.
- If unexpectedly severe adverse impacts are identified during the course of the investigation, which are difficult to mitigate, alternatives rejected in the earlier planning phases should be re-appraised.

Scope of effectiveness of mitigation measures.

- The mitigation of all significant adverse impacts should be considered and, where practicable, specific mitigation measures should be put forward. Any residual or unmitigated impacts should be indicated and justification offered as to why these impacts should not be mitigated.
- Mitigation methods considered should include modification of the project, compensation, and the provision of alternative facilities as well as pollution control.
- It should be clear to what extent the mitigation methods will be effective when implemented. Where the effectiveness is uncertain or depends on assumptions about operating procedures, climatic conditions, etc., data should be introduced to justify the acceptance of these assumptions.

Commitment to mitigation.

- There should be a clear record of the commitment of the developer to the mitigation measures presented in the statement. Details of how the mitigation measures will be implemented and function over the time span for which they are necessary should also be given.
- Monitoring arrangements should be proposed to check the environmental impacts resulting from the implementation of the project and their conformity with the predictions within the statement. Provision should be made to adjust mitigating measures where unexpected adverse impacts occur. The scale of these monitoring arrangements should correspond to the likely scale and significance of deviations from expected impacts.

(d) Communication of results

Layout.
- The layout of the statement should enable the reader to find and assimilate data easily and quickly. External data sources should be acknowledged.
- There should be an introduction briefly describing the project, the aims of the environmental assessment, and how those aims are to be achieved.
- Information should be logically arranged in sections or chapters and the whereabouts of important data should be signalled in a table of contents or index.
- Unless the chapters themselves are very short, there should be chapter summaries outlining the main findings of each phase of the investigation.
- When data, conclusions, or quality standards from external sources are introduced, the original source should be acknowledged at that point in the text. A full reference should also be included either with the acknowledgement, at the bottom of the page, or in a list of references.

Presentation.
- Information should be presented so as to be comprehensible to the non-specialist. Tables, graphs, and other devices should be used as appropriate. Unnecessarily technical or obscure language should be avoided.
- Technical terms, acronyms, and initials should be defined, either when first introduced into the text or in a glossary. Important data should be presented and discussed in the main text
- The statement should be presented as an integrated whole. Summaries of data presented in separately bound appendices should be introduced in the main body of the text.

Emphasis.
- Prominence and emphasis should be given to potentially severe adverse impacts as well as to potentially substantial favourable environmental impacts. The statement should avoid disproportionate space to impacts which have been well investigated or are beneficial.
- The statement should be unbiased; it should not lobby for any particular point of view. Adverse impacts should not be disguised by euphemisms or platitudes.

Non-technical summary.
- There should be a non-technical summary of the main findings and conclusions of the study. Technical terms, lists of data, and detailed explanations of scientific reasoning should be avoided.

- The summary should cover all the main issues discussed in the statement and contain at least a brief description of the project and the environment, an account of the main mitigation measures to be undertaken by the developer, and a description of any significant residual impacts. A brief explanation of the methods by which these data were obtained, and an indication of the confidence which can be placed in them, should also be included.

8.3 Preparing terms of reference for consultants or contractors

Many EIAs are performed by consulting companies for the project proponents. The tasks to be carried out by the consultant are best directed and judged by terms of reference (TOR). To develop an optimum TOR, the project proponent needs to have their own team and brainstorm on some of the major environmental issues, options, and alternatives. A well placed TOR often provides much of its solution and reduces the cost of consultancy services. However, additional studies may be suggested during negotiations or during execution of the study.

The clarity and comprehensiveness of the TOR is a crucial step in determining the nature of the EIA report, which is the final communiqué of the entire study to the decision makers and the various stakeholders in the project. The EIA report is eventually a reflection of the requirements and studies specified in the TOR.

8.3.1 Checking out the consulting organization

The consulting organization should be checked for the presence of a multi-disciplinary team of subject experts. The expertise generally needed should encompass areas such as:
- civil and environmental engineering;
- chemical and environmental engineering;
- environmental monitoring;
- life sciences with training in ecology;
- air pollution meteorology and modelling;
- social sciences.

Preferably, much of the above expertise should be in-house, employed by the consulting company, and not in the form of associates. Associates may be available to handle specialized areas such as risk assessment and design of green belts. In the case of associates, institutional support may be preferred. If institutional support is cited for environmental monitoring, then it is advisable to check out the status of the laboratories in terms of equipment and analytical expertise available.

The interdisciplinary team set up should have prior experience of the EIA process in the developing countries concerned and the methodology and tools used in EIA. The project manager must have formal exposure to the subject and should have completed/supervised a minimum of two or three EIA studies.

It is important to check on the manpower planning proposed by the consulting company vis-à-vis their on-going commitments to ensure they meet their schedules. Some companies have excellent interdisciplinary teams and a project manager on paper, but the team may be already booked on other EIA contracts.

There are two possible methods to choose a consultant. One method is to hire consultant A for the project contract and consultant B for the EIA. The proponent in this case needs to orchestrate a coordination between the two consultants to achieve an effect of concurrent EIA. This requires good coordination skills with the team of the project proponent.

The other method is to include EIA in the scope of consultant A and provide a "turn key" assignment to engineer and clear the project. The responsibility of conducting an EIA study is thus assigned to consultant A. Here, the proponent has relatively less interaction with the environmental consultant unless this is mentioned in the TOR for consultant A.

In either of the methods, the make-up of the team for an EIA study is as follows. An EIA advisor/consultant hired by the project proponent to protect the project's interests and do coordination, supervision, and review, attend meetings, etc. An EIA consulting company which would do the tasks of running the EIA study, prepare reports, attend meetings, and do any follow-up studies, etc. A network of experts and institutions may be identified which would provide support to the EIA consulting company for specialized activities such as monitoring of specific pollutants, carrying out flora and fauna related studies, carry out risk assessments, etc. These institutions should be reputable and of high standing.

8.3.2 Strategy for formulating TOR

It is a good idea to develop an initial TOR with the help of the project team and EIA advisor. To make such a formulation the team must visit the project site, carry out a scoping exercise, list all the alternatives, and identify issues of concern. (Alternatives generally refer to different project sites and options refer to possibilities in selecting production technologies, etc.) Unless such an exercise is performed, it is difficult to develop a well focused, balanced, and optimum TOR for the EIA study.

The EIA advisor should then be asked to step up the exercise from scoping level to IEE level, but only to scrutinize the alternatives and options. This step is necessary to arrive at a few potential alternatives and options which may need further evaluation. In this step, the project team which is responsible for the technical/engineering design of the project would play a very crucial role. In most situations, the latter is not done and hence "real alternatives" and "real options" are never produced.

For the examination of alternatives and options, some background information is needed on the environmental settings of the project sites, which is collected through secondary sources of information and site visits. Much depends here on the experience of the EIA advisor.

After the basic alternatives and options have been debated, on both the environmental and technical angles, a TOR for further studies is written. Here the project proponent may consider engaging the consultant with the help of the EIA advisor.

The EIA process that follows typically has two components. One is procedural and follows the table of contents and documents listed under the respective legislation. The second is analytical, where interpretations and conclusions drawn from the information collected in the procedural sequence are put to the best use, that is, to develop sound environmental management plans. It is important that this spirit of the EIA exercise is conveyed to the consultant. Many consultants follow only the procedural process to obtain the clearance for the project proponent, but fail to produce a workable and environmentally sound management plan to address the environmental issues. In fact, the latter is the principle objective of the EIA exercise.

To get the best results from the consultant, therefore, the project proponent needs to set several milestones of reports/workshops in the TOR to increase the interaction with the environmental consultant. In each of these interactions, the proponent should insist that the consultant comes for the meeting with specified data/results with its entire team and should ask that the company's project team is present. Eye to eye contact is most important here. The meeting should be chaired by the chief executive officer (CEO) of the company in assistance with the EIA advisor.

In many cases, the TOR for EIA are not specifically written and a reference is made to the various requirements of the EIA notification. The ultimate objective of obtaining environmental clearance is thus governing the TOR. Most consulting companies are familiar with filling up the EIA questionnaire, but translation of the questionnaire into an EIA study to develop an EMP is the crucial step.

One of the ways to guide the consultant for the preparation of the study is to provide a sample table of contents for the EIA report.

Many EIAs are performed by consulting firms under contract to environmental agencies or project proponents. The consultant proposes a statement of work in response to a request for a proposal which contains instructions or TOR. After negotiation of the scope, schedules, and price, a contract is executed. A good definition of a problem often provides much of its solution and reduces the cost of contract services. It is essential that the major environmental concerns be identified and a search for other likely consequences of development be specifically requested in the TOR. For competitively bid contracts, the consultant will seldom add tasks, for fear that the resulting costs will keep the firm from being awarded the job. During negotiations, however, additional studies may be suggested. Hence, the buyer must have an understanding of what is needed in order to avoid paying for unnecessary services. It is also important to request the form of analysis and presentation appropriate to the use of the EIA (i.e., extended benefit/cost analysis, comparative risk assessment, cost effectiveness).

The clarity and comprehensiveness of the TOR is a crucial step in determining the nature of the EIA report, as this is the final communiqué of the entire study to decision makers and the various stakeholders in the project. The EIA report is eventually a reflection of the requirements and studies specified in the TOR.

The technical contents of a TOR typically include:

* the objective of the EIA – what decisions will be made, by whom, a timetable, what kinds of advice are required, what is the stage of the project?
* components of the project – sites, technologies, inputs of energy, and materials anticipated;
* preliminary scope of EIA – should include geography, region, lifetime of project, externalities, and major anticipated concerns about environmental changes and consequences;
* impacts – major anticipated impacts on human health and welfare and on ecosystems;
* mitigation – mitigation measures possible, including reasonable alternative project designs for achieving the development objective;
* monitoring – estimated monitoring necessary for feedback of operations, for detecting environmental consequences, and judging whether mitigation measures have been implemented;
* type of study required (e.g., benefit/cost analysis, land-use plan, pollution control regulation, simulation model, comparison of sites or technologies, risk assessment);
* staff level of effort, skills required, cost estimate, and deadlines for completion of tasks.

The preliminary environmental assessment prepared by the project proponent should have most of the preceding information in qualitative form and may be appended to the TOR for guidance.

Non-technical requirements in the TOR include:

* stipulation of references and data to be provided by the buyer;

- frequency and subject of meetings and progress reports;
- opportunities for review and comment on draft reports;
- prior approval of changes in contractor personnel;
- payment schedules;
- liability insurance;
- printing, distribution of reports; and
- coordination requirements.

FURTHER READING

Reviewing the Quality of Environmental Statements Part B – Environmental Statement Review 1, N. Lee and R. Colley, EIA Centre, Department of Planning and Landscape, University of Manchester.

How to Assess Environmental Impacts on Tropical Islands and Coastal Areas, eds. R. A. Carpenter and J. E. Maragos, prepared by Environment and Policy Institute East-West Center, October 1989.

9

Emerging developments in EIA

9.1 Introduction

Traditionally, in the practice of EIA there has always been a bias towards project EIA. However, all development projects have far reaching impacts. As a result, there is a need for a more holistic approach. Regional and global implications of impacts due to projects therefore need to be examined. Apart from the projects *per se*, the policies of governments also need to be assessed since they will determine the trends of implementation of various types of projects. Emerging areas which may be used to assess such impacts include cumulative effects assessment (CEA) to assess regional impacts and strategic level EIA (SEA) to assess the impacts of policies. The other aspects of EIA which have been emerging as specific areas in their own right, which were earlier considered as a section of an EIA, are social impact assessment (SIA), environmental risk assessment (ERA), and environmental health impact assessment (EHIA).

9.2 Cumulative effects assessment

Cumulative effects refer to the accumulation of changes in environmental systems over time and across space in an additive or interactive manner.

Changes may originate from actions that are single or multiple, and similar or different in kind. A unit of environmental change attributable to an individual action may be considered insignificant because of confined spatial and temporal scales. However, environmental changes originating from repeated or multiple human actions can accumulate over time and across space, resulting in cumulative effects deemed significant.

CEA is the process of systematically analysing and assessing cumulative environmental change. The practice of CEA is complex because of the need to consider multiple sources of change, alternative pathways of accumulation, and temporally and spatially variable effects. CEA can be guided by an approach that recognizes the components of sources, pathways, and effects and distinguishes attributes specific to each component. Such guidance is particularly relevant in Canada where enactment of the Canadian Environmental Assessment Act in 1992 has simulated inquiry into the theoretical and methodological bases of CEA.

Some countries have incorporated an explicit requirement to address cumulative environmental effects in their EA legislation, for example, Canada and the United States. The requirements to analyse and assess cumulative effects reflects a broadened perspective on the nature of environmental change. This perspective acknowledges multiple perturbations, complex causation, interactive processes, expanded and permeable spatial boundaries, and extended time horizons and time lags. These attributes characterize cumulative effects, or cumulative environmental change.

CEA literature generally concentrates on pervasive, regional environmental problems. Examples include acid rain, agricultural land loss, and watershed management. Clearly there is a need for regional planning and management initiatives to address such matters, but a CEA perspective can also be incorporated into individual project EIAs. Indeed, it is essential because EIA requirements usually focus on individual projects. Such requirement, and the desirability of placing project EIAs within a broader environmental management perspective, contribute to an urgent need for practical, project-level CEA approaches.

Table 9.1 highlights the major differences between conventional EIA and CEA. The distinctions listed in the table create something of a false dichotomy; in practice, it is more a question of emphasis. Conventional EIA can be applied at the policy and programme levels in ways that mirror CEA characteristics. Similarly, project-level planning can apply many CEA properties. Thus, there is considerable fertile ground within the overlap between these two related fields. A careful attention to this middle ground will both renew EIA and ground the largely conceptual field of CEA.

Table 9.1 Characteristics of conventional EIA and CEA

Aspects	Conventional EIA	CEA
Purpose	Project evaluation	Management of pervasive environmental problems
Proponent	Single proponent	Multiple projects and/or no proponents
Sources	Individual projects with high potential for adverse environmental impacts	Multiple projects and/or activities
Disciplinary perspective	Disciplinary and, to a lesser extent, interdisciplinary	Transdisciplinary and, to a lesser extent, interdisciplinary
Temporal perspective	• Short to medium term • Continuous dispersion over time • Proposed activity	• Medium to long term • Discontinuous dispersion over time (e.g., time lags) • Past, present, and future activities
Spatial perspective	• Site-specific • Focus direct on-site and off-site impacts • Continuous dispersion over space	• Broad spatial patterns • Wide geographic areas (e.g., cross-boundary impacts)
Systems perspective	• Tendency – single ecological system • Tendency – single socio-economic system	• Multiple ecological system • Multiple socio-economic systems
Interactions	• Interactions among project components • Interactions among components of environment • Interactions between project and environment • Primarily major, direct interactions • Assumption that interactions are additive	• Also interactions among projects and other activities • Also interactions among environmental systems • Also interactions between activities and environmental systems • Major and minor, direct and indirect interactions • Expectation that some interactions are non-additive (e.g., synergistic, antagonistic)
Significance of interpretations	• Significance of individual effects interpreted • Assumption that if individual impacts are insignificant, combined impacts are also insignificant	• Significance of multiple activities interpreted • Expectation that combined impacts may be significant even though individual impacts may be insignificant

Table 9.1 (cont.)

Aspects	Conventional EIA	CEA
Organizational level	• Intraorganizational	• Interorganizational
Relationship to planning	• Weak links to comprehensive environmental objectives • Project-level planning • Incremental project evaluation	• Explicit links to comprehensive environmental objectives • Programme and policy-level planning • Middle ground project evaluation and comprehensive planning
Relationship to decision-making	Reactive; after initial decision to initiate activity	Proactive; anticipates future actions
Impact management	Monitoring and management of major, direct impacts	Comprehensive impact monitoring and management system

9.2.1 Concepts and principles relevant to CEA

Several concepts and principles contribute to the development of a conceptual framework of cumulative environmental change.

9.2.1.1 Model of causality

A cause and effect relationship exists between the perturbation and the response of the system. This causal model is fundamental to a framework of cumulative environmental change. The nature of the cause and effect relationship is complex because of multiple causation, feedback mechanisms, and variable system response.

9.2.1.2 Input–process–output model

An input–process–output model provides the elemental structure for a framework of cumulative environmental change. The three elements of input, process, and output are inherent in the notion of environmental systems, and parallel the basic parts of a stress response model. Each component is briefly elaborated on below.

Input refers to a stimulus which acts as the causative agent of change. Inputs may be differentiated by type, magnitude, and frequency. Key considerations for cumulative environmental change include whether inputs are single or multiple, similar or different in kind, continuous or discrete, short or long term, and concentrated (i.e., point source) or dispersed (i.e., non-point source).

Process alludes to the pathway or mechanism followed to transfer a unit of input into a unit of environmental change. It determines a system's ability to resist, absorb, or adapt to perturbation. Processes of accumulation may be additive or interactive. The latter implies feedback mechanisms, a concept to be included in a framework of cumulative environmental change.

Output or response represents a change in system structure (e.g., hierarchy, spatial) or system function (e.g., primary production, nutrient cycling) after perturbation. A typology of cumulative effects should distinguish changes in structure and function.

9.2.1.3 Temporal and spatial accumulation

Time and space are generic to each of the components of the input–process–output model of cumulative environmental change. A temporal perspective recognizes that in an environmental system exposed to continuous or repeated inputs, the interval between each input may be insufficient for system recovery before the next input occurs, resulting in temporal accumulation. Processes with lengthy feedback loops may contribute to time delays. The output or system response may differ over the short and long term, as the response frequently requires critical thresholds to be reached before cumulative effects are apparent.

A spatial dimension is also evident. In environmental systems subjected to multiple inputs, such as those from non-point sources, the spatial proximity between inputs may be too small to disperse each input, resulting in spatial accumulation. The additive and interactive mechanisms of environmental processes at local scales may increase and contribute to regional environmental change. System responses may also involve cross-boundary movement or alter the spatial pattern of a landscape.

9.2.1.4 Control factors

Several factors control the components of input, process, and output. They are not mutually exclusive and may act dependently or independently of each other. The factors listed below are described briefly in terms of their influence on system response to perturbation.

Boundaries. Spatial and temporal dimensions define the perimeter of a system and so distinguish it from the external environment. Boundaries determine whether inputs are foreign or internal to the system, and also establish margins to identify cross-boundary flows between systems. Cumulative effects assessments are generally characterized by broad temporal and spatial boundaries to incorporate the accumulation of environmental changes over long time frames (i.e., decades, centuries) and among spatial scales (i.e., local, regional, global).

Hierarchy. Each level of organization (e.g., individual, population, community, ecosystem) within a system operates with a degree of autonomy by functioning at time and space scales which differ from other levels in the hierarchy. Different levels of organization may be associated with varying types of system response. For example, a perturbation such as cultural eutrophication may eliminate or replace a single fish species (e.g., trout), but the aquatic system as a whole may remain intact. Thus, cumulative effects assessment investigates environmental changes within and among various levels of organization.

Organizational complexity. The degree of organizational complexity also influences the capacity of a system to respond to varying amounts of stress. Mature and complex organizations tend to resist cumulative effects characterized by small and short-term stress, but are more likely to succumb to severe and prolonged stress. Immature stages of organization are more likely to absorb or adapt to extreme events by rapid rebuilding of system structure and function. The response to cumulative effects differs between mature and rudimentary systems because as organizational complexity increases, the degree of specialization and connectivity among elements usually increases, and dynamic variability of system processes generally decreases.

Assimilative capacity. All environmental systems possess an assimilative capacity that regulates the amount of input a system can receive without degradation to a system component or process. A stress of high intensity and short duration may quickly exhaust the assimilative capacity of a system, resulting in sudden system response. A stress of low magnitude and frequent repetition may deplete assimilative capacity at a gradual rate. Low levels of repeated stress may result in increments of environmental change which accumulate over time and delay the system's response (i.e., time delay).

Thresholds. Accumulation of environmental change can result in a critical threshold. This is the point at which the intensity or duration of an input is sufficient to result in system response. Thresholds control the response function by defining the level at which a system can no longer resist or absorb inputs. Perturbations that exceed the critical threshold result in adaptation or breakdown. Analogous to assimilative capacity, critical thresholds may be reached quickly under high level of stress or incrementally under low stress levels.

Dynamic variability. Perturbation may force an environmental system or a system variable to function outside its normal operating range. Dynamic variability is a measure of the amplitude or degree of fluctuation beyond this range. It determines the capacity of a system to adapt to stress, whether extreme events or the accumulation of incremental environmental changes. Systems with high dynamic variability generally have a greater capacity to adapt to severe stress than systems with low variability.

Stability and resilience. Closely related to dynamic variability, the factors of stability and resilience also influence the manner in which systems respond to perturbation. Stability is characterized by a low degree of fluctuation around an equilibrium state and a rapid return to this state following stress. Resilience is distinguished by high variability and the ability of a system to maintain its structure and function. A system with low stability and high resilience is more likely to persist in the face of extreme stress than a system with high stability and low resilience. The latter can absorb incremental cumulative effects, but is vulnerable to change when thresholds are reached.

The influence of the control factors varies among the three components of input, process, and output so that some govern inputs (e.g., boundaries, assimilative capacity), others regulate processes (e.g., thresholds, dynamic variability), and still others determine the type of output response (e.g., hierarchy, organizational complexity, stability, and resilience).

9.2.2 Conceptual framework

Building on the above concepts and principles, a conceptual framework of cumulative environmental change can be developed. The framework is based on an input–process–output model.

- Input is represented by sources of cumulative environmental change (i.e., human actions). Sources are characterized by time, space, and the nature of the perturbation.
- Process is manifested in pathways of cumulative environmental change which are distinguished as additive or interactive.
- Output is exemplified by the resulting cumulative effects, broadly differentiated as structural or functional.

There are three components of the conceptual framework, that is the source, pathways, and effects. They are interconnected in as much as there is a cause and effect relationship between components, together with feedback mechanisms. The various pathways may stimulate other sources of cumulative environmental change and an effect itself may become a source, or activate other pathways, of cumulative environmental change. The following discussion briefly elaborates on each of the three components of the conceptual framework.

Table 9.2 A typology describing the source of cumulative environmental changes applied to three examples of human–environment interactions

Attribute		Construction of Hydro-electric dam	Forestry clear-cutting	CO$_2$ emissions (from fossil fuels)
			Examples	
Temporal				
Scale	short	$\frac{1}{4}$		
	long		$\frac{1}{4}$	$\frac{1}{4}$
Frequency	discontinuous	$\frac{1}{4}$		
	continuous		$\frac{1}{4}$	$\frac{1}{4}$
Spatial				
Scale	local	$\frac{1}{4}$		
	regional		$\frac{1}{4}$	
	global			$\frac{1}{4}$
Density	clustered	$\frac{1}{4}$		
	dispersed		$\frac{1}{4}$	$\frac{1}{4}$
Configuration point	linear	$\frac{1}{4}$		
	areal		$\frac{1}{4}$	$\frac{1}{4}$
Perturbation				
Type	similar	$\frac{1}{4}$	$\frac{1}{4}$	
	different			$\frac{1}{4}$
Quantity	single	$\frac{1}{4}$		
	multiple		$\frac{1}{4}$	$\frac{1}{4}$

9.2.2.1 Sources of cumulative environmental change

A typology to describe and classify various sources of cumulative environmental change is shown in Table 9.2. The typology differentiates sources according to temporal, spatial, and perturbation attributes. Three examples illustrate various ways in which the typology can be applied to different sources. Construction of a hydroelectric dam is typically viewed as a single, discontinuous event at the local scale. However, dam construction is a potential source of cumulative effects when characterized by multiple perturbations of the same type (e.g., several hydroelectric projects) or different type (e.g., access roads, transmission corridors), expanded spatial scales (e.g., loss of upstream terrestrial habitat as the impoundment fills, altered downstream flow), and extended temporal bounds (e.g., eventual release of methyl mercury and the gradual deposition of sediment in the reservoir).

It could also be argued that clear-cutting of a forest is a single, discontinuous event at the local scale. However, once a particular stand of trees is cut, the operators move elsewhere. Clear-cutting is a potential source of cumulative effects because the action is repeated over time and across space (see Table 9.2).

Finally, CO_2 emissions are also representative of cumulative effects. The increasing accumulation of CO_2 in the atmosphere has occurred over the long term (i.e., since the pre-industrial era) and at a global scale. CO_2 emissions come from diverse and multiple sources (e.g., thermal power plants, transportation, heating) (see Table 9.2).

This typology broadens the consideration of sources (i.e., human actions) beyond the bounded projects typically appraised by environmental assessments to include activities which are repeated over time and dispersed across space.

9.2.2.2 Pathways of cumulative environmental change

Environmental changes accumulate through different processes or pathways. As with sources of change, these pathways vary by number, type, and temporal and spatial attributes. A perturbation may follow single or multiple pathways and involve additive or interactive processes. Additive pathways are summative because one unit of environmental change can be added or subtracted from a previous unit of environmental change. Interactive pathways are multiplicative, or synergistic, in that the nett accumulation is more or less than the sum of all environmental changes. Temporally, pathways may be characterized by instantaneous processes or involve time lags. From a spatial perspective, pathways may function at local, regional, or global scales, and involve cross-boundary movement among systems at the same scale.

Cumulative environmental change generally involves processes that are characterized by a series of incremental changes in environmental components or relationships. These incremental changes are categorized into four types by Sonnatag *et al.*

1 Linear additive changes are distinguished by a series of small, incremental additions to, or removals of, energy or materials from a fixed large storage (e.g., a lake). Each addition or removal has the same effect as the previous increment. A linear dose–effect relationship between a contaminant and a fish species exemplifies this category of change.

2 Amplifying or exponential changes involve a series of incremental additions to or removal from a seemingly limitless storage (e.g., atmosphere). Each increment of change has a greater effect than the previous one so that system response increases over time. An example is the steady release of CO_2 into the atmosphere and the associated change in global temperature.

3 Discontinuous changes involve incremental additions or removals that

are assimilated until a threshold is reached. Each increment of change that exceeds the threshold results in a response. An example is the addition of nutrients into a lake which triggers algae blooms once critical concentrations are attained.

4 Structural surprises refer to a process whereby increments of local and slow environmental changes gradually accumulate so that spatial scales are increased (i.e., local to regional to global) and temporal scales are intensified (i.e., slow to rapid rates). The result is a collection of various effects on system structures. These effects are measured by spatial homogenization of key system variables and a loss of major system functions. The spatial and temporal accumulation of wetland loss, and the subsequent change in wetland functions (e.g., groundwater recharge, biotic diversity, floodwater storage), is an example of structural surprise.

This categorization describes various mechanisms involved in the accumulation of incremental environmental changes. The categories increase in complexity as the mechanisms shift from linearity to non-linearity, continuity to discontinuity, and uniform spatial and temporal scales to hierarchical scales. They also question a common premise that an incremental change in an environmental component or process is similar to the previous unit of change. The above categories recognize that non-linear processes, trigger mechanisms, and surprise events can intensify and amplify the effect of each successive increment. Controlling factors such as assimilative capacity, thresholds, and dynamic variability regulate the accumulation of incremental environmental changes.

9.2.2.3 Cumulative effects

Cumulative effects have been categorized in various ways. Lane *et al.* characterized four types of cumulative effects by their primary driving force (cause) and their basic spatial pattern (effect).

1 Type A effects are proponent-driven, large, single projects that induce environmental change over a large region (e.g., NATO low-level aircraft flights over Labrador).

2 Type B effects are proponent-driven, multiple projects (related or unrelated) that interact, resulting in spatially diffuse and complex environmental change (e.g., shoreline development along the Great Lakes).

3 Type C effects are ecosystem-driven (no identifiable proponent), catastrophic, or sudden events (natural or anthropogenic origin) with abrupt environmental changes (e.g., eruption of Mount Pinatubo in the Philippines, pollution from oil well fires in Kuwait during Operation Desert Storm).

4 Type D effects are incremental and widespread ecosystem-driven (no

Table 9.3 A typology of cumulative effects

Type	Main characteristics	Example
Time crowding	Frequent and repetitive impacts on an environmental system	Forest harvesting rate exceeds regrowth
Time lags	Delayed effects	Exposure to carcinogens
Space crowding	High spatial density of impacts on an environmental system	Pesticides in streams from non-point sources
Cross-boundary movement	Impacts occur away from the source	Acid rain deposition
Fragmentation	Change in landscape pattern	Fragmentation of wetlands
Compounding effects	Effects arising from multiple sources or pathways	Synergism among pesticides
Indirect effects	Secondary impacts	Release of methyl mercury in reservoirs
Triggers and thresholds	Fundamental changes in system behaviour or structure	Global climate change

identifiable proponent) environmental changes attributed to diverse temporal and spatial processes (e.g., increase in the atmospheric concentration of carbon dioxide).

The emphasis here is on the spatial pattern and minimizes the recognition of temporal attributes. Also, effects are distinguished according to the source of the cumulative environmental change rather than characteristics inherent to different types of cumulative effects. Nevertheless, it makes a useful contribution by discriminating cumulative environmental change according to their cause–effect relationships.

A typology of cumulative effects which incorporates temporal and spatial attributes more explicitly is shown in Table 9.3. These effects can be broadly grouped into two categories. Functional effects refer primarily to the accumulation of time-dependent cumulative environmental changes. Temporal accumulation occurs when the interval between perturbations is less than the time required for an environmental system to recover after each perturbation. An example is harvesting renewable resources, such as forests and fish, at rates that exceed those of replacement. Time lags are exemplified in the continuous exposure to toxins in a food chain which may contribute to intergenerational genetic abnormalities.

Structural effects are primarily spatially oriented (e.g., space crowding, cross-boundary movement, fragmentation). Spatial accumulation is where the spatial proximity between each perturbation is smaller than the distance required to remove or disperse each perturbation. Space crowding is evident in the systematic collection of pesticide residues by farm drainage systems and its movement at a higher concentration into an aquatic system. This movement also demonstrates cross-boundary flow from one environmental system to another (i.e., agroecosystem to aquatic system). Spatial fragmentation is manifested in changes in size, shape, and contiguity of forests and wetlands in intensely farmed rural landscapes.

Other types of cumulative effects such as compounding, indirect effects, and triggers and thresholds are indicative of the manner of accumulation (Table 9.4). These types generally contribute to or manifest themselves as functional or structural effects, or both.

An attempt has been made to relate the types of cumulative effects to specific pathways of accumulation. Although all cumulative effects are potentially associated with each pathway to a certain degree, some effects are potentially more related than others. For example, time crowding, space crowding, and fragmentation are usually dominated by additive pathways. Time lags and cross-boundary movements are likely to also involve interactive processes. Compounding by definition is interactive.

Linking types of cumulative effects to pathways of accumulation enhances the understanding of system response to perturbation in two ways. First, it provides an indicator of potential cumulative effects in the future when unwanted changes in pathways occur. For example, incremental increases (additive processes) in the area and density of agricultural land drainage within a region might signify future cumulative effects such as fragmentation of wetlands. Similarly, drainage can result in space crowding by the systematic gathering of leached residue from widely dispersed farm inputs (e.g., fertilizers, pesticides), and cross-boundary movements by transporting contaminants downstream. Thus, linkage provides the basis for a predictive tool of analysis. Second, when a cumulative effect is observed and the cause is largely unknown (e.g., change in waterfowl migration, loss of ecosystem functions in a regional landscape), the association among effects and pathways can be used to trace and identify sources of cumulative environmental change. In this case, the association provides the basis for a form of hindsight analysis.

9.2.3 Conclusion

Cumulative environmental problems can be desegregated by distinguishing their sources, pathways, and effects. Application of the typology specific to each component provides a basis for identifying and analysing perturbations, mechanisms of accumulation, and temporally and spatially differentiated effects. The framework can provide guidance to conventional CEA practice characterized by multiple projects bound in time and space, as well as to innovative CEAs of temporally repetitive and spatially dispersed human actions of a non-project nature. Such CEAs can

Table 9.4 Characterizing cumulative effects

Characteristics	Examples
Sources	
Action quantity	Single, multiple, global, cause unknown
Action type	Similar or different, common or uncommon, human or natural, additions to or removal from environment
Temporal characteristics	Historical, existing, or future; short, medium, or long term; low, moderate, or high frequency; continuity of actions over time
Spatial characteristics	Local, regional or global; small or large scale; continuity of actions over space
Proponents	Single or multiple; public or private
Source connections	Connected, unconnected, uncertain connections
Pathways to the environment	
Environmental media	Groundwater, surface water, air, energy
Degree of concentration	Concentrated or dispersed over time and space
Degree of continuity	Continuous or discontinuous over time or space (e.g., time or space lags)
Pathway connections	Connected pathways, unconnected pathways, uncertain connections across pathways
Environment	
System type	Number, type, components, structure, and function of ecological, social, economic, institutional and political systems
Resources	Number, type and significance
Significance	Number and type of valuable ecosystem and other ecological components
State of environment	Healthy, impaired, or collapsed; stable or unstable; resilient or not resilient
Environmental connections	Connected components, unconnected components, uncertain connections
Interactions	
Connection to sources	Connected, not connected, connections uncertain
Strength of connections	Strongly connected, weakly connected
Direction of connection	Direct, indirect, feedback
Temporal distribution	Concentrated or dispersed; continuous or discontinuous distribution of effects
Special distribution	Concentrated or dispersed; continuous or discontinuous distribution of effects
Nature of connections	Additive or interactive, reversible or irreversible
Significance of connections	Significant, insignificant, uncertain significance

generate new information and insights about environmental changes too frequently deemed insignificant.

There remain challenges to conduct a CEA focused on sources, pathways, and effects. Sources of cumulative environmental change that are non-project in nature are likely to involve numerous "proponents", if they can even be identified.

The least understood of the three components of the framework is pathways of accumulation. The complexity of these pathways is evident in multiple routes, feedback loops, and processes that are interactive, synergistic, or involve compounding. Theoretical understanding and tools to identify, monitor, and analyse these pathways are not readily available.

Finally, while cumulative effects can be analysed using available information sources, empirical evidence is often scanty, and quantitative analyses of effects are hindered by insufficient data. CEA requires a temporal scan of long duration and geographic representation at various scales. The limited time span and local focus of many existing databases impede analyses at broader temporal and spatial scales. Rigorous analysis of cumulative effects requires building up the empirical base.

The field of CEA is still in its infancy, so there are few cases where CEAs for major projects have been completed. In general, thus, there is more agreement on the concept of CEA than there is on practical methodologies and techniques.

9.3 Sectoral environmental assessment

The benefits of EIA are now widely accepted and there is a growing belief that the EA of policies, plans, and programmes may also be necessary to ensure that alternatives and impacts which cannot be fully considered at project level are adequately evaluated. This is a consequence of the growing belief that project EIA may occur too late in the planning process to ensure that all the relevant alternatives and impacts are adequately considered. Such an assessment of policies, plans, and programmes is termed strategic environmental assessment (SEA). It can also be applied to enable cumulative impacts between projects, policies, and programmes to be taken into consideration.

Partly because the advantages of project EIA are so widely recognized, the desirability of taking the environment into account earlier in the planning process has gained acceptance worldwide. The tasks involved in SEA are similar to those in EIA and many EIA methods can be adapted to SEA methods. There exists a tiered forward-planning process which starts with the formulation of a policy at the upper level, is followed by a plan at the second stage, and by a programme at the end. The tiered EA process can permit relevant alternative approaches and cumulative, synergistic, global, and non-project impacts to be assessed. The tiered

Table 9.5 Potential benefits of SEA

- Encourages the consideration of environmental objectives during policy, plan and programme making activities within non-environmental organizations.
- Facilitates consultations between authorities on, and enhances public involvement in evaluation of environmental aspects of policy, plan and programme formulation.
- May render some project EIAs redundant if impacts have been assessed adequately.
- May leave examination of certain impacts to project EIA.
- Allows formulation of standard or generic mitigation measures for later projects.
- Encourages consideration of alternatives often ignored or not feasible in project EIA.
- Can help determine appropriate sites for projects subsequently subject to EIA.
- Allow more effective analysis of cumulative effects of both large and small projects.
- Encourages and facilitates the consideration of synergistic effects.
- Allows more effective consideration of ancillary or secondary effects and activities.
- Facilitates consideration of long range and delayed impacts.
- Allows analysis of the impacts of policies which may not be implemented through projects.

process can be applied at the national as well as local levels. It can apply to sectoral actions and physical planning actions.

9.3.1 Need for SEA

There are several reasons for the perceived need for SEA. Alternative approaches, cumulative impacts, and synergistic impacts (which may be cross-sectoral in nature), ancillary impacts, regional or global impacts, and non-project impacts (for e.g., impacts resulting from management practices) may all be better assessed initially at policy, plan, or programme level rather than at the project level. The various benefits of SEA are summarized in Table 9.5 and the direct and indirect impacts of higher order actions are shown in Figure 9.1.

9.3.2 Differences between project level EIA and SEA

The main elements of the EIA process and its most tangible output (the EIA report) are in principle applicable to all levels of decision-making including policies, plans, and programmes. However, in practice, it is likely that the scope and purpose of the EA of policies, plans and programmes will be different from that of projects in five main ways:

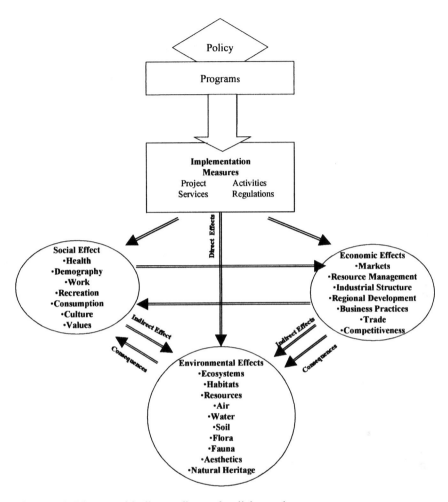

Figure 9.1 Direct and indirect effects of policies and programmes
Source: Wood, C. In: Proceedings of the Indo-British Workshop on Environmental Impact and Risk Assessment of Petrochemical Industry and Environmental Audit, Nagpur, January 8–10, 1994.

- the precision with which spatial implications can be defined is less;
- the amount of detail relating to the nature of physical development is less;
- the lead time is greater;
- the decision-making procedures and the organizations involved may differ, requiring a greater degree of coordination;
- the degree of confidentiality may well be greater.

These variations indicate that the nature of SEA will differ in detail from the nature of EIA of projects. It is apparent that the likely significant environmental impacts of higher-order actions can only be assessed at a most strategic level.

When certain alternatives and significant environmental impacts cannot be adequately assessed at the project level, it may well be possible to assess them at the programme, plan, or policy level utilizing a form of SEA basically similar in nature to that employed for projects. Thus SEA would involve screening, scoping, prediction, consultation, public participation, mitigation of impacts, and monitoring.

If project alternatives are adequately assessed in project level EIA and if all the various significant impacts are adequately examined then there is no need to carry out SEA. However, by definition, this is seldom the case. In many countries where there is already a project-level EIA system, the most logical course of action might be to supplement these EIAs with higher tier SEAs largely confined to issues such as cumulative impacts which cannot be adequately assessed at the project level.

9.3.3 Methodologies for SEA

SEA methodologies are not well developed. However, nearly all the tasks involved in SEA are similar to those in project-level EIA. As with project EIA, the skill of the assessor comes to bear in selecting an appropriate mixture from different approaches, tools, and techniques available. The key considerations that assessors should bear in mind in designing their approach to SEA are listed in Table 9.6.

9.3.4 Status of SEA

In principle, the pioneering 1969 US NEPA contained provision for the environmental assessment of policies, programmes, and plans. However, only recently has attention been focused on SEA with the preparation of EAs of programmes and plans. The status of SEAs in various countries is summarized in Table 9.7.

9.3.5 Effectiveness of SEA

Like EIA, SEA faces a number of important political and institutional barriers, in fact more so since setting policies is a political issue. Currently, SEA processes vary considerably. They may be formal or informal, comprehensive or more limited in scope, and closely linked with or unrelated to either policy or planning instruments. As shown in Table 9.7, in some cases SEA has been introduced as a relatively separate, distinct

Table 9.6 Key considerations in choosing SEA techniques

1 Will this technique or approach help achieve the objectives of this step of the process? What is the best technique at this stage for:
  • identifying linkages?
  • estimating and forecasting effects and consequences?
  • assessing significance?

2 Does the magnitude and potential significance of the impacts warrant the level of effort required by the technique?
  • cost?
  • timing?
  • involvement of key personnel?
  • involvement of peers, outside experts, and public stakeholders?

3 Is it possible and practical to utilize the techniques under consideration?
  • are peers, experts, and stakeholders available and willing to participate?
  • do adequate and reliable data exist?

4 Are there any other factors that may influence selection of approaches and techniques?
  • structures of confidentiality?
  • skill levels and capacity to design and implement given techniques?
  • personal preferences of parties involved?

Table 9.7 Summary of the SEA situation in various countries

Jurisdiction	Comments
Federal USA	1969 Act provides clear legal provisions for SEA. SEA practice developing steadily: several hundred programatic EISs prepared
California	1971 Act interpreted to include provisions for SEA. SEA practice developing steadily especially in regard to land-use plans (several hundred plan EISs prepared)
United Kingdom	No formal requirement for SEA. Guidance on environmental appraisal of both central government policy and of local land-use plans exist. Little practice.
Canada	Non-legislated SEA process applies to cabinet proposals. SEA research and guidance commissioned but little practice.
Commonwealth of Australia	1974 Act provides powers to undertake SEA but no SEA reports prepared to date. Commitment to undertake SEA of policies and programmes in future.
Western Australia	Australia 1986 Act provides clear legal provisions for SEA. SEA practice developing, with a small number of SEA reports prepared.
New Zealand	1991 Act requires SEA of certain regional and local policies and plans to be undertaken. Some guidance but little practice.

process (e.g., in Canada) or, as in the UK, incorporated into more integrated forms of environmental policy appraisal.

Eventually, in order to make SEA effective, the following courses of actions may need to be considered:

- increasing the general understanding of SEA; for example, the types of actions to which SEA could usefully be applied and its relation to existing EIA and sustainable development policies;
- clarifying procedural issues; for example, at which decision points in a planning process should SEA be applied, and how should SEA findings be integrated with other policy and planning considerations in decision-making?
- clarifying methodological issues by adapting existing EIA methods for SEA use;
- strengthening the capacity for the practical application of appropriate SEA methods; for example, undertaking trial runs adapting existing methods (including EIA methods) for SEA, diffusing examples of good SEA practice, preparing SEA guidance, and providing training in its use;
- reviewing existing environmental data sources to assess their potential use in SEA and prioritizing measures for correcting any deficiencies.

SEA, if implemented judiciously and at the appropriate level in the various planning processes, would establish itself as a cost-effective tool of environmental management.

9.4 Environmental risk assessments

9.4.1 What is environmental risk assessment?

Environmental risk assessment (ERA) is a qualitative and quantitative evaluation of environmental status performed in an effort to define the risk posed to human health and the environment by the presence, potential presence, or use of specific pollutants. ERA should be conducted when it is determined that a management action may have consequences to either humans or the environment. Effective conducting of ERA entails adopting a systematic approach, as shown in Figures 9.2 and 9.3.

ERA is comprised of two related disciplines; that is, human health risk assessment (HHRA) and ecological risk assessment (EcoRA).

The process for HHRA often involves the following steps:

- hazard identification – the determination of whether a particular chemical is or is not causally linked to a particular health effect on human beings;
- dose–response assessment – the determination of the relationship be-

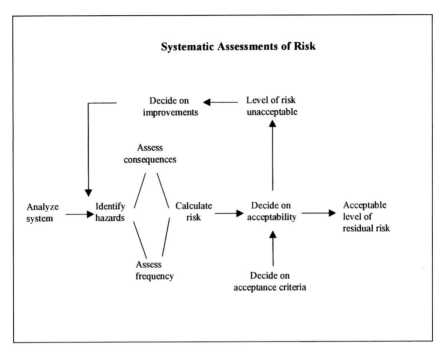

Figure 9.2 Systematic approach to risk assessment
Source: Environmental Risk Assessment for Sustainable Cities, Technical Publication Series [3], International Environmental Technology Centre, Osaka, 1996.

tween the magnitude of the exposure and the probability of occurrence
of the health effects in question;
• exposure assessment – determination of the extent of exposure;
• risk characterization – description of the nature and often the magnitude of risk including attendant uncertainty.
  EcoRA is conceptually similar to the approach used for HHRA. During this assessment, the likelihood of the occurrence/non-occurrence of
adverse ecological effects as a result of exposure to stressors is determined. The term "stressor" here may be defined as any chemical, physical, or biological entity that can induce adverse effects on individuals,
populations, communities, or ecosystems. The various components are
schematically represented in Figure 9.4 for both HHRA and EcoRA.

9.4.2 Terminology associated with ERA

Risk. The probability of an adverse effect, direct or indirect, on human
health or the environment. It is, in fact, a combination of the probability

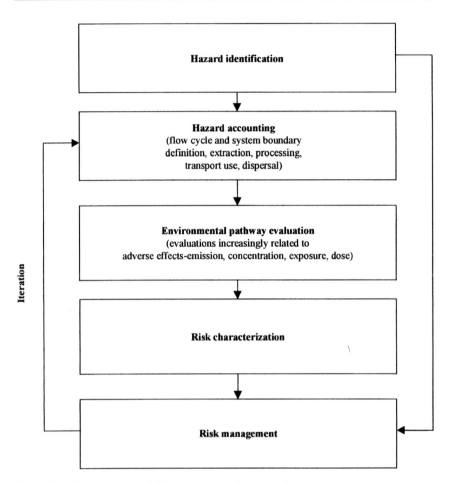

Figure 9.3 Recommended risk assessment framework
Source: Environmental Risk Assessment for Sustainable Cities, Technical Publication Series [3], International Environmental Technology Centre, Osaka, 1996.

of occurrence of an event and the possible extent of that event's adverse effects and consequences, in terms of human injury or adverse effects on the ecosystem. In a more mathematical sense, risk can be expressed as:

the probability of an event occurring × the seriousness of its consequences

Hazard. The innate properties (biological, chemical, or physical) of a substance to cause harm.

Uncertainty. Doubt, lack of assurance as to the true value of a variable, considering all the possible values attributed to data or information.

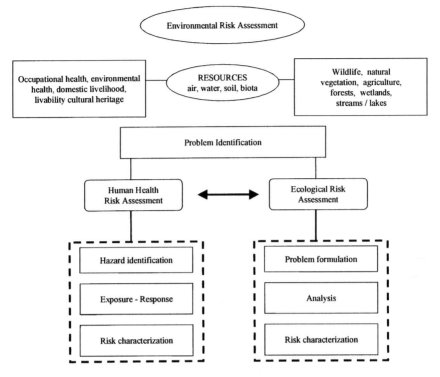

Figure 9.4 Components of human health risk and ecological risk assessment
Source: Environmental Risk Assessment for Sustainable Cities, Technical Publication Series [3], UNEP International Environmental Technology Centre, Osaka/Shiga, 1996.

Assessment. Appraisal or evaluation in some prescribed endpoints in order to judge an activity.

Analysis. Detailed examination or thorough study in order to understand.

Exposure. The condition under which an organism comes into actual contact with a stressor. In site-specific considerations, the exposure value is substantially less than the quantity in the environment although sometimes it is assumed, under conservative assumptions, to be the amount of contaminant in the environment.

9.4.2.1 Hazards and uncertainties

The inquiry into the presence of hazards is also part of the preliminary assessment for EIA. It is by the explicit identification of significant uncertainties that the need to extend an EIA to include ERA is determined. Of course, if uncertainties can be resolved by readily acquiring more information, then the assessor should proceed to do so (Table 9.8).

Table 9.8 Major hazards associated with development projects

Types of project hazard	Toxic chemical	Flammable or explosive material	Highly reactive or corrosive material	Extreme conditions of temperature or pressure	Large mechanical equipment	Collision
Cement		X		X		
Dam and reservoir				X	X	
Fertilizer (N&P)	X	X	X	X	X	
Hazardous materials handling, transport, and disposal		X	X	X		X
Highway	X	X			X	X
Iron and steel	X		X			
Metal finishing	X		X			
Pesticide	X	X				
Petrochemical	X	X	X	X	X	X
Petroleum production and refining	X	X	X	X	X	
Ports and harbours	X	X	X		X	X
Pulp and paper	X		X			
Railroad	X	X			X	X
Smelting	X		X	X	X	
Textiles	X	X				
Thermal power		X		X	X	
Waste management	X	X	X			

The hazards of concern in economic development projects include:
- chemicals toxic to humans, animals, and plants;
- materials that are highly flammable or explosive;
- mechanical equipment, the failure of which would endanger persons and property;
- structural failure (e.g., dam or containment vessel);
- natural disasters that exacerbate technological hazards;
- ecosystem damage (e.g., eutrophication, soil erosion).

Examples of information about these hazards that, if uncertain, might trigger an ERA are:
- potential release of hazardous chemicals (rate and amount);
- accidental fires and explosions;
- transport and fate of pollutants in the environment;
- dilution–dispersion mechanisms and rates;
- exposure to toxins (who, how many, how much);
- dose–response predictions based on animal tests;
- failure rates of mechanical equipment or structures;
- human behaviour (errors by workers, public reaction);
- natural hazards (earthquake, tsunami, typhoon);
- alterations in drainage patterns, water table, vegetation, microclimate.

Uncertainties arise from:
- lack of understanding of important cause–effect relationships, lack of scientific theory (e.g., bioaccumulation of toxic chemicals in a food chain, pharmacokinetic mechanisms, reaction of crops to air pollutants);
- models that do not correspond to reality because they must be simplified and because of lack of understanding (see above);
- weaknesses in available data due to sampling and/or measurement problems, insufficient time-series of data, lack of replication;
- data gaps such as no measurements on baseline environmental conditions at a project site;
- toxicological data that are extrapolated from animals to humans and from high-dose experiments to low-dose exposures;
- natural variation in environmental parameters due to weather, climate, stochastic events;
- necessary assumptions on which estimates are based, and the sensitivity of the resulting estimates to changes in the assumptions;
- novelty of the project in terms of technology, chemicals, or siting, and lack of experience and historical data.

9.4.3 ERA and the project cycle

The condition of the environment is evaluated as part of the ERA. If the condition of the environment is already stressed or degraded, further stress produced by development will be detrimental. In order to weigh the various management options available to the project proponent that will minimize the damage to the environment and maximize the benefits from the project, it is essential that ERA be integrated at the appropriate stage in the project.

In the project cycle, ERA begins at the fact finding/preparation stage when the IEE indicates a potential problem. If plausible risk scenarios (what can go wrong?) are considered likely to be unacceptable, then provisions for ERA may be prescribed and included in the TOR for EIA.

In the pre-appraisal/appraisal stage, the results of ERA suggest risk reduction and risk management measures to be incorporated into the detailed project design. Agreements may be sought on the most cost-effective strategies for achieving acceptable risk using technological and other approaches. At the negotiation stage, remaining issues concerning environmental risk are resolved and appropriate assurances of mitigation incorporated in the project. The implementation and supervision stage monitors installation and operation of risk management measures, and effectiveness of the prescribed risk-reduction strategies.

Finally, the project compilation report and the post-project audit report evaluates the accuracy of predicted environmental impacts and risks and the actual experience as to frequency and severity of both anticipated and unanticipated adverse consequences. Also, compliance with implementation of required risk-reduction measures will be monitored. These findings are used to improve future EIAs and ERAs by being assembled into a database for project staff and consultants.

9.4.4 ERA builds upon EIA

Environmental risk assessment addresses three questions.

1   *What can go wrong with the project?* What impacts might occur to human health and welfare that arise in, or are transmitted through, the environment (i.e., air, water, soil, food, and other plants or animals)? What are some reasonable scenarios (environmental sequences of cause and effect) for the project to result in damage to human health, environment, or equipment (e.g., excess deaths, exceedance of standards, catastrophic accident)?

2   *What is the range of magnitude of these adverse consequences?* With what frequency might they occur? What historical or empirical evidence is available to judge their likelihood? What data are available on failure rates of processes or components in the project technology?

3   *What can be done and at what cost to reduce unacceptable risk and damage?* What are the mitigation measures that need to be adopted?

What are the costs involved vis-à-vis the benefits derived by implementing these measures?

An EIA answers the first question and usually gives at least a qualitative expression of the magnitude of impacts, while ERA complements and extends the environmental review process. The major additional consideration is frequency of occurrence of adverse effects and how this relates to their magnitude. Risk is evaluated in terms of both frequency and severity (and the level of confidence in quantitative measures of these parameters).

9.4.5 Basic approach to ERA

The process by which an ERA proceeds involves several successive interactive stages. The first and probably the most important activity is "problem identification" in which the resources that may be affected and the possible consequences of the proposed action are described. Key issues and concerns, such as the possible impact on human health and environmental resources, are provided. The concerns identified during this stage become the focus of the next step which involves parallel evaluation of risks to human health and to the ecosystem through the use of HHRA and EcoRA.

In order for the assessments to be efficient, the processes of EcoRA and HHRA should proceed in a stepwise iterative fashion, as shown in Figure 9.5.

As seen in the figure, scoping forms the first tier and the output of this activity, as in the case of EIA, and identifies issues and concerns that have potential risks. In the event of indications of there being unacceptable risks, more detailed studies need to be done. The scoping activity proceeds by choosing from various options for levels of analysis, system boundaries, and types of risk expression.

Levels of analysis. Micro, systems, or national?

System boundaries. Routine releases and/or accidents? Which population? Which parts of the flow cycle? Which geographic boundaries for each? Which phases of the project? Effects for how long into the future? Which health endpoints? Which ecosystem risk endpoints? Which parts of the causal chain? Interaction with other projects, existing or planned?

Risk expressions. Which risk indicators? Which methods of exposure determination? Which environmental concentrations will be used? Which final risk measures? Which confidence levels?

Scoping is essentially a process of choosing system boundaries, units of measurement, and the level of analysis that are relevant to the management questions of concern. Consequently, the process requires the input of all those groups that will be using the results.

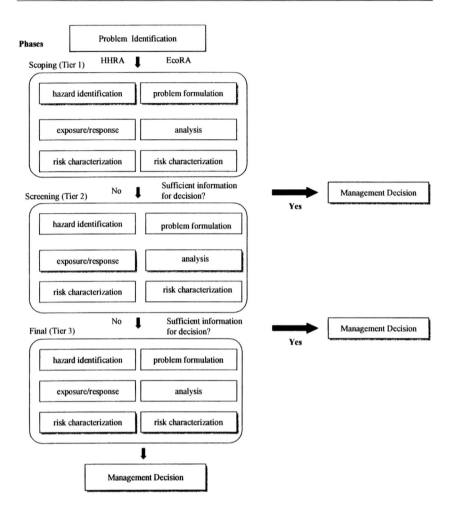

Phases

Figure 9.5 The interactive nature of environmental risk assessment
Source: Environmental Risk Assessment for Sustainable Cities, Technical Publication Series [3], International Environmental Technology Centre, Osaka. 1996.

There is a direct linkage between the hazard identification/accounting stages and risk assessment. During this stage the questions of concern are used to set the boundaries of the risk assessment steps to follow. Since the design of the risk assessment will depend on the type of questions being asked, there is no universal risk assessment method independent of the use for which it will be put. This means that in practice project officers will engage in an ERA scoping process with the project proponents, the risk consultants, and other affected and concerned parties, preferably together, to establish a mutually agreed upon and practical set of system boundaries, units of measurement, and level of analysis. Guidance may also be available from the EIA that led to the ERA.

These decisions make up the accounting step and establish priorities as to which hazards need to be evaluated first and to identify linkages leading to mitigation measures. In some cases, failure to think carefully through the scoping decisions can lead to quite misleading conclusions and suboptimizations (i.e., a focus on relatively unimportant risks or even promoting actions that increase overall risk).

In order to evaluate hazards at this stage, a number of methods exist, summarized in Table 9.9.

The screening tier is an intermediate level ERA that incorporates greater rigour than the scoping tier in describing hazards and exposure. In this tier, the greatest effort is placed on analysis of data describing the dose–response relationships of exposure scenarios. In cases where the estimates of risk are unusually or inexplicably high a more rigorous estimation of likely exposure and a review of existing hazard information is warranted. The methodology for hazard evaluation is as used in scoping, relying on conservative estimates and deterministic approaches to estimating risk. The main objective at this stage is to identify major outstanding risk issues and, if possible, eliminate some of the lesser issues before proceeding with detailed investigations.

The final tier involves more sophisticated modelling of exposure and direct measure of effect where possible. Exposures may be quantified in a probabilistic manner. Hazards are reviewed in-depth for more accurate estimations appropriate to the exposure or species in question. Rather than relying on conservative assumptions of exposure and hazard, this tier of risk characterization provides a more realistic quantification of potential risks associated with the relevant exposures.

9.4.6 Characterization of risk

There are two main purposes in performing ERA: the first to learn about the risks and the second to reduce them. The organization of this information is done through characterization of risks. Risk characterization integrates the information from hazard identification, dose–response relationships, and exposure estimates to determine the probability of risk to humans or to the ecosystem. The risk characterization should consist of discussion, analysis, and conclusions that synthesize the results from the hazard and exposure assessment, present a balanced representation of the available data and its relevancy to the health effects of concern, and identify key assumptions and major areas of uncertainty. All this information must be presented in a manner that can easily be interpreted and used by the relevant personnel.

Table 9.9 Characteristics of hazard evaluation procedures

Procedure	Use	Approach	Performed by	Event scenario	Advantages	Limitations	Information/data requirements
Process or system checklists	Compliance with minimal standards; identify areas requiring further evaluation	Answer questions on previously prepared checklist	Engineer with moderate experience	Not identified	Rapid assessments of hazards	Identifies only hazards previously recognized	Detailed checklist
Safety review	Periodic safety or loss control inspections	Checklists, worker interviews, records review, visual inspection	Team with complementary skills and backgrounds	Normally not identified	–	Primarily for existing facilities	Checklists, detailed facility information
Relative ranking; Dow and Mond hazard indices	Provides relative ranking of hazards and estimates in-plant consequences	Scoring procedure based on credits and penalties for observed conditions	Engineer with moderate experience	Limited identification	Rapid semi-quantitative estimate of relative risks	Primarily for hazards previously recognized	Calculational parameters based on previous accidents

Method	Purpose	Procedure	Team	Output	Advantages	Limitations	Data needed
Preliminary hazard analysis	Precursor to subsequent hazard prevention analysis	Early in design stage, identify broad hazard categories and potential initiating events	Engineer with considerable experience	Potential scenarios identified, but not design specific	Early identification of potential hazards	Dependent on experience and knowledge of analyst	Preliminary plant designs
"What if" method	Identification of potential accident scenarios	Formulate possible deviations in operation and project consequence	Team of experts	Scenarios identified	Can provide thorough evaluation of hazards	Highly dependent on skill of analyst	Detailed facility design information
Hazard and operability studies (HAZOP)	Investigations of possible deviations from design intent	Structured meetings of analysis team to review plant design; use of "guide words"	Multi-disciplinary team of experts	Many scenarios identified for consideration through use of guide words	Procedure stimulates identification of all credible scenarios	Time consuming; only qualitative likelihood of scenarios occurring	Detailed plant designs and operating characteristics

Table 9.9 (cont.)

Procedure	Use	Approach	Performed by	Event scenario	Advantages	Limitations	Information/data requirements
Failure modes, effects, and criticality analysis (FMECA)	Identify modes and effects of equipment failure; possible design improvements input to other analyses	Evaluation and ranking of the effect of each failure independent of other failures	Engineer(s) with considerable experience	Cause of failure is not identified	Thorough evaluation of all equipment failures, their probabilities and effects	Does not consider scenarios with multiple failures	Detailed facility design information; probabilities for equipment failure
Fault tree analysis	Evaluation of alternative sequences of failures and consequences	Accident evaluated in "reverse", to identify possible causes; graphical representations	Engineer(s) with considerable experience	Defined in detail	Thorough identification of all event scenarios	Extensive analysis required to identify scenarios of greatest significance	Detailed facility design information; probabilities for failure modes

Technique	Purpose	Description	Personnel	System definition	Advantages	Disadvantages	Requirements
Event tree analysis	Evaluation of alternative sequences of failures and results	Evaluation of single and combinations of events "forward" to identify results; graphical representations	Engineer(s) with considerable experience	Defined in detail	Thorough identification of all event scenarios	Extensive analysis required to identify scenarios of greatest significance	Detailed facility design information; probabilities for failure modes
Cause–consequence analysis	Evaluation of alternative sequences of failures and consequences	Combines "reverse" and "forward" analyses of fault tree and event tree analyses	Engineer(s) with considerable experience	Defined in detail	Graphical method that can proceed forward to consequences and reverse to causes	Extensive analysis required to identify scenarios of greatest significance	Detailed facility design information; probabilities for failure modes
Human error analysis	Evaluate role of human error as contributing factors in event scenarios	Various techniques; usually interactive with other hazard analysis techniques	Experts in human performance technology	Contributes to defining scenarios, if conducted as part of other analyses	Provides evaluation of often significant role of human error	Difficulty in transferring results to other contexts	Role of human intervention in specific operations; level of training

In HHRA both individual risks and risks to the population should be characterized. In order to characterize risk to the individual, differences in susceptibility and exposure of individuals must be taken into account. The hypothetical maximally exposed individual is frequently of primary concern. There are two possible descriptors of population risks. The first is the probabilistic number of health effect cases estimated in the population of interest over a specified time. The second type is an estimate of the percentage of the population that would receive exposures greater than the reference dose.

In EcoRA, characterization describes risk in terms of assessment end points, discusses the ecological significance of the effects, and summarizes overall confidence in the assessment.

Risk characterization also contains a description and estimate of the uncertainity of the assessment.

9.4.7 Risk comparison

Risk assessments typically involve analysis of a specific substance or problem area. Another way to use risk assessment is to compare risks from multiple problems. Various expressions allow for comparison of risks during comparative risk assessment.

- Probability of frequency of events causing one or more immediate fatalities. One of the most valuable potential contributions of ERA is an idea of the range of possible outcomes and their respective probabilities. Although it is possible to present results in the form of a mean or medium, giving some idea of the distribution is also important in most cases.
- Chance of death for an individual within a specified population in each year, or risk of death per person per year.
- Number of deaths from lifetime exposure. This is expressed as excess deaths per million persons. For example, the chance of a person in the United States dying from cancer is 1 in 4 or 250,000 in 1 million. A lifetime exposure to a carcinogen can be predicted from cancer potency data (derived from animal tests) to cause, say, 10 additional deaths per million (10^5 risk) for a total of 250,010 deaths per million.
- Loss of life expectancy considers the age at which death occurs.
- Deaths per tonne of product, or per facility, are expressions that, while often encountered, are not recommended.

There is, of course, no risk-free lifestyle or location, but often the natural background level of risks is unrecognized. If the new risk is relatively small in relation to that already and unavoidably accepted, then a more "correct" perception may occur. The number of days per year that an air pollutant exceeds the ambient air quality standard for the project site may be 10 at present and 15 after the project begins operation. The reduction of better-than-standard days from 355 to 350 offers a useful comparison. If the excess cancer deaths or days of pollution were obviously nontrivial, the comparisons would also serve to more closely correlate perception and objective assessment results more closely.

Risks of alternative technologies, sites, or projects that might provide the same economic growth benefits are a useful comparison. For example, a hydroelectric dam could be compared with a coal-fired power plant as to the different risks to human health and the environment. Improving a rail transport system for hazardous chemicals could be compared to truck transport over highways. In the case of a pulp and paper mill, the disposal of organic wastes may be compared in three ways: oxidation ponds, discharge to a stream, and use as irrigation water.

Familiar risks are an important reference point in interpreting new risks but only if they are truly comparable (i.e., they must not compare risks that have opposite aspects of the psychological factors previously mentioned, such as voluntary/involuntary). Comparison of the same risk at two different times is particularly effective (e.g., before and after installation of some pollution abatement equipment). If a standard exists, the new risk can be expressed as a percentage of the allowable amount of contaminant. If the same industrial process is used at another location, the actual experience can be used as a comparison for the predicted new risk. Risks from pesticide residues in food can be compared with risks from naturally occurring carcinogens such as aflatoxin in peanuts.

Benefits of development projects are usually so large and obvious that the accompanying risk may be acceptable if those at risk share the benefits. The risks to health and environment of not developing are also great (i.e., continued poverty, workplace risks elsewhere). The risks of a dam for irrigation should be compared with the benefits of additional agricultural production. The risks from sulphur oxide particulate pollutants from a coal-fired power plant contrast with the benefits of increased electricity. The risks of improved roads should be offset by the benefits of productivity and communication.

A final, useful type of comparison is with the costs and benefits of risk reduction. Risk assessment will usually recommend changes in the project in order to lower unacceptable risks. Where this decision is made, the remaining task is to find the most cost-effective means of achieving the goal. Usually, risk levels are sought that provide the lowest total or nett risk for the least cost: a sort of optimum allocation of risk-reduction efforts among different sources and target populations.

9.4.8 Quantitative risk assessments

The quantitative risk assessment process typically involves identifying the possible scenarios, estimating the likelihood (or frequency) of occurrence for each one, projecting the range of possible impacts given that the scenario occurs, and quantifying the uncertainty (or conversely, the confidence) in these evaluations. Mathematically combining these results for all scenarios provides risk curves that can be displayed, for example, as curves of event frequency versus number of individuals affected (or other adverse effects) per event.

A typical quantitative risk assessment process can be illustrated with a hypothetical industrial facility that includes use of a toxic gas in the proposed manufacturing process. It is assumed for this hypothetical analysis that a previous hazard identification (screening) pointed to storage of the on-site inventory of this toxic material in a single above-ground steel tank as a hazard requiring ERA. The subsequent hazard accounting process (scoping) specified that the risk assessment should evaluate the likelihood, over the 30-year facility operational lifetime, of accidental release of the stored toxic gas, and estimate the expected number of persons, both facility workers and the public in surrounding areas, that would be adversely affected by such accidents. The scoping process in the hypothetical analysis specified as an "adverse effect level" the exposure of individuals for 15 minutes or more to a concentration of 10 percent of the LC_{50} concentration (concentration which is lethal to 50 percent of the exposed persons). The risk assessment is to provide estimates of the expected (mean) number of persons exposed at this level per year and the upper bound number of persons affected at the 90% confidence level.

It is important that the boundary conditions and scope specified for the risk assessment be recognized in conducting the risk management decisions. For example, the specified risk assessment considers only acute effects of accidents from the toxic gas release, so this assessment should not be interpreted as the overall facility risk level. Also, the estimate of number of persons exposed at the specified adverse effect concentration level does not mean that all of those persons will suffer adverse health effects.

The objective of the quantitative risk assessment in this hypothetical example is to obtain the probability of annual consequences being within a specified range. The typical method for obtaining this approximation is first to describe all possible sequences of events or scenarios for the components in the environmental pathway that will lead to the defined adverse consequence. This answers the question, "What can go wrong?"

An example of one possible scenario for these pathway components might be:
- quantity of toxic material in the inventory is hazardous;
- overpressure in the storage tank in combination with failure of the relief valve leading to tank rupture;
- combination of wind speed and atmospheric stability leading to an estimated spatial and temporal distribution of toxic material concentration;
- population distribution based on night-time occurrence.

9.4.9 Risk communication

The results of a competently prepared EIA are relatively easy to express (i.e., a potentially adverse impact is identified and mitigation measures are prescribed). An ERA, in contrast, results in probabilistic expressions that highlight uncertainties about the outcome of a project. To technical and managerial experts, the quantification of risks is an aid in decision-making, even though these "real" risks are still bounded by confidence limits (the degree of belief in the numbers). But the response of the public to a risk that has been identified, analysed, and characterized depends on how they perceive and interpret the information.

Psychologists studying risk perception find that fears are heightened beyond what the objective facts would warrant when:
• risks are involuntary or controlled by others;
• the consequences are dread and delayed;
• the benefits and risks are inequitably distributed;
• the proposed project is unfamiliar and involves complex technology;
• basic needs such as clean air, drinking water, or food are threatened.
Combinations of these factors can lead to intense opposition to projects by local citizens or environmental groups. Ultimately, the political process in a developing country must deal with risks as they are perceived rather than as they "really are".

Risk perception, however, can be made more congruent with the objective findings about risk by appropriate and effective communication, not a one-way transfer of information but a dialogue between the project proponent and affected parties. The worldwide trend toward involving and informing those who are affected by economic development in the planning and implementation of projects is probably a good thing and in any event, it is irresistible. Thus, risk communication must be incorporated into the use of ERA.

In summary, the communication of risk information should take the form of decision analysis. What options are available and, for each option, what is the set of risks, costs, and benefits? How are these risks, costs, and benefits distributed within the society? These comparisons can actually change the perception of risks so that participative decision-making may proceed on a more rational basis.

9.4.10 Risk management

Risk management is the evaluation of alternative risk reduction measures and the implementation of those that appear cost-effective. It is essentially the decision-making process in which an action or a policy is developed once a risk has been determined to exist. The general process of risk management can be subdivided in three main phases.

- Phase 1 – risk analysis and assessment – involves the identification of hazards to people and the environment, the determination of the probability of occurrence of these hazards, and the magnitude of the events.
- Phase II – risk limits – entails defining the acceptability of the risk which can be classified as acceptable or in need of reduction.
- Phase III – risk reduction – involves the design and implementation of risk-reducing measures and controls.

Management concerns that arise because of substantial uncertainties about major environmental consequences determine the scope of detailed risk assessment. Projects are undertaken for obvious and direct benefits of economic growth, employment, and exploitation of natural resources in a developing country. Achievement of these benefits always entails risks, but the risks must be acceptable to the funding agency and the country. Reduction of risks costs money but so does incurring the unwanted impacts. Avoiding one risk may create a new risk; hence, nett risk is always a consideration. Thus, a risk assessment analyses trade-offs, compares risk levels, and evaluates cost-effectiveness of risk-reduction alternatives.

Risk management integrates ERA with technical, political, social, and economic issues to develop risk reduction and prevention strategies. Figure 9.6 illustrates the relationship between the elements of risk assessment and risk management for human health considerations. A similar model would be applicable for EcoRA too. As indicated by the figure, different types of information are used in ERA.

As an illustration of the various activities which constitute the process of ERA, the case study of a petroleum terminal and distribution project is provided as Annex 9.1 (page 272), which traces the risk assessment process through scoping and screening to the final decision.

In the case of industrial projects, a significant outcome of the risk management is the development of a disaster management plan (DMP) in the case of projects involving manufacture of potentially hazardous products. Recommendations for a typical DMP are given in the next section.

9.4.11 Guidelines for disaster management planning

The disaster management plan (DMP) should generally include the following:
- details of the specification of equipment and machineries, plot plan, and hazardous areas classifications;
- details of the risk assessment procedure adopted;
- details of the on-site and off-site emergency plan;
- details of the fire extinguishers and foams.

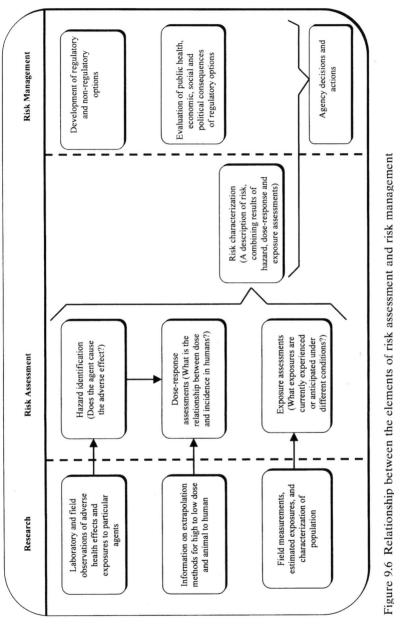

Figure 9.6 Relationship between the elements of risk assessment and risk management
Source: Environmental Risk Assessment for Sustainable Cities, Technical Publication Series [3], International Environmental Technology Centre, Osaka, 1996.

9.4.11.1 Specification

The first step in the design of any plant is the preparation of specifications of equipment and machinery for safety considerations in the design. For example, in general for catalytic reactors the design temperature should take into account the rise in catalyst bed temperature when it becomes old or that the temperature may shoot up due to operation of the plant.

9.4.11.2 Plot plan

Safety considerations are taken into account while finalizing the plot plan of an industrial plant producing chemicals. Sufficient spacing should be provided between the boundaries of different sections of the plant, and the distances between individual pieces of equipment in each section should be well within boundaries limit. The distances between individual pieces of equipment bear in mind accessibility, safe maintenance space, and safety from the adjacent equipment.

9.4.11.3 Hazardous area classification

To determine the suitable type of electrical installation, the entire plant area is classified into different zones according to the hazardous material likely to be present.

9.4.11.4 P & I diagrams

P & I diagrams are the documents which are prepared at the earliest stage of the design of a plant. It shows all the equipment in position, process and utility valves, instruments, control system, safety valves and other safety devices. After the zero revision, the P & I is reviewed in great detail taking all aspects into consideration, regarding safety of the plant under all eventualities. One of the methods used for the process may be a hazard and operability study (HAZOP study).

9.4.11.5 Storage of inflammable liquids

Safety considerations include the location of the tank farm, alternative access, the allowable number of tanks in a tank farm, proper spacing between tanks, proper height of the dike wall, adequate tank farm enclosure capacity, minimum distance between the tank and nearby vicinity to be conformed to, emergency venting in fixed roof tanks, provision of a pump house, provision of floating roof tanks on top of the naphtha and methanol storage tanks, proper velocity at the inlet of methanol or naphtha tanks, provision of nitrogen blanketing for the naphtha or methanol tanks, and, in case of more than one tank, provision of double block and bleed valves with spectacle fluid.

"Non-pressure" fixed roof tanks should be suitable for working at

Table 9.10 Recommended types of cylindrical tanks for petroleum liquids

Petroleum liquid	Type of tank
Class "I" petroleum (flashpoint below 21 °C/70 °F), e.g., motor and aviation gasolines	(a) Floating roof (b) "Non-pressure" fixed roof with internal floating deck (c) "Pressure" fixed roof
Class "II" petroleum (flashpoint above 55 °C/131 °F) e.g., kerosene, special boiling point liquids	(a) Floating roof (b) "Non-pressure" fixed roof with internal floating deck (c) "Non-pressure" fixed roof with "atmospheric" vents
Class "III" petroleum (flashpoint above 55 °C/131 °F), e.g., diesel and gas oils, medium and heavy fuel oils, lubricating oils and bitumens	"Non-pressure" fixed roof with "atmospheric" vents. Tanks which contain heavy fuel oils or bitumen are insulated and heated

atmospheric pressure, but be designed for an internal pressure of 7.5 mbar and a vacuum of 2.5 mbar. "Low-pressure" fixed roof tanks should be designed for an internal pressure of 20 mbar and a vacuum of 6 mbar. "High-pressure" fixed roof tanks should be designed for an internal pressure of 56 mbar and a vacuum of 7 mbar. See Table 9.10.

9.4.11.6 Risk assessment

(i) Hazard analysis : risk assessment of plants
Hazard analysis should answer these questions:
1 Which materials or process streams are flammable or combustible?
2 What is their ignition temperature or what is their ignition energy requirement?
3 How fast will they burn?
4 How much heat can be generated per unit?
5 How much quantity will be available in any one area?
6 Will it explode?

(ii) Scope and objectives of risk assessment of industries
(a) To develop a risk hazard checking system.
(b) To rank the plant layout on the hazard potentials.
(c) To remodify the plant layout and identify safety measures to be undertaken within the industry, so as to minimize the on-site economic damage as well as off-site risks to the society and environment.
(d) To assist the regulatory authorities, planners, and designers to investigate plant accidents and predict the possible consequences for decision-making.

(e) To make decisions on industrial clearance swiftly and on a more rational basis.

(iii) Total risk assessment

Risk assessment consists of the following four steps:

1 Identification of possible hazardous events.
2 Consequence analysis.
3 Quantitative analysis of system failure probability from their component failure or frequency assessment.

(a) Hazard identification procedures. Effective hazard identification depends primarily upon two factors: data and organization. For well-tried processes and common materials this data will be readily available when required. However, if new conditions, chemicals, and materials are involved it may take several months to design and carry out experiments to produce the required data.

Types of hazard identification methods are comparative methods which rely upon comparing the design with some recognized code or set of design practices and fundamental methods such as HAZOP, which can be applied in almost any situation.

Comparative methods use engineering codes and practices as the standards against which the acceptability of a design is evaluated. Comparisons with codes and practices generate questions such as "Shouldn't the design be like...?", "Why is this different from previous proven practice?", and "Will this change cover the hazard at the same risk level?" If the designer is unable to demonstrate that he has covered the hazard, the question is recorded for further study. Equipment checklists used by the equipment designers are also used by the hazard identification (HAZID) team to re-check critical aspects of the design.

Fundamental methods can be further subdivided.

Hazard and operability studies use guide words such as "too much" and "too little", which can be applied to the process parameters to generate questions such as "What if there is too much flow?"

Failure modes and effects analysis (FMEA) is based on identifying the possible failure modes of each component of a system and predicting the consequences of the failure. The method is especially useful for the analysis of very critical processes but is extremely time consuming if applied on too broad a scale.

Fault tree analysis works from a chosen "top event" such as "explosion in Reactor 1" and then considers the combination of failures and conditions which could cause the event to occur. Both failure modes and effects analysis are useful aids to hazard identification as they both structure and document the analysis. However, because they involve very detailed analysis of components and operations, their use in the process industry is mainly limited to the identification of special hazards where they form the basis of qualification of risks.

Hazard indices, such as those developed by Dow Chemical company and extended by Lewis, are methods which are designed to give a quantitative indication of the potential for hazardous incidents associated with a given design of plant. They require a minimum of process and design data and can graphically demonstrate which areas within the plant require more detailed information.

Event tree analysis works from a chosen event called the initiating event and is a systematic representation of all the possible states of the system, conditional to the given initiating event and relevant for a given type of consequence.

The given event may be the top event in a fault tree as well as the initiating event in an event tree. The main problem is at which level an event has to be regarded as the top event, for example, initiating event. Too high will lead to an extensive fault tree and small event trees; too low will lead to the reverse.

(b) Consequence analysis. There are three categories of dispersion model: simple "passive", moment jet, and dense vapour cloud.

Simple "passive" dispersion involves neutral buoyancy and plume rise for heat and momentum. It is used for those phases of gas dispersion dominated by atmospheric turbulence.

Moment jet dispersion covers high velocity release, when the released gas can be denser or lighter than air, and involves simple horizontal jet models, and complex plume path models. Moment jet dispersion is for vapour only. The jet dispersion model does assume a Gaussian concentration profile. However, the rate of dilution in jet dispersion is greater than the rate in neutral dispersion. Hence, by using the true release rate and source in the neutral dispersion model, calculations will result in concentrations which are too high.

Dense vapour cloud dispersion deals with clouds heavier than air, cold clouds, for example, LNG vapour, and liquid and vapour clouds, for example, ammonia.

Vulnerability model or probit equations have been derived for estimating, from dose relationships, the probability of affecting a certain proportion of the exposed population. These have been based almost exclusively on animal test data. The probit equation is:

$$\Pr = A_t + B_t \ln(C_n t_e)$$

where $\Pr$ = probability function, A_t, B_t, and n are constants, C is the concentration of pollutant to which exposure is made (in ppm v/v), and t_e is the duration of exposure to the pollutant, measured in minutes.

The consequences for toxic releases are expressed in terms of distances to specific concentrations. These are then translated into effects on people or property by means of vulnerability models, which may also require the duration of the effect.

(c) Frequency assessment and quantitative analysis.   What is the probability that the system will fail on demand? What is the frequency of occurrence of the top event? Does a change in the system design improve or reduce the system reliability?

Given the "top event", the analyst has to work logically and systematically through the system to determine how each top event can occur. Here, the required numerical information is obtained, for example the probability and/or frequency of the top event.

The application of event tree in this analysis can be illustrated diagrammatically. The nodal events in these (plant) event trees mainly concern the functionality of the engineered safety features. The next set of pinch points occur when the fault progression can determine the type and quantity of release of material from the containment. The nodal event in these (containment) event trees are mainly phenomenological questions. The probabilities are generated from the subjective assessments of accident conditions prevailing in the various fault conditions. Another set of event trees deal with the transport of hazardous chemicals in the environment and the system, when outcomes are the environmental consequences.

Hence, the frequency of any outcome is equal to the frequency of the initiating event multiplied by the probability of outcome or accident sequence.

The derivation of nodal probabilities is crucial to both on-site and off-site emergency planning and requires works managements to identify systematically what emergencies could arise in their plants. These should range from small events, which can be dealt with by works personnel without outside help, to the largest event for which it is practical to have a plan. Experience has shown that for every occasion that the full potential of an accident is realized, there are many occasions when some lesser event occurs or when a developing incident is made safe before reaching full potential.

Most major hazard accidents involve either flammable or toxic materials.

Events involving flammable materials can be broken down into (a) major fires with no danger of explosion, with hazards from prolonged high levels of thermal radiation and smoke; (b) fire threatening items of plant containing hazardous substances, with hazards from spread of fire, explosion, or release of toxic substances; and (c) explosion with little or no warning, with hazards from blast wave, flying debris, and high levels of thermal radiation.

Events involving toxic materials can be broken down into (a) slow or intermittent release of toxic substances, for example, from a leaking valve; (b) items of plant threatened by fire, with hazards from potential loss of containment; (c) rapid release of limited duration, due to plant failure, for example, fracture of pipe, with hazards from a toxic cloud, limited in size, which may quickly disperse; (d) massive release of a toxic substance due to failure of a large storage or process vessel, an uncontrollable chemical reaction and failure of safety systems, with the exposure hazard affecting a wide area.

The assessment of possible incidents should produce a report indicating: (a) the worst events considered; (b) the route of those worst events; (c) the timescale to lesser events along the way; (d) the size of lesser events if their development is halted; (e) the relative likelihood of events; and (f) the consequences of each event. This report may be part of the hazard assessment report or may be a separate exercise produced specifically for the purposes of emergency planning.

The following elements should be included in an on-site emergency plan: (a) proper alarm and communication mechanisms; (b) appointment of personnel; these include: (i) the site incident controller who will take care of the area around the incident when the emergency occurs and who will arrange the required rescue operations and (ii) a site main controller who will direct operations from the emergency control centre after relieving the site incident controller of the responsibility for overall control; and (c) details of the emergency control centres.

Off-site emergency planning takes care of the area outside the works. The responsibility for the off-site plan will be likely to rest either with the works management or, as is the case under European Community legislation, with the local authority. Aspects to be included in an off-site emergency plan are as follows.

(i) Organization: details of command structure, warning systems, implementation procedures, emergency control centres; names and appointments of incident controller, site main controller, their deputies, and other key personnel.

(ii) Communications: identification of personnel involved, communication centre, call signs, network, lists of telephone numbers.

(iii) Specialized emergency equipment: details of availability and location of heavy lifting gear, bulldozers, specified fire-fighting equipment, fire boats.

(iv)   Specialized knowledge: details of specialist bodies, firms and people upon whom it may be necessary to call, for example, those with specialized chemical knowledge, laboratories.

(v)   Voluntary organizations: details of organizers, telephone numbers, resources, etc.

(vi)   Chemical information: details of the hazardous substances stored or processed on each site and a summary of the risks associated with them.

(vii)   Meteorological information: arrangements for obtaining details of weather conditions prevailing at the time and weather forecasts.

(viii)   Humanitarian arrangements: transport, evacuation centres, emergency feeding, treatment of injured, first aid, ambulances, temporary mortuaries.

(ix)   Public information: arrangements for (a) dealing with the media press office and (b) informing relatives, etc.

(x)   Assessment: arrangements for (a) collecting information on the causes of the emergency and (b) reviewing the efficiency and effectiveness of all aspects of the emergency plan.

9.5   Environmental health impact assessment

Human health is influenced not only by the physical environment, but also by social and economic factors. Traditionally, it has been the practice to include health-related risks as part of EIA studies. However, it is being increasingly recognized that a more comprehensive and rigorous approach needs to be adopted to identify and appraise those environmental factors which may affect human health, in the form of an environmental health impact assessment (EHIA). The various factors influencing human health can include geology, vegetation, demography, economics, pollutants, as well as the availability of health services.

The World Health Organization (WHO) has undertaken a great deal of fundamental research on EHIA, holding regular seminars, publishing documentation, and developing methodologies.

9.5.1   Need for EHIA

The WHO has identified a number of reasons for the need to undertake an EHIA. They include: prevention is better than cure, as with other forms of assessment; it is specified in many forms of EIA legislation; environmental degradation is linked to health impacts; the methodology can be incorporated in EIA; systematic inclusion of health impacts improves the legitimacy of the decisions made and the process by which they are taken; human health issues often prompt a public response and/or involvement; and there is no argument against it!

Although the need for EHIA is self-evident and is clearly spelt out by the WHO, there are some inherent difficulties in undertaking an EHIA: lack of baseline data on humans in local communities; the timescale for health effects to show up is very long; the interaction of different chemical, physical, and biological agents, their synergistic/antagonistic effects, etc., make it difficult to isolate the individual agent or group of agents responsible for the adverse impact – in other words, a clear cause/effect relationship is difficult to determine; the variety of human responses and exposures; limited knowledge of dose–response relationships; and planners and decision makers may feel that health is not their responsibility.

9.5.2 Potential methodologies and approaches for addressing health impacts

Given that health impacts need to be addressed and integrated in EIA studies, and they often are not given sufficient attention or analysis, the question then becomes "What methodologies and/or approaches exist that might be used to facilitate the integrated consideration of health impacts?"

9.5.2.1 Adapt EIA study activities

Adapt the typical activities in an EIA study (listed below) to systematically include attention to health impacts.
(i)   Preparation of description of projects.
(ii)   Review and analysis of pertinent institutional information.
(iii)   Identification of impacts.
(iv)   Description of effected environment.
(v)   Predictions of impacts.
(vi)   Interpretation of predicted impacts.
(vii)   Identification and evaluation of mitigation measures.
(viii) Selection of proposed action.
(ix)   Written documentation.
(x)   Monitoring of environmental impacts.

9.5.2.2 Integrate health impacts into EIA

Integrate an existing health impact methodology into the typical activities in an EIA study or use the health impact methodology as the focus of the EIA study. To serve as an example, a generic methodology for EHIA has been suggested by the WHO. It consists of the nine steps listed in Table 9.11. Steps 1 and 2 are related to the normal EIA process in which primary, secondary, and tertiary impacts on environmental parameters

Table 9.11 Steps in EHIA methodology

Item number	Steps to be taken	Tools to be used
Step 1	Assessments of primary impacts on environmental parameters	Regular impact assessments process
Step 2	Assessments of secondary and tertiary impacts on environmental parameters	Regular impact assessments process
Step 3	Screening of impacted environmental parameters of recognized health significance (EH factors)	Epidemiological knowledge
Step 4	Assessments of the magnitude of exposed population for each group of EH factors	Census, land use planning
Step 5	Assessments of the magnitude of risk groups included in each group of exposed population	Census
Step 6	Computation of predicted health impacts in terms of mortality and morbidity, if possible	Results from risk assessments studies
Step 7	Definition of acceptable risk (or of significance of adverse health impacts)	Assessments of trade off between human and economic requirements
Step 8	Identification of mitigation measures to prevent or reduce significant adverse health impacts	Abatement of EH factors? Magnitude reduction of exposure, reduction of exposed populations, protection of risk groups
Step 9	Final decision on whether or not the project should proceed	

Source: Giroult, 1988, *WHO Interest in EHIA*, In: Wathern, P. (Ed.) *Theory and Practice*, Routledge: London.

are assessed. Step 3 is derived from information given in the EIA and for which environmental health factors can be identified. Methods for identification of environmental health factors could be based on epidemiological and/or toxicological evidences of causal links between environmental parameters and health effects. Step 4 involves the study of exposure pathways. Steps 5 and 6 use epidemiological and toxicological information on dose–incidence and dose–response relationships between environmental parameters and specific health effects. Step 7 can be used to evaluate significance and acceptability of adverse health effects, and step 8 focuses on mitigation measures. Finally, step 9 involves appropriate decision-making. This generic EHIA methodology has been modified to allow its use for chemical manufacturing facilities.

9.5.2.3 Use a targeted approach

A targeted approach can be used, in which one or more empirical indices depict the relative health-related concerns associated with pollutant emissions (e.g., stress related to physical, chemical, biological, and/or radiological emissions), environmental transport and their pathways, environmental media contamination potential, and/or potential remediation measures and their effectiveness in reducing existing contamination.

Information on other targeted approaches is also available. These results of targeted approaches could then be integrated into the appropriate activities associated with the EIA study.

9.5.2.4 Probabilistic risk assessment

A probabilistic risk assessment can be conducted using the four major steps typically associated with health-related risk assessments; these steps include hazard identification, dose–response assessments, exposure assessments, and risk characterization.

9.5.3 Proposed methodology

Considering the above methodologies or approaches in terms of their advantages and limitations, including such issues as data and personnel requirements and scientific credibility, it was determined that an integrated health impact prediction and assessment methodology should be based on an amalgam of selected features of each methodology or approach. A generic methodology will be effective only if it can take account of the broader policy-making context represented by the EIA process.

Figure 9.7 shows a flow diagram of the generic health impact prediction and assessment methodology. Each of the boxes represents an EIA activity, with the three activities representing the fundamental functions of the EIA process enclosed in a larger box. The activities corresponding to the description of the project and the environment are represented in the same box because in a health impact assessment they serve the same purpose. Information related to the description of the project and the environment can be used to identify and predict impacts.

9.5.3.1 Determining the need for health impact assessment

A preliminary task involves determining whether or not a health impact assessment is necessary. This task should consider in broad terms whether the possibility exists that health impacts will result from the proposed

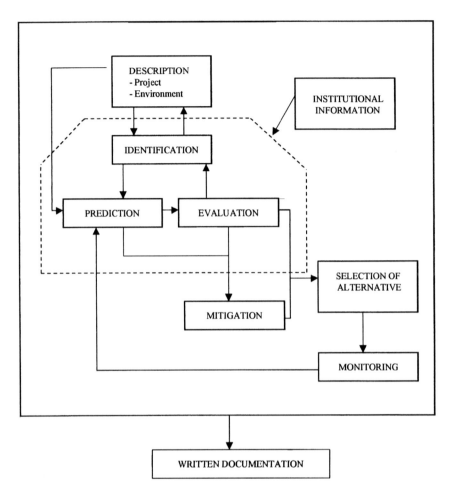

Figure 9.7 Conceptual framework for health impact prediction and assessment methodology
Source: Arquiaga, M. C., Canter, L. W., Nelson, D. I. Integration of health impact considerations in enviromental impact studies. *Impact Assessment*, Vol. 12, No. 2. 1994, p. 175–197.

action. To conduct this task, potential health impacts should be analysed according to the nature of agents that may cause them. Depending on whether the agent is a chemical, a radionuclide, an organism, or a physical phenomenon, health impacts can be classified in the following categories: (1) chemical health impacts, (2) radiological health impacts, (3) biological health impacts, and/or (4) physical health impacts.

If the need for a health impact assessment is shown, then a more exhaustive analysis of the health effects that could result from the project should be conducted. This analysis may start with the review and analysis of pertinent institutional information, which should be conducted prior to an extensive effort in an environmental impact study. The identification of pertinent legislation or regulations that address health effects should provide information helpful for one or more of the three analytical functions in the EIA process. The main use of institutional information will be for the interpretation of health impacts.

The task of describing the proposed action and its alternatives, and the environmental setting that will be affected, is the next activity in the methodology. The information related to the description of the project and the environment serves two purposes. The first is to identify project components and/or environmental features that may give rise to health impact concerns, and to use these to identify specific health impacts likely to occur. The second purpose is to record information regarding the project and the environment that may be useful in predicting (quantifying where possible) the identified health impacts.

9.5.3.2 Identify health impacts

Identifying health impacts is approximately equivalent to the hazard identification component of a conventional health risk assessment. It consists of determining whether exposure to the elements of the project and/or the environment may or may not cause a change in the incidence of a health condition. This activity, which may require an extensive review of information regarding human and animal studies, also involves identifying the nature of the health condition affected, if any, and the evidence that such a condition occurs in humans. The nature of the health condition affected should include not only the description of the condition, but also the classification of the potential impact in terms of its adverse/beneficial, reversible/irreversible, short-term/long-term, direct/indirect, and cumulative characteristics. These classifications, besides being important for the identification of health impacts, are relevant to their interpretation.

Another task associated with the identification of health impacts is that of defining those circumstances or scenarios, for example, routine operations versus accidents, under which health impacts may occur. This task provides a basis for assessing potential human exposure to the health impact causing agents. Examples of health hazards associated with various development projects are given in Table 9.12 parts (a) to (f), which may be used as guidelines during screening of projects for their potential health impacts.

9.5.3.3 Prediction of health impacts

The prediction of impacts represents the key technical steps in the EIA process, with qualitative information needed on types of impacts and

Table 9.12(a) Mining and mineral processing: screening for health hazards

Project	Health hazards	Causes
Location	Malnutrition	Loss of common property resources
	Vector-borne disease	Endemic disease foci
	Poisoning	Pollution from spoil deposits
Planning and design	Dust-induced lung disease	Excessive dust
Construction	Poisoning, injury	Inadequate occupational safety measures
	Communicable disease	Poor sanitation, poor water supply, poor food hygiene
	STDs	Labour camps
	Vector-borne disease	Exposure to vectors in endemic disease foci
Operation	Dust-induced lung disease, infectious respiratory disease	Poor protection from dust, poor ventilation
	STDs	Labour camps, unaccustomed wealth, poor health education
	Injury, poisoning, deafness, drowning	Poor occupational safety, abandoned mine workings, dam failure

Table 9.12(b) Coastal zone development: screening for health hazards

Project stage	Health hazards	Causes
Location	Malnutrition	Loss of common property resources by fisher folk
	Poisoning and excreta-related disease	Water-based pollution
Planning and design	Poisoning and excreta-related disease	Effluent disposal
Construction	Poisoning, injury, miscarriage	Inadequate occupational safety measures
	Communicable diseases associated with poor living conditions	Poor sanitation, poor water supply, poor food hygiene
	STDs	Labour camps
Operation	Injury	Storm and flood
	Poisoning and excreta-related disease	Pollution

Table 9.12(c) Thermal power: screening for health hazards

Project stage	Health hazards	Causes
Location	Injury	Fire, explosion, road haulage of fuel
	Respiratory disease	Air pollution
	Excreta-related disease	Use of contaminated water supplies following loss of water sources
Planning and design	Injury	Traffic routing
	Heavy metal poisoning	Fly ash disposal, leachates
Construction	Poisoning, injury	Inadequate occupational safety measures
	Communicable diseases associated with poor living conditions	Poor sanitation, poor water supply, poor food hygiene
	STDs	Labour camps
Operation	Respiratory disease, eye disease, injury, cancers, deafness	Air pollution, fly ash, explosion, noise, and vibration

quantitative information needed on unit impact factors and/or relevant impact models. Prediction methods are being improved as their predictive capabilities are verified and new technology and scientific knowledge become available. Since risk assessments techniques represent the state-of-the-art for the prediction of health effects resulting from environmental insults, and since these techniques are being extensively used in several regulatory areas, this generic methodology incorporates the use or adaptation of existing risk assessments techniques for the prediction of health impacts.

Except for the prediction of health impacts involved caused by mechanical effects, which are generally predicted by extrapolating statistical data from similar types of actions, the risk assessment techniques for assessing the effects of the four categories of health impact causing agents considered in this generic methodology are similar, in that all consist of four well-defined steps. These steps (which in existing risk assessment techniques are hazard identification, dose–response assessments, exposure assessments, and risk characterization) could be perceived as health impact identification, dose–response assessments, exposure assessments, and health impact characterization when they are integrated in the EIA process.

The first step, which consists of establishing the relationship between a suspected health impact causing agent and a health condition, was

Table 9.12(d) Highways and roads: screening for health hazards

Project stage	Health hazards	Causes
Location	Vector-borne disease	Endemic disease foci Access to forested hinterlands
	Malnutrition	Loss of common property resources, increase in land values, change of livelihood
Planning and design	Injury	Roads with poor safety features
	Communicable disease	Burrow pits, pooling, interrupted surface flows
Construction	Poisoning, injury	Inadequate occupational safety measures
	Communicable diseases associated with poor living conditions	Poor sanitation, poor water supply, poor food hygiene
	STDs	Labour camps
	Vector-borne disease	Exposure to vectors in endemic disease foci
Operation	Vector-borne diseases	Roadside squatters using surface water supplies
	Communicable diseases associated with poor living conditions	
	Respiratory disease	Dust
	Injury	Poor vehicle and road maintenance, poor traffic regulation, poor driver education, increasing vehicle density
	STDs	Long distance truck drivers

described earlier. The dose–response assessment, which is closely related to the health impact identification, consists of describing the relationship between the dose of the health impact causing agent and the predicted occurrence of a health effect in an exposed population. The health effects that may result from exposure to health impact causing agents may fall into two categories: (1) those for which a range of tolerance exists in which no health effects are observed; and (2) those for which any dose is able to cause the health effect. For the former category, a threshold is

Table 9.12(e) Ports and harbours: screening for health hazards

Project stage	Health hazards	Causes
Location	Malnutrition	Loss of communal fisheries
	Poisoning	Leakage of hazardous materials during transit
	Excreta-related diseases	Poor waste disposal facilities
Construction	Poisoning, injury	Inadequate occupational safety measures
	Communicable diseases associated with poor living conditions	Poor sanitation, poor water supply, poor food hygiene
	STDs	Labour camps
Operation	Exotic communicable diseases, including bubonic plague	Accidental shipment of infected rodents, vectors, or pathogens
	STDs	Transit of single males
	Injury	Poor operation and maintenance

Table 9.12(f) Urban development: screening for health hazards

Project stage	Health hazards	Causes
Location	Communicable diseases associated with poor living conditions	Displacement through slum clearance, excreta disposal, water supply
	Injury	Steep hillsides, flood-prone valleys, poor access to and for emergency services
	Non-communicable disease	Pollution, hazardous waste, hazardous occupation
Planning and design	Excreta-related disease, vector-borne disease	Water supply and sanitation problems
	Injury	Traffic
Construction	Poisoning, injury	Inadequate occupational safety measures
	Communicable diseases associated with poor living conditions	Poor sanitation, poor water supply, poor food hygiene
Operation	Vector-borne diseases Excreta-related disease	Blocked drainage, domestic water storage, solid waste management
	Injury	Traffic

typically defined that determines the upper level of the tolerance range. For the latter, a value defining the probability of incremental risk per dose unit is calculated. Depending on the nature of the health impact causing agent and the scenario defined for this agent, one or both types of dose–response relationship can be defined for a particular health impact causing agent.

The main features of exposure assessment and health impact characterization in an EIA study is that exposures to the health impact causing agents and their subsequent effects must be determined for the no action alternatives (the project is not implemented) and the proposed action and its alternatives. Thus, the health effects characterized for the no action alternative provide the baseline condition against which the health effects characterized for the proposed action and its alternatives can be compared. The information obtained during the description of the project and the environment is critical to these steps. An important consideration in assessing exposures within the EIA process is that many of the methods, tools, and techniques used to predict other biophysical environmental impacts may be used to determine exposure to health impact causing agents.

Finally, health impact characterization consists of two parts. The first part combines the environmental doses estimated in the exposure assessment and the dose–response values determined in the dose–response assessment. The results, depending on the health impact being assessed, can be expressed as probabilities of the health impact occurring for non-threshold effects, and hazard indices or margins of safety indices for threshold effects. This characterization of health impacts assumes that exposure to the health impact causing agent has occurred only sporadically (e.g., an accident). Therefore, the probability of occurrence of such events also needs to be considered and/or calculated and combined with the results of the first part as necessary.

9.5.3.4 Interpreting health impacts

The activity that follows prediction of health impacts is their evaluation or interpretation. For many health impacts, appropriate standards do not exist for determining whether the predicted effects are acceptable or not. In the context of the EIA process the evaluation of health impacts can be performed by taking into consideration several factors, including regulatory criteria, institutional information that might be relevant to the health effects or health impact causing agents being considered, the repercussions of the health effects at the individual and populational levels, the evidence that the health effect occurs in humans, the level of confidence in the quantitative and qualitative information used to estimate dose–

response relationships, the level of confidence in the exposure estimates, and, finally, the public perceptions related to the health effects.

9.5.3.5 Mitigation, monitoring, and reporting

Depending on the evaluation of health impacts some may be found to be objectionable; therefore, mitigation measures may be needed. The mitigation process involves two tasks: (1) identifying the appropriate mitigation measures or measures, and (2) estimating the magnitude by which the health impact will be reduced. For most projects, mitigation measures to minimize undesirable health effects fall into one or more of three categories: (a) mitigation through control of sources, (b) mitigation through control of exposure, and (c) mitigation through health service development.

Information regarding the evaluation of health impacts and mitigation measures, together with the information on other environmental impacts should then be used by decision makers to select the proposed action from the alternatives evaluated. A number of more or less complex decision-making procedures have been developed to assist at this stage in the EIA process. In terms of health impact assessment methodology, the aim of this activity is not the selection process itself, but the organization and presentation of the health impact information, integrated with other environmental impact information, in a way that is most useful to the decision makers.

The selection of the proposed action should be accompained by the design of a health monitoring programme if potentially significant health impacts are expected to result from the implementation of the action. One objective of monitoring is to check predicted impacts, thereby allowing responsible entities to validate, modify, and/or adjust the prediction techniques used. Monitoring could also be used in project management decisions. The health monitoring system should be designed in coordination with other environmental monitoring systems in order to minimize resources and avoid duplication of efforts.

The preparation of the written documentation may be the last activity to be completed, but not necessarily the last to be initiated. As a part of this health assessment methodology, it is recommended that the previous activities be documented. This information should then be integrated in the EIS in such a way that it reflects that the health impact assessment was conducted with due consideration in the overall EIA process. Thus, each of the sections of the EIS should contain succinct information pertinent to the assessment of health impacts, which are extensive material generated in connection with the health impacts assessment incorporated as appendices, and with external supporting data and literature adequately referenced.

9.6 Social impact assessment

9.6.1 What is SIA? Why SIA?

Social impact assessment (SIA) is intended to identify and quantify the impacts on human populations resulting from changes to the natural environment. The term "social impact assessment" was first introduced in 1973 to refer to changes in the indigenous Inuit culture due to the construction of the trans-Alaska pipeline. The technique has now developed as a discipline in its own right and is applied in many countries.

SIA is predicated on the notion that decision makers should understand the consequences of their decisions before they act, and that the people affected will not only be appraised of the effects, but have the opportunity to participate in designing their future.

Social impacts may be taken to mean the effects of an action on human populations that alter the ways in which people live, work, meet their basic needs, and interact with each other. As a minimum, SIA should take into account:

- demographic impacts – including labour force, population shift, employment, displacement and relocation effects, change in population make-up;
- socio-economic impacts – including income and income-multiplier effects, employment rates and patterns, prices of local goods and services, and taxation effects;
- institutional impacts – including demands on government and social service NGOs in areas such as housing, schools, criminal justice, health and welfare, and recreation;
- cultural impacts – including those on traditional patterns of life and work, family structure and authority, religion and tribal factors, archaeological features, social networks, and community cohesion; and
- gender impacts – including the implications of development projects on women's role in society, income-generating opportunities, access to resources, and employment opportunities.

As with impacts on the physical environment, factors of scale, duration, and severity of impacts also need to be considered during SIA.

9.6.2 Identifying social impact assessment variables

SIA variables point to measurable changes in human populations, communities, and social relationships resulting from a development project or policy change. After research on local community change, rural industrialization, reservoir and highway development, natural resource development, and social change in general, we suggest a list of social variables under the general headings of: (1) population characteristics; (2) community and institutional structures, (3) political and social resources, (4) individual and family changes, and (5) community resources.

Population characteristics means present population and expected change, ethnic and racial diversity, and influxes and outflows of temporary residents as well as the arrival of seasonal or leisure residents.

Community and institutional structures mean the size, structure, and level or organization of local government including linkages to the larger political systems. They also include historical and present patterns of employment and industrial diversification, the size and level of activity of voluntary associations, religious organizations, and interest groups, and finally, how these institutions relate to each other.

Political and social resources refer to the distribution of power authority, the interested and affected publics, and the leadership capability and capacity within the community or region.

Individual and family changes refer to factors which influence the daily life of the individuals and families, including attitudes, perceptions, family characteristics, and friendship networks. These changes range from attitudes toward the policy to an alternation in family and friendship networks to perceptions of risk, health, and safety.

Community resources include patterns of natural resource and land use, the availability of housing and community services to include health, police, and fire protection, and sanitation facilities. Keys to the continuity and survival of human communities are their historical and cultural resources. Under this collection of variables we also consider possible changes for indigenous people and religious subcultures.

At this point in discussion of an SIA model, we demonstrate a conceptual procedure for both examining and accumulating information about social impacts. We also outline a matrix which demonstrates that social impacts will be different depending upon the project type and the stage of development. The next step in the development of the SIA model is to suggest the social impact variables for each stage in project development given different project types and settings.

9.6.3 Combining social impact assessment variables, project/policy stage, and setting

The four stages of project/policy development affect the social processes which produce changes in characteristics of the community or region. SIA specialists must construct a matrix to direct their investigation of potentially significant social impacts. Sample matrices are shown in Tables 9.13 and 9.14.

For each project/policy stage, the assessor should identify potential

Table 9.13 Matrix relating project stage to social impact assessment variables

Social impact assessment variable	Planning/policy development	Implementation/ construction	Operation/ maintenance	Decomissioning/ abandonment
Population characteristics				
Population change				
Ethnic and racial distribution				
Relocated populations				
Influx or outflow of temporary workers				
Seasonal residents				
Community and institutional structures				
Voluntary association				
Interest group activity				
Size and structure of local government				
Historical experience with change				
Employment/income characteristics				
Employment equity of minority groups				
Local/regional/national linkages				
Industrial/commercial diversity				
Presence of planning and zoning activity				
Political and social resources				
Distribution of power and authority				
Identification of stakeholders				
Interested and affected parties				
Leadership capability and characteristics				

Individual and family changes
Perceptions of risk, health, and safety
Displacement/relocation concerns
Trust in political and social institutions
Residential stability
Density of acquaintanceship
Attitudes toward policy/project
Family and friendship networks
Concerns about social wellbeing

Community resources
Change in community infrastructure
Native American tribes
Land use patterns
Effects on cultural, historical, and archaeological resources

Table 9.14 SIA variables, by project/policy setting (type) and stage

Project/policy settings (type)	Planning/policy development	Construction/ implementation	Operation/ maintenance	Decommission/ abandonment
Hazardous waste site	Perceptions of risk, health, and safety	Influx of temporary workers	Trust in political and social institutions	Alteration in size of local government
Industrial plant	Formation of attitudes toward the project	Change in community infrastructure	Change in employment/income characteristics	Change in employment equity of minority groups
Forest service/park service management	Interested and affected parties	Trust in political and social institutions	Influx of recreational users	Distribution of power authority

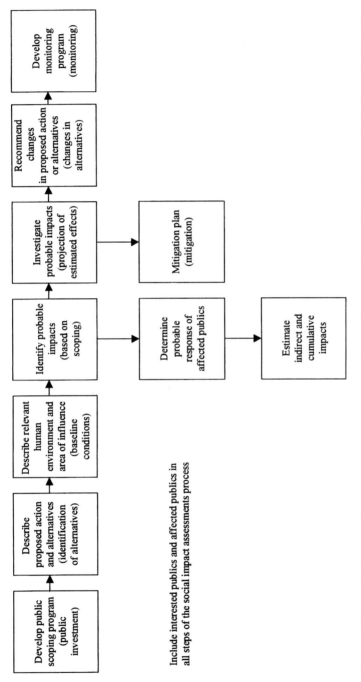

Figure 9.8 Steps in the social impact assessment process after the Interorganizational Committee on Guidelines & Principles for Social Impact Assessment, 1994

Source: Guidelines and Principles for Social Impact Assessment. Interorganizational Committee on Guidelines and Principles. *Impact Assessment*, Vol. 12, No. 2, 1994, p. 107–152.

impacts on each social variable identified in the matrix. This approach ensures that no critical areas are overlooked. It must be emphasized that Table 9.13 does not represent all SIA variables that may be of interest for any project. It is presented to illustrate the issues which represent the beginning of such a task. The task for the assessor is to spell out the magnitude and significance of impacts for each cell identified in the illustrations.

Table 9.14 provides an abbreviated illustration of how SIA variables (as suggested in Table 9.13) might be applied within the context of both the setting type and the stage in a project. The first example is the siting of a hazardous waste facility. Perceptions about problems of public health and safety could emerge during the early planning stage. If a decision is made to go ahead, construction would be accompanied by an influx of temporary workers. In the case of the industrial plant, community infrastructure support might be needed during construction, while changes in the industrial focus of the community might occur during the operational stage. These analytical procedures would be repeated for each of the SIA variables for each stage of the project.

9.6.4 Steps in the social impact assessment process

The SIA process is based on the steps in the EIA process as outlined below. It should contain the 10 steps described in Figure 9.8. These steps are logically sequential, but often overlap in practice. This sequence is patterned after the EIA steps as listed in the Council for Environmental Quality (CEQ) guidelines.

9.6.4.1 Public involvement

• Develop an effective public involvement plan to involve all potentially affected publics.

This requires identifying and working with all potentially affected groups, starting at the very beginning of planning for the proposed action. Groups affected by proposed actions include those who live nearby; those who will hear, smell, or see a development; those who are forced to relocate because of a project; and those who have an interest in a new project or policy change but may not live in proximity. Others affected include those who might normally use the land on which the project is located (such as farmers who have to plough around a transmission line). Still others include those affected by the influx of seasonal residents who may have to pay higher prices for food or rent, or pay higher taxes to cover the cost of expanded community services.

Once identified, representatives from each group should be systematically interviewed to determine potential areas of concern/impact, and ways in which each representative might be involved in the planning decision process. Public meetings by themselves are inadequate for collecting information about public perceptions. Survey data can be used to define the potentially affected population. In this step, the pieces are put in place for a public involvement programme which will last throughout the EIA and SIA processes.

9.6.4.2 Identification of alternatives

• Describe the proposed action or policy change and reasonable alternatives.

In the next step, the proposed action is described in enough detail to identify the data requirements needed from the project proponent to frame the SIA. At a minimum, this includes: locations, land requirements, needs for ancillary facilities (roads, transmission lines, sewer and water lines), construction schedule, size of the work force (construction and operation, by year or month), facility size and shape, need for a local work force, and institutional resources.

The list of SIA variables shown in the subsequent section is a guide for obtaining data from policy or project proponents. Sometimes the descriptions of the proposed alternatives may not include all the information needed for an SIA. Another problem is the provision of total numbers when breakdown numbers are needed. For example, the social assessor may be given numbers for the total peak work force of a construction project when information is needed on local, immigrating, and non-local commuting workers for each phase of construction.

9.6.4.3 Baseline conditions

• Describe the relevant human environment/area of influence and baseline conditions.

The baseline conditions are the existing conditions and past trends associated with the human environment in which the proposed activity is to take place. This is called the baseline study. For construction projects, a geographical area is identified along with the distribution of special populations at risk. However, for programmes, policies, or technology assessments, the relevant human environment may be a more dispersed collection of interested and affected publics, interest groups, organizations, and institutions. The generic set of dimensions for investigation listed below would include the following aspects of the human environment for construction projects and geographically located programmes and policies.

• Relationships with the biophysical environment, including ecological setting; aspects of the environment seen as resources or problems; areas having economic, recreational, aesthetic, or symbolic significance to specific people; residential arrangements and living patterns, including relationships among communities and social organizations; attitudes toward environmental features; and patterns of resource use.

- Historical background, including initial settlement and subsequent shifts in population; developmental events and eras, including experience with boom–bust effects, as well as discussions of broader employment trends; past or on-going community controversies, particularly those involving technology or the environment; and other experiences likely to affect the level or distribution of the impacts on local receptivity to the proposed action.

- Political and social resources, including the distribution of power and authority; the capacities of relevant systems or institutions (e.g., the school system); friendship networks and patterns of cleavage or cooperation among potentially affected groups; levels of residential stability; distributions of sociodemographic characteristics such as age and ethnicity; presence of distinctive or potentially vulnerable groups (e.g., low income); and linkages among geopolitical units (federal, state, county, local, and interlocal).

- Culture, attitudes, and sociopsychological conditions, including attitudes toward the proposed action; trust in political and social institutions, perceptions of risks, relevant psychological coping and adjustment capacity; cultural cognition of society and environment; assessed quality of life; and important values that may be relevant to or affected by the proposed action.

- Population characteristics, including the demographics of relevant groups (including all significant stakeholders and sensitive populations and groups); major economic activities; future prospects; the labour markets and available work force; unemployment and underemployment; population and expected changes; availability of housing, infrastructure, and services; size and age structure of households; and seasonal migration patterns.

The level of effort that is devoted to the description of the human environment should be commensurate with the size, cost, and degree of expected impacts of the proposed action. At a minimum, the existing literature on comparable or analogous events, knowledge experts, and readily available documents, such as government reports, should be consulted. On-site investigations and the use of previous field surveys are recommended, as well as rapid appraisals and mini-surveys.

9.6.4.4 Scoping

- After obtaining a technical understanding of the proposal, one needs to identify the full range of probable social impacts that will be addressed, based on discussion or interviews with some of all those potentially affected.

After initial scoping, the social impact assessor selects the SIA variables for further assessment situations. Consideration needs to be devoted both to the impacts perceived by the acting agency and to those perceived by affected groups and communities. The principal methods to be used by experts and interdisciplinary teams are reviews of the existing social literature, public scoping, public surveys, and public participation techniques. It is important for the views of affected people to be taken into consideration. Ideally, all affected people or groups contribute to the selection of the variables assessed, through either a participatory process or by review and comment on the decisions made by responsible officials and the interdisciplinary team.

Relevant criteria for selecting significant impacts include the following: probability of the event occurring; number of people including indigenous populations that will be affected; duration of impacts (long-term versus short-term); value of benefits and costs to impacted groups (intensity of impacts); extent that the impact is reversible or can be mitigated; likelihood of causing subsequent impacts; relevance to present and future policy decisions; uncertainty over possible effects; and presence or absence of controversy over the issue.

9.6.4.5 Projection of estimated effects

- Investigate the probable impacts.

The probable social impacts will be formulated in terms of predicted conditions without the actions (baseline projection), predicted conditions with the actions, and predicted impacts that can be interpreted as the differences between the future with and without the proposed action.

Investigation of the probable impacts involves five major sources of information: (1) data from project proponents; (2) records of previous experience with similar actions as represented in reference literature as well as other EISs; (3) census statistics; (4) documents and secondary sources; and (5) field research, including informant interviews, hearings, group meetings, and surveys of the general population. The investigation of the social impacts identified during scoping is the most important component.

Methods of projecting the future lie at the heart of social assessment, and much of the process of analysis is tied up in this endeavour. In spite of the long lists of methods available, most fall into the following categories:
- straight-line trend projects (taking an existing trend and simply projecting the same rate of change into the future);
- population multiplier methods (each specified increase in population

implies designated multiples of some other variable, for example, jobs, housing units);

- scenarios (1) logical – based on construction of hypothetical futures through a process of mentally modelling the assumptions about the variables in question; and (2) fitted empirical – similar past cases used to analyse the present case with experts adjusting the scenario by taking into account the unique characteristics of the present case;
- expert testimony (experts can be asked to present scenarios and assess their implications);
- computer modelling (involving the mathematical formulation of premises and a process of quantitative weighing of variables);
- calculation of "futures foregone" (a number of methods have been formulated to determine what options would be given up irrevocably as a result of a plan or project, for example, river recreation and agricultural land use after the building of a dam).

The record of previous experiences is very important to estimate future impacts. This record is largely contained in case reports and studies and the experience of experts. Variations in the patterns of impacts and responses in these cases also should be registered. Expert knowledge is used to enlarge this knowledge base and to judge how the study case is likely to deviate from the typical patterns. The documents and secondary sources provide information on existing conditions, plans, reported attitudes, and opinions, and contribute to the case record. The field research involves interviews with people who have different interests at stake, different perspectives, and different kinds of expertise. Wherever feasible, it should also involve a search through a wide range of documentation that is often available (in forms that range from official statistics and the minutes of meetings to the patterns of coverage and letters to the editor).

The opinions of various individuals and groups toward the proposed change should also be part of the record. Surveys are valuable to assess public opinion properly, because spokespersons for groups do not always represent the views of the rank-and-file. Statements at public meetings and by spokespersons should not be used as projections, but as possible impacts to be evaluated through other means.

9.6.4.6 Predicting response to impacts

- Determine the significance of the identified social impacts.

This is a difficult assessment task often avoided, but the response of affected parties will frequently have significant subsequent impacts. After direct impacts have been estimated, the assessor must next estimate how the affected people will respond in terms of attitude and actions. Their attitudes before implementation predict their attitudes afterwards, though increasingly data show that fears are often overblown and that expected (often promised) benefits fail to meet expectations. This literature should be consulted.

The action of affected groups are to be estimated using comparable cases and interviews with affected people about what they expect to do. So much depends on whether local leadership arises (and the objectives and strategies of these leaders), that this assessment step often is highly uncertain, but at least policy makers will be notified of potential problems and unexpected results. This step is also important because the adoption and responses of affected parties can have consequences of their own, whether for the agency that proposes an action (as when political protest stalls a proposal) or for the affected communities, whether in the short term or in the longer term.

Patterns in previous assessments guide this analysis, and expert judgement and field investigations are used to see whether the study case is following the typical patterns or if it is developing uniquely. Being able to show potentially affected people that significant impacts are being incorporated into the assessment is critical to the success of this step.

9.6.4.7 Indirect and cumulative impacts

• Estimate subsequent impacts and cumulative impacts.

Indirect impacts are impacts caused by direct impacts; they often occur later than the direct impact, or farther away. Cumulative impacts are those impacts that result from the incremental impacts of an action added to other past, present, and reasonably foreseeable future actions, regardless of which agency or person undertakes them. A community's residential and retail growth and pressures on government services following the siting of a major project are examples of indirect and cumulative impacts. While they are more difficult to estimate precisely than direct impacts, it is very important that indirect and cumulative impacts be clearly identified in the SIA.

9.6.4.8 Change in alternatives

• Recommend new or changed alternatives and estimate or project their consequences.

Each new alternative or recommended change should be assessed separately. The methods used in the estimation step (Section 9.6.4.5) apply here but usually on a more modest scale. More innovative alternatives and changes probably should be presented in an experimental structure. Expert judgements and scenarios are helpful in developing project and policy alternatives. The number of iterations here will depend upon time, funding, and the magnitude of the project or policy changes.

9.6.4.9 Mitigation

• Develop a mitigation plan.

A social impact assessment not only forecasts impacts, it should identify means to mitigate adverse impacts. Mitigation includes avoiding the
impact by modifying or not taking an action; minimization, rectifying, or
reducing the impacts through the design or operation of the project or
policy; or compensating for the impact by providing substitute facilities,
resources, or opportunities.

Ideally, mitigation measures are built into the selected alternative, but
it is appropriate to identify mitigation measures even if they are not
immediately adopted or if they would be the responsibility of another
person or government unit.

We suggest a sequencing strategy to manage social impacts that is
modelled on a strategy used with wetland protection and other natural
resources issues. During the first sequence, managers strive to minimize
any adverse impacts that cannot be avoided. During the third sequence,
managers compensate for adverse impacts. Compensation for the loss of
a wetland, for example, could be to acquire a different wetland, enhance
a degraded site, or create a new wetland. The amount of compensation
can be based on the type of wetland or resource lost, the severity of the
impact, and the location of the wetland mitigation site.

The first two steps of sequencing (avoiding and minimizing) can apply
to the project itself or to the host community or the impacted region. For
example, the project may be revised to avoid or minimize adverse social
impact (e.g., extend the construction period to minimize immigration), or
the community may be able to take steps to attenuate, if not avoid, any
adverse effects. Application of the sequencing concept for the mitigation
of adverse social impacts requires that the assessor first rank the level of
importance of each significant SIA variable determined during estimated
effects step (Section 9.6.4.5).

The first step in evaluating potential mitigation for each variable is to
determine whether the proponent should modify the project or proposed
policy to avoid the adverse effects. For example, a road that displaces
families might be rerouted. The next step in the sequencing process is to
identify ways to minimize adverse social impacts. For example, most citizens are uncomfortable with the idea of locating a facility perceived as
undesirable near their community. Attitudes (particularly negative ones)
formed about the project cannot be eliminated, but might be moderated
if the public has complete information about the proposed development,
if they are included in the decision-making process, or are provided with
structural arrangements that assure safe operations.

There are at least three benefits of identifying unresolvable social impacts that may result from a proposed project. The first is identifying methods of compensating individuals and the community for unavoidable impacts. The second occurs when the community may identify ways of enhancing other quality-of-life variables as compensation for the adverse effects. The third happens when the identification of unresolvable social impacts makes community leaders and project proponents more sensitive to the feeling of community residents.

By articulating the impacts that will occur and making efforts to avoid or minimize the adverse consequences, or compensating the residents or the community for the losses, benefits may be enhanced and avoidable conflicts managed or minimized.

Examples of some mitigation measures recommended for specific adverse impacts are given in Table 9.15.

9.6.4.10 Monitoring

• Develop a monitoring programme.

A monitoring programme should be developed. It must be capable of identifying deviations from the proposed action and any important unanticipated impacts. A monitoring plan should be developed to track project and programme development and compare real impacts with projected ones. It should spell out (to the degree possible) the nature and extent of additional steps that should take place when unanticipated impacts or impacts larger than the projections occur.

Monitoring programmes are particularly necessary for projects and programmes that lack detailed information or that have high variability or uncertainty. It is important to recognize, in advance, the potential for "surprises" that may lie completely outside the range of options considered by the SIA. If monitoring procedures cannot be adequately implemented, then mitigation agreements should acknowledge the uncertainty faced in implementing the decision.

It is generally only at this stage that the community or affected group has the influence to "get it in writing". A recent example of a monitoring programme with subsequent provision for mitigation was negotiated between the US Department of Energy, the state of Texas, and the Super Conduction/Super Collider Laboratory. The process allowed for the payment of approximately $800,000 to local jurisdictions to monitor the impacts of the construction activity.

9.6.5 Principles for SIA

In order to make SIA effective, the SIA practitioner should focus on the most significant impacts in order to use appropriate measures and information, to provide quantification where feasible and appropriate, and

Table 9.15 Suggested mitigation measures for specific project based impacts

Results from project activities	Environmental effects	Recommended mitigative measures
Environmental examination of project location		
Loss of land	• Economic loss • Hardship to affected people • Social resentment	Cash compensation and/or resettlement
Loss of housing	• Economic loss • Hardship to affected people • Social resentment	Cash compensation and/or resettlement
Loss of roads, bridges, irrigation weir	• Economic loss • Hardship to affected people • Social resentment	Construction of replacement
Loss of raw material for brick making	• Economic loss	No measure required, minor loss, existing brick-making kiln is temporary
Resettlement	• Hardship • Loss of kinship coherence • Change in way of living	Assistance in skill training, poverty alleviation, infrastructure development
Encroachment into precious ecology	• Loss of ecological values	Environmental management programme
Encroachment on religious values	• Social resentment	Reconstruction of religious establishments
Encroachment on historical/ cultural values	• Loss of human values • Social resentment	
Scenic values	• Loss of human values	Avoid destruction whenever possible
Watershed erosion silt run-off	• Shortened reservoir life • Costly water treatment	Environmental management programme
Impairment of navigation	• Economic loss	
Effect on groundwater hydrology	• Economic loss	
Impairment of fish migration	• Economic loss • Ecological damage	
Inundation of mineral resources	• Economic loss	
Impairment of wildlife movement	• Ecological damage	

Table 9.15 (cont.)

Results from project activities	Environmental effects	Recommended mitigative measures
Encroachment of outsiders	• Social problems • Ecological damage • Impaired reservoir water quality	Environmental management programme; regulation and enforcement
Seismic activity	• Economic loss • Downstream destruction	Proper structural design of project facilities; contingency plans
Road erosion	• Impairment of water quality • Reduced land values	Common precaution and control measures; rehabilitation of damaged roads
Reservoir site preparation	• Impaired water treatment plant • Impaired downstream water quality	Common prevention, precaution, and control measures
Water rights conflicts	• Social conflicts	
Fish screens	• Economic loss	
Environmental examination of project construction		
Dust/fumes	• Human nuisance and hazard	Common prevention, precaution, and control measures
Noise	• Human nuisance and hazard	Common prevention, precaution, and control measures
Soil erosion/silt run-off	• Impaired downstream water quality • Impaired downstream land values	Common prevention, precaution, and control measures
Workers' safety	• Human safety	Common prevention, precaution, and control measures
Sanitation at field office and campus	• Public health hazard	Provision of sanitation and waste management
Quarrying hazards	• Human hazard	Common prevention, precaution, and control measures
Presence of labour force	• Community nuisance • Community resentment • Ecological damage	Education of workforce Regulation and enforcement
Borrow areas	• Loss of land values • Ecological damage • Public health hazard • Loss of aesthetic values	Common prevention, precaution, and control measures
Environmental aesthetics	• Loss of scenic values	Alternative site of borrow area if affordable

Table 9.15 (cont.)

Results from project activities	Environmental effects	Recommended mitigative measures
Environmental examination of project operations		
Downstream flow variations	• Impaired downstream irrigation	Provision in design of adequate downstream irrigation regime
Reduced downstream inundation of fisheries	• Economic loss	
Downstream erosion	• Damage to downstream riverside facilities	
Lack of reservoir management	• Social conflicts	
Eutrophication (aquatic weeds)	• Impairment of fishery	
Reduced downstream nutrients	• Economic loss	Compensation, assistance to affected farmers
Insect and vector disease hazards	• Community health hazards	
Reservoir bank stability	• Impaired reservoir uses and water quality	
Sludge from water treatment plant	• Environmental pollution	Common prevention, precaution, and control measures
Environmental examination of spin-off development		
Employment opportunities	• Income generation	Encouragement of local employment
	• Inequitable benefit sharing	Equitable employment
Reservoir fishery enhancement	• Income generation	Planning for fishery project to offset losses
	• Nutritional improvement	Avoid middlemen
	• Inequitable benefit sharing	Community management
Drawdown agriculture	• Extra agricultural production	Appropriate management of drawdown agriculture
	• Economic development	
Improved water supply	• Improved quality of life for community	Provision of water to community
	• Increased wastewater generation	Sanitation improvement
Agro-forestry	• Income generation	Planning for agro-forestry project to offset losses
	• Economic development	
	• Inequitable benefit sharing	Community management

Table 9.15 (cont.)

Results from project activities	Environmental effects	Recommended mitigative measures
Wildlife reserves	• Environmental conservation	Use of project for raising environmental awareness
Improved access roads	• Improved quality of life for community	Use of project for road construction to offset losses
	• Loss of ecological values	Environmental management programme
Reservoir as recreational site	• Economic development in community	Use of project for promoting tourism
	• Loss of ecological values	Regulations and enforcement
	• Inequality in benefit sharing	Community management
Women in development	• Improved women's quality of life	Use of project for enhancing women's roles and benefits
	• Women suffer more from negative impacts	Mitigative measures with focus on women

Critical review criteria
Loss of irreplaceable natural resources
Accelerated use of resources for short-term
  gains
Endangering of species   Environmental manage-
  \   ment programme
Undesirable rural to urban migration
Increase in affluent/poor people gap

finally to present the social impacts in a manner that can be understood by decision makers and community leaders.

The principles outlined in Table 9.16 augment the ideas and concepts discussed in the earlier sections. These principles are benchmarks for conducting a SIA.

9.6.6 TOR for consultants

The concepts, principles, and methods discussed in the proceeding sections only serve as guidelines to carry out an SIA. If a well-prepared SIA is integrated into the decision-making process, better decisions will result. One of the key factors to ensure that a SIA is carried out thoroughly is to make sure that the SIA practitioner (the project developer or a

Table 9.16 Principles for SIA

1 Involve the diverse public
   Identify and involve all potentially affected groups and individuals.
2 Analyses impact equity
   Clearly identify who will win and who will lose and emphasize vulnerability of
      under-represented groups.
3 Focus the assessment
   Deal with issues and public concern that "really count" not those that are "easy
      to count".
4 Identify methods and assumptions and define significance in advance
   Define how the SIA was conducted, what assumptions were used, and how
      significance was selected.
5 Provide feedback on social impacts to project planners
   Identify problems that could be solved with change to the proposed action or
      alternatives.
6 Use SIA practitioners
   Trained social scientists employing social results methods will provide the best
      results
7 Establish monitoring and mitigation programmes
   Manage uncertainty by monitoring and mitigating adverse impacts.
8 Identify data sources
   Use published scientific literature, secondary data, and primary data from the
      affected area.
9 Plan for gaps in data

consultant) knows exactly what is required. This can be best achieved by preparing a precise TOR clearly delineating the various activities that are essential for the SIA study of a particular project.

FURTHER READING

Cumulative Effects Assessment: Concepts and Principles, Harry Spaling.

Cumulative Effects Assessment at the Project Level, David P. Lawrence.

Environmental Assessment of Programmes, Plans and Policies: A Comparative Review, Christopher Wood, 1994.

Environmental Risk Assessment for Sustainable Cities, IETC, Technical Publications Series (3), UNEP, Osaka, 1996.

Guidelines and principles for SIA, interorganizational committee on guidelines and principles, *Impact Assessment*, 12(2), 107–152, 1994.

ESCAP, Environment and Development Series, Environmental Impact Assessments Guidelines for Agricultural Development.

M. C. Arquiaga, L. W. Canter, and D. I. Nelson, Integration of health impact considerations in environmental impact studies, *Impact Assessment*, 12(2), 175–197, 1994.

G. W. Barrett, and R. Rosenbers (eds.), *Stress Effects on Natural Ecosystems*, Wiley, Chichester, 1981.

G. W. Barrett, G. M. Van Dyne, and E. P. Odum, Stress ecology, *Bioscience*, 26, 192–194, 1976.

R. J. Bennett, and R. J. Chorley, *Environmental Systems: Philosophy, Analysis and Control*, Princeton University Press, Princeton, 1978.

Canadian Environmental Assessment Research Council (CEARC) and United States National Research Council (USNRC), *Proceedings of the Workshop on Cumulative Environmental Effect. A Binational Perspective*, Hull, Quebec, CEARC, 1986.

Canadian Environmental Assessment Research Council (CEARC), *The Assessment of Cumulative Effects: A Research Prospectus*, Hull, Quebec, CEARC, 1988.

C. Cocklin, S. Parker, and J. Hay. Notes on cumulative environmental change 1: concepts and issues, *Journal of Environmental Management*, 35, 31–49, 1992.

A. Hill, Ecosystem stability: some recent perspectives, *Progress in Physical Geography*, 11, 315–333, 1987.

C. S. Holling, Resilience and stability of ecological systems, *Annual Review of Ecological and Systematics*, 4, 1–23, 1973.

C. S. Holling, (ed.) *Adaptive Environmental Assessment and Management*, Wiley, New York, 1978.

C. S. Holling, The resilience of terrestrial ecosystems: local surprise and global change, in *Sustainable Development of the Biosphere*, ed. W. Clark and R. Munn, Cambridge University Press, pp. 292–320, 1986.

R. Huggett, *Systems Analysis in Geography*, Clarendon, Oxford, 1980.

P. A. Lane, R. R. Wallace, R. J. Johnson, and D. Bernard, *A Reference Guide to Cumulative Effects Assessment in Canada*, Volume 1, Hull, Quebec, Canadian Environmental Assessment Research Council, 1988.

E. B. Peterson, Y. H. Chan, N. M. Peterson, G. A. Constable, R. B. Caton, C. S. Davis, R. R. Wallace, and G. A. Yarranton, *Cumulative Effects Assessment in Canada: An Agenda for Action and Research*, Hull, Quebec, Canadian Environmental Assessment Research Council, 1987.

D. J. Rapport, H. A. Regier, and T. C. Hutchinson, Ecosystem behaviour under stress, *American Naturalist*, 125, 617–640, 1985.

H. Selye, The evolution of the stress concept, *American Scientist*, 61, 692–699, 1973.

N. C. Sonntag, R. R. Everitt, L. P. Rattie, D. L. Colnett, C. P. Wolf, J. C. Truett, A. H. J. Corcey, and C. S. Holling, *Cumulative Effects Assessments. A Context for Further Research and Development*, Hull, Quebec, Canadian Environmental Assessment Research Council, 1987.

H. Spaling, and B. Smit, Cumulative environmental change: conceptual frameworks, methodological approaches and institutional perspectives, *Environmental Management*, 17, 587–600, 1993.

H. Spaling, and B. Smit, *Classification and Evaluation of Methods for Cumulative Effects Assessments*. Paper presented at the Conference on Cumulative Effects in Canada: From Concept to Practice, Calgary, Alberta, and Canadian Societies of Professional Biologists, April 13–14, 1994.

H. Van Emden and G. Williams, Insect stability and diversity in agroecosystems, *Annual Review of Entomology*, 19, 445–475, 1974.

Annex 9.1: Case study for risk assessments

Petroleum terminal and distribution project

Project description

The project involves upgrading an operational oil terminal facility through the addition of new storage tanks, improvement of tank foundations, and construction of a new pipeline. The terminal receives various petroleum products by ship. It stores the products and subsequently distributes them to the domestic market by barge, tank trucks, drums, and cylinders. At present, the main activities in the terminal include unloading of the products from ships, loading of liquid products into barges, loading of liquid products and liquefied petroleum gas (LPG) into tank trucks, blending and loading of lubricating oils in drums, and filling of LPG cylinders.

The proposed 50 km pipeline will be used to transport LPG and light petroleum products to a pumping station in another city, and then to another terminal in a port. The pipeline will pass a populated area, highways, rivers, a railroad, mangrove areas, and energy transmission lines.

The terminal is in a commercial/industrial area on the edge of an island. Adjacent facilities include shipyards, other industrial plants, and office buildings. Strong typhoons average two per year. The population around the terminal consists mostly of about 2000 workers in the area. Similar terminals operated by the same company can be found in many other countries, although the distribution system varies in each case.

ERA screening

An EIA with ERA is proposed to be conducted for the project. The EIA will assess the impact of the project to the population and the natural ecosystem. EIAs for similar facilities have identified the following as the major sources of environmental concerns: fuel spills and leakages, fires, explosions, vapour clouds, and pollution from the storage or accidental spills and leaks of the petroleum products. The ERA is expected to investigate these concerns where significant consequences and uncertainties warrant. The major hazard is large quantities of motor gasoline and LPG, which have low flash points. Spills and leakages could cause fires, explosions, or vapour clouds and could lead to catastrophic consequences, but the actual risk depends on how and when the spills and leakages would occur and what their magnitudes or sizes are.

Potential spills during operations are most likely during the transfer of products from one location or from one transport mode to another, such as from barge to tank truck. Those transferred at temperatures below their flash points may burn but will not create a flammable vapour cloud. Those liquids with high flash points (e.g., in excess of 80 °C) will be difficult to ignite but may add fuel to a fire. The liquid products, which have flash points lower than ambient temperature, could produce vapour clouds under normal conditions.

Calculation of risk and presentation

The usual method of calculation of individual risk is to calculate the risk of a specified level of harm occurring to an individual who is assumed to be at a particular point 100% of the time. The calculation is summed for all hazardous events which can give that level of harm at that particular point, and this gives the total individual risk at that point from the hazardous source. By repeating the calculations for a series of points in a radial direction from the source, a risk profile can be generated. If a grid of points is considered, a series of contours can be produced around the source by interpolating between the risk values in the grid.

The distance from the release point to the location of interest is determined and then the concentration and cloud width at this downwind distance from the release point is calculated from either the concentration or the duration of exposure (release duration for a continuous release and the time for the cloud to pass over for an instantaneous release) using a probit function.

Emergency planning – definition

A major emergency is one which has the potential to cause serious injury or loss of life. It may cause extensive damage to property and serious disruption both inside and outside the works. It would normally require the assistance of outside emergency services to handle it effectively. While an on-site plan will always be the responsibility of the works management, different legislations may place the responsibility for the off-site plan elsewhere. For example, the EC Seveso Directive requires the local authority to prepare the off-site plan.

Emergency planning – objectives

The overall objectives of an emergency plan are: (a) to localize the emergency and, if possible, eliminate it, and (b) to minimize the effects of the accident on people and property. Elimination will require prompt action by operators and works emergency staff using, for example, fire-fighting equipment, emergency shut-off valves, and water sprays. Minimizing the effects may include rescue, first aid, evacuation, rehabilitation, and giving information promptly to people living nearby.

Identification and assessment of hazards

Overfilling of tanks could lead to large spills. The tanks are equipped with liquid indicators and vents to prevent spillage. But the alarms may fail or may be ignored by operators. Leakage from the pipeline may occur from operational errors, faulty systems, or damage to the pipeline from external sources. As the pipeline gets older, the frequency of leaks may increase.

Another possible catastrophic event is called BLEVE (boiling liquid expanding vapour explosion). This is the sudden failure of a tank when the contained liquid is at a temperature well above its atmospheric pressure boiling point. The usual cause of a BLEVE is the exposure to fire of the dry portions of a tank.

Additional matters that need further investigation are presented in the risk screen report (see below).

Accidents while transporting petrochemical products have occurred in many countries. Recent accidents in developing countries have caused many fatalities. In 1983, a train transporting gasoline in Pojuca, near Salvador, Bahia, derailed and caused the death of about 100 people. In the same year, a big rock from the construction of a highway damaged an oil pipeline in the state of Sao Paulo. The spilled oil polluted about 20 kilometers of estuarine mangroves and several beaches. In 1984, leakage from a pipeline transporting gasoline and other light petroleum products in Cubatao, Sao Paulo, caused a fire that killed 100 people and destroyed houses.

Pipelines will be equipped with protection systems and instruments for controlling internal conditions. Line pressure, temperature, flow rate alarm system, and shutdown devices will be triggered if abnormal transmission conditions occur. It will also have safety valves for the upstream and downstream parts of the zone. In each of the populated areas it will pass through, an emergency management system will be installed. This will include warning signs with clear instructions to people on what to do in case of an emergency.

Tanks are fitted with fire extinguishers, external water spray systems for exposure protection, and liquid level indicators and alarms. The terminal is provided with a manually operated emergency shutdown system with actuators strategically located in various areas in the terminal.

There is a need to evaluate probable accident scenarios with the use of fault and event tree analysis, failure modes and effect analysis, and common model failures. The contractor must identify probable initiating events. The analysis must consider similar accidents already experienced in similar facilities. The maximum credible spill, leakage, fire, and explosion and their adverse consequences must be assessed.

Physical risk screen

The physical risk screen was conducted to identify hazards other than those related to hazardous chemicals that could lead to impacts or public and occupational safety, physical damage to ecosystems, or monetary and disruptive impacts on project or community facilities. The following were identified: transportation risks; ship traffic accidents near the terminal or while docking; natural disasters; typhoon, which could cause some damage to the terminal and the distribution system; other on-site and off-site hazards; workers in the project, in general, may be compared with workers in a petrochemical plant for which the British Standard of the Advisory Committee on Major Hazards defines the total accident frequency rates (TAFR) to be equivalent to a death risk probability of 3×10^5 per person-year; the project involves use of barges, tank trucks, drums, and cylinders, and in addition to the distribution pipeline, the terminal itself has a piping system; the project does not involve complex human operations; the system within the terminal and the distribution system is simple – some parts of the pipeline, however, may be more difficult to monitor because they pass through rivers; the island has been peaceful because the entire system is secured from trespassers; the project is not highly dependent on the reliability of an electricity supply.

ERA scoping

1   Categories of adverse events: accidents, spills, leakages, fires, explosions, vapour clouds; natural disasters (typhoons) affecting the project.

2   Population at risk: workers in and around the terminal; residents of communities where the pipeline will pass through; residents of communities along the route of tank trucks; public within 500 m of the terminal.

3   Flow cycle: unloading of ships and barges; additional processing (i.e., mixing of products, enhancing of products with additives); storage; transport from the terminal to various distribution sites.

4   Geographic boundary: terminal project site, plus surrounding commercial/industrial area.

5   Time period: the operating lifetime of the facility.

6   Human health endpoints: deaths.

7   Risk indicators: inventory; routine emissions and leaks.

Terms of reference for the contractor

The contractor is to conduct the ERA in accordance with the following terms of reference.

1   The feasibility study for the project includes an EIA, which covers all the environmental effects found by initial examination to be of significant importance. This EIA will be performed simultaneously with the ERA.

2   The objective of the ERA is to advise management on the risks to human health, the ecosystem, and welfare from the major hazards encountered in the proposed petroleum terminal and distribution project. The consultant will conduct studies sufficient to:

- identify major hazards, including those in the attached screening checklist;
- construct plausible risk scenarios within the boundaries suggested in the attached scoping summary;
- characterize the risks as quantitatively as possible;
- compare the risk with alternative means of accomplishing the project or with abandonment of the project or of any aspect of it (e.g., the pipeline);
- describe the feasible risk reduction actions and estimate their costs; and
- recommend the most appropriate risk-reduction measures and project alternatives.

3   Description of the project.

4   The concerns of management centre on the risks from fuel spills, leakages (mainly from the proposed pipeline), fires, explosions, and vapour clouds, and their impact on populations within and around the terminal site and distribution routes, on property, on other industrial facilities, and on community infrastructure.

The screening process shows the following: significant quantities of flammable products shall be stored, handled, and transported and increased levels of transportation accident hazards. Scenarios include transportation accidents from the terminal to the distribution sites using various transportation routes and modes. These include accidents on highways, railroad crossings, and in rivers, and spills and leaks of hazardous products stored. The maximum credible accident (BLEVE) should be evaluated, including its likelihood of occurrence.

5   The scope of the ERA is detailed in the attached report of the scoping meeting.

6   Constraints and opportunities for risk reduction are foreseen to include the following.

- The terminal was moved only a year ago from a previous site. The move required substantial investment. Hence it is unlikely that any alternative terminal site will be considered at this point.
- Alternative transportation routes have been considered for each of the destinations of the petroleum products and the ones proposed have been found by the proponent to be the best, based on both economic and safety considerations. The contractor must confirm this finding, as it may be possible to reroute the pipeline to the least populated areas.
- Relocation of populations near the terminal and along the chosen transportation routes will be expensive and politically unacceptable.
- Workers and engineers trained to prevent and handle spills and leakages can be supplied as required by the project.

- Other possibilities for reducing risk from spills and leakages are using equipment with low failure rates, redundancy in critical equipment, installing spill detection and emergency shutdown systems to reduce the size of spills, and using drainage and diking systems to reduce the spread of spills.
- Community emergency response plans have been designed and may be reviewed further for additional improvements.
- Emergency response and safety features in the facility may be strengthened further.

7   Risks should be characterized as:

- plot of frequency versus severity for different designs and operations that would achieve the project objective;
- the severity should be measured in terms of deaths of workers or residents;
- individual risk of premature death for workers and residents in and around the terminal and near the transportation routes from accidents involving spills, leakages, fires, explosions, and vapour clouds;
- damage to surrounding facilities from terminal or transportation accidents.

8   Study constraints.

- The estimated cost of the ERA is _____, of which _____% is allocated for technology transfer and training of local staff.
- The estimated time required to conduct the ERA is _____.
- The proposed payment schedule is as follows: _____.
- The specialist staff requirements are _____.
- The contractor is expected to coordinate closely with the project proponent and the ADB project manager during the conduct of the ERA.

10

Case studies to illustrate environmental impact assessment studies

Case study 10.1 Tongonan Geothermal Power Plant, Leyte, Philippines

Source: ESCAP Environment and Development Series, Environmental Impact Assessment, Guidelines for Industrial Development, p. 52.

Notes: The case can be used to show how environmental aspects have not been costed

The complete case study, of which this is a part, was adapted by Somluckrat Grandstaff from materials prepared by Beta Balagot, and may be found in Dixon and Hufschmidt (1986). It presents the analysis of the cost-effectiveness of various options for disposing of wastewater from a geothermal power plant built on the island of Leyte in the Philippines. The decision to build the power plant and to tap the local geothermal energy had already been made; it was necessary to decide which means of wastewater disposal from the plant would protect the environment in the most cost-effective manner.

Seven ways of disposing of wastewater are considered in the full case study; the costs of building and operating each are different and each has a different effect on the environment. The analysis examines each option in turn, determining its monetary values and, where possible, its environmental effect.

Not all of the effects on the environment can be quantified and given a monetary value, but those which cannot be quantified should not be

278

ignored in the analysis. These effects are listed in a qualitative manner and taken into consideration when the final decision is made. In this way the decision maker or project designer is presented with a range of information on the actual costs of construction and operation of each option as well as the various effects of each upon the environment.

While each option is subjected to a complete benefit-cost analysis, a more complete presentation would include a benefit-cost analysis of the entire project including the differing options for design of the power plant as a whole as well as those for disposing of wastewater. In this way the economic worth of the entire project, not just one part of it, could have been explored and then compared with other ways of producing electricity.

Background information

In the past the Philippines has been highly dependent on imported crude oil to meet its energy requirements and so has adopted an energy policy which will promote various forms of domestic energy production. These include nuclear energy, hydroelectric power, coal, petroleum, natural gas, and geothermal energy. Geothermal energy is derived from the natural heat of the earth. With existing technology only geothermal reservoirs associated with recent hot intrusive rocks and with vulcanism can be harnessed for the generation of electrical power. High temperature geothermal energy is found in two forms: dry-steam fields, as seen in the geysers of the United States, and hot-water (wet) fields, as seen at Wairakei and Broadland in New Zealand. At present, the Philippines is exploiting only the wet fields, which produce a mix of steam and water.

Exploration at Tongonan in Leyte started in 1973, and in 1978 a potential productive capacity of 3000 MW of geothermal electricity was confirmed. This case study considers Phase 1 of the Tongonan Geothermal Power Plant (TGPP) which has a capacity of 112.5 MW. This power station relies on a wet-steam geothermal resource and produces residual liquids and gases. These have chemical and thermal characteristics that may affect the environment adversely; the degree to which they might do so depends on the rate and frequency of discharge and the method of disposal.

Environmental dimensions

An environmental impact report prepared by Kingston, Reynolds, Thom, and Allardice Limited (KRTA), consultants to the Ministry of Energy and the Philippine National Oil Corporation, indicated that the major adverse effects on the environment would be caused by the disposal of the geothermal waste fluids. The fluids from the Tongonan wells contain more dissolved solids than those from most other geothermal fields; these include chloride, silica, arsenic, boron, and lithium. Arsenic, boron, lithium, and mercury all have known toxic effects on plants, animals, and people, and the full case study examines these effects. The indiscriminate disposal of geothermal wastewater would have severe effects on health and productivity and, to minimize these, the government has set limits to its discharge. Concentrations of arsenic, boron, and lithium in water from the Tongonan wells were found to exceed the limits recommended by the National Pollution Control Commission.

Although the full case study examined the costs and benefits of all seven methods of disposing of the wastewater, our abbreviated version will outline the analysis of only four of them; the analysis of the remainder may be found in Dixon and Hufschmidt (1986).

The data

Seven options for disposal for the wastewater of the plant were proposed:
1. Reinjection
2. Discharge into the Mahiao river without treatment
3. Discharge into the Mahiao River after treatment for the removal of arsenic
4. Discharge into the Bao River without treatment
5. Discharge into the Bao River after treatment for the removal of arsenic
6. Discharge at sea without treatment through an outfall at Lao Point
7. Discharge at sea without treatment through an outfall at Biasong Point.

In option 1, geothermal fluids from separator stations would be piped to reinjection wells within the field. At full capacity the 112.5 MW power plant would need seven such wells. A standby disposal system consisting of thermal ponds and other contingency structures would also be needed. They would be used while the reinjection system was temporarily shut down either for maintenance or for some limited emergency. When the system is shut down for longer periods the stand-by scheme would permit the discharge of chemically treated waste fluids into the river.

Options 2 and 3 involve the direct discharge of waste fluids into the Mahiao River. Before being discharged, the fluids would be retained for a few days in a thermal pond where they may be treated with chemicals to remove arsenic.

In options 4 and 5 waste fluids would be discharged into the Bao River through a pipeline. A thermal pond would also be required for cooling the fluids before releasing them into the river. Option 5 would entail treatment of the fluids in the pond in order to precipitate the arsenic.

Options 6 and 7 involve the selection of an outfall at sea through which to discharge the wastes. Two possible sites have been studied: Lao Point

and the Biasong Point. An outfall at the former would involve 22 km of pipeline and at the latter 32 km.

Costs and environmental effects of the options

Each of the seven options has different capital and operations, maintenance, and replacement (OM&R) costs, as well as different effects on the environment. They are briefly described here and 1980 prices are used in the analysis.

1   Reinjection. The construction of seven reinjection wells and the stand-by waste disposal system will take two years. Each well will cost P10 million, or P70 million in all. The construction of a system of pipelines for the separator stations to the reinjection wells will cost P20 million. The stand-by waste disposal system will involve another P17 million. The annual operation and maintenance costs will total P104 million.

Although reinjection is seen as the most ecologically sound method of disposal, it is not yet a well-established technology. In areas where water supplies are drawn from underground aquifers, as in the site of this project, it is important to know the local groundwater hydrology and to monitor carefully any effects of injecting geothermal wastewater.

Reinjection may also lower the temperature and hence the potential energy of the sub-surface geothermal water. In addition, the geothermal liquids at Tongonan contain large amounts of dissolved solids like silica which may clog the reinjection pipes. Such problems could be dealt with by adding chemicals to keep the solids in solution, but the effect of these chemicals may be to create other environmental problems.

2   Discharge into the Mahiao River without treatment. The construction of a thermal pond would take one year and cost P7 million. Operation and maintenance costs are estimated at P43,300 per year.

High levels of arsenic and boron in the untreated waste fluids discharged into the river would affect adversely the productivity of 4,000 hectares of rice fields served by the Bao River Irrigation System. If the irrigation waters are heavily polluted, farmers will probably not irrigate their crops; the consequence is a severe reduction in productivity. Irrigated rice fields yield an average of 61 cavans (1 cavan = 50 kg) per hectare against a yield of 37.9 cavans from unirrigated fields (NIA Region 8 Office, 1980). Production would also be reduced to one crop a year. However, since the rice produced in the Bao River Irrigation System is only a small part of the regional total, it can safely be assumed that these changes in production will not affect local rice prices.

Based on the cost of production data for the area over the 1975–78 period, the nett return per hectare for irrigated rice was estimated at P346 and for unirrigated rice P324, less if irrigation water were made unusable for the entire 4,000 hectares, the economic loss would be as follows:

$$4{,}000 \text{ ha} \times \text{P346 per ha} \times 2 \text{ crops} = \text{P2,768,000}$$

One crop of unirrigated rice could be grown, yielding the following nett return:

$$4{,}000 \text{ ha} \times \text{P324} = \text{P1,296,000}$$

The annual loss, therefore, would be the difference, P1.47 million.

An added environmental cost of discharging untreated wastewater into the river system is the risk to human health and livestock. To evaluate this, the cost of a water purification system that will render the river water safe for domestic use and for drinking was also estimated. The construction of such a system would cost P50 million and cost P15 million annually to operate and maintain.

Estimating the costs to the freshwater ecosystem is more difficult, since there are no data on the economic value of the fishing along the river. However, another environmental cost which can be estimated will be the pollution of the delta, which will affect the marine fisheries of the area. The delta or mangrove area of Ormoc Bay plays an important role in sustaining productivity in the adjoining fishing grounds because it is the feeding and spawning ground of several species of fish.

Fishing is an important industry in the Ormoc Bay and Camotes Sea area. Based on 1978 figures, the nett return from fishing was estimated at 29 percent of the gross return from the catch. Although the annual value of the fish catch varied from year to year depending on the actual size of the catch and on market prices, a gross value of P39.4 million was taken as representative. If this fishery was lost as a consequence of heavy-metal contamination, the annual economic loss would be about P11.4 million (P39.4 × 0.29). It is assumed that the capital equipment could be sold or shifted to other areas, but that the lost catch would not be replaced by additional fish catches elsewhere.

3   Discharge to Mahiao River after treatment. A thermal pond will be constructed at a cost of P7 million and completed in one year. In addition to the regular operation and maintenance costs of the pond itself, there will be further costs for the treatment of arsenic. These will amount to P4 million per year for each of the 15 producing wells. There are no scientific studies of the interactive effects of boron and arsenic on a rice field: hence there is no basis at this point for determining whether or not the effects on productivity will be less severe if the arsenic is removed. There may also be some residual effects on the aquatic ecosystems, but these are not identifiable.

Capital costs for a water purification system are estimated at P25 million and annual operating and maintenance costs at P7.5 million.

4   Discharge of untreated effluent into the Bao River. A thermal pond

will cost P7 million. A pipeline some 6 or 7 km long would take two years to build at a cost of P13 million. Operation and maintenance costs will be P6.2 million a year. Since the point of discharge will be downstream from the diversion for irrigation, the area of the Bao River Irrigation System will not be affected by the waste fluids.

A water purification system will be needed to serve the residents along the reaches of the Bao River below the point of discharge. Its construction will take two years at a cost of P15 million. Annual operation and maintenance costs are estimated at P4.5 million. The information on fishery productivity used in option 2 will be used in this option to estimate the costs to the marine environment.

5   Discharge of treated effluent into the Bao River. The capital costs will be the same as in option 4. However, the operation and maintenance costs will be higher. The annual cost of treating the waste fluids for arsenic is estimated at P4 million per producing well. The cost of establishing a water purification system will be lower when the fluids are treated for arsenic. The capital cost is estimated at P7.5 million, but the time needed for construction remains the same. Operation and maintenance costs of P2 million are expected.

6   Discharge into the sea with an outfall at Lao Point. This scheme will need a 22 km pipeline which will take two years to build at a cost of P45 million. Its annual operating and maintenance cost will be P41.8 million. The disposal of wastewater at sea may affect the productivity of coastal fishing as well as the commercial fishing in Ormoc Bay and the Camotes Sea. Not enough information is available, however, to quantify these effects.

7   Disposal at sea with an outfall at Biasong Point. For this option a 32 km pipeline would be constructed. This would take two years and would cost P65 million. Operation and maintenance costs would come to P60.8 million per year. The productivity of marine fishing may be affected. In estimating the effects of options 6 and 7 on marine productivity, hydrological and dispersal patterns in Ormoc Bay and the Camotes Sea should be taken into account.

Analysis of the options

There is enough information available to carry out an analysis of some of the major environmental effects of the various options. While the overall approach is that of cost effectiveness analysis, individual effects are usually valued using direct productivity changes based on market prices.

The assumption is therefore that market prices can be used to value agricultural and fishery production: that is, that there are no major distortions requiring the use of shadow prices. This may or may not be correct for the Philippines, but in this example no price adjustments are made. A similar assumption is made in the case of imported capital equipment used in the disposal systems and for petroleum products used to power the pumps and other equipment involved. Again, if major distortions like subsidies, foreign exchange controls, or capital rationing exist, then shadow prices would be needed.

The present value of the direct costs and the associated environmental costs for each of the proposed wastewater disposal schemes are calculated with a discount rate of 15 percent and an estimated project life for the geothermal power plant of 30 years. Table 10.1 presents the calculations of direct capital, OM&R costs for options 1, 2, 3, and 6. Table 10.2 presents the calculation of environmental resource costs for the same options.

The results of these calculations for all seven options are summarized in Table 10.3, without including the values of environmental costs. Option 4, in which untreated waste fluids are discharged into the Bao River, would have been chosen because it entailed the lowest direct cost. Once the environmental effects are valued and added to the direct cost, the total direct and indirect measurable costs are obtained.

Options 3, 5, 6, and 7 can be rejected because they are all relatively costly compared to options 1, 2, and 4, among which the choice would now seem to lie. If the decision is based strictly on measurable costs, then option 4 is the cheapest scheme. However, both options 4 and 2 may seriously contaminate the marine ecosystem with unknown and unquantifiable results. Option 2, which calls for the discharge of untreated waste into the Mahiao River, is rejected because not only does it pollute, like option 4, but it is also more expensive. In contrast, the main nonquantifiable effect of option 1 is the possible loss of energy from the lowering of the steam temperature. Hence reinjection becomes the most desirable method, although its total measured costs are slightly higher than for option 4. In this case a slightly larger measured cost in option 1 is preferred over the greater environmental uncertainty inherent in option 4, the least cost alternative.

Further Reading

J. A. Dixon and M. M. Hufschmidt, eds., *Economic Valuation Techniques for the Environment: A Case Study Workbook*, Johns Hopkins University Press, Baltimore, 1986.

Case study 10.2 Accelerated Mahaweli Development Programme

Notes: This case study can be used to make matrices and grade them.
   Name of project: Accelerated Mahaweli Development Programme.

Table 10.1 Calculation of direct capital and OM&R costs of alternative wastewater disposal options (in Pesos)

	Part of project				Cost
Option 1 – Reinjection	1 Construction (2 years)				Million Pesos
	(a) reinjection wells				70
	(b) pipeline				20
	(c) stand-by system				17
					107
	Construction cost per year				53.50
	2 Operation and maintenance per year				10.4
	Cash flow:				
	Year	1	2	3–30	
	million Pesos	53.5	53.5	10.4	
	Present value at 15 percent discount rate				
	Year 1 = 53.5 × 0.8696				46.5
	Year 2 = 53.5 × 0.7561				40.4
	Years 3–30 = 10.4 × 4.9405				51.4
	Present value of total direct cost				138.30
Option 2 – Discharge to Mahiao River without treatment	1 Construction				
	(a) thermal pond (1 year)				7
	(b) Water supply system (2 years)				50
	2 Operation and maintenance per year				
	(a) thermal pond				0.0433
	(b) water supply system				15.0
	Cash Flow:				
	Year	1	2	3–30	
	million Pesos	25	25	15	
			7	0.0433	
	Cost/year	25	32	15.0433	
	Present value at 15 percent discount rate				
	Year 1 = 25 × 0.8696				21.74
	Year 2 = 32 × 0.7561				24.20
	Years 3–30 = 15.0433 × 4.9405				74.32
	Present value of total direct cost				120.26

Table 10.1 (cont.)

Part of project				Cost
Option 3 – Discharge to Mahiao River without treatment	1 Construction (a) thermal pond (1 year) (b) Water supply system (2 years)			7 25
	2 Operation and maintenance per year (a) thermal pond (b) arsenic removal for 15 steam producing wells (at 4 million Pesos each) (c) water supply system			0.0433 60 7.5

Cash flow:

Year	1	2	3–30
million Pesos	12.5	12.5	0.0433
		7	60
			7.5
Cost/year	12.5	19.5	67.5433

Present value at 15 percent discount rate

Year 1 = 12.5 × 0.8696	10.87
Year 2 = 19.5 × 0.7561	14.74
Years 3–30 = 67.5433 × 4.9405	333.7
Present value of total direct cost	359.3

Part of project				Cost
Option 6 – Discharge at sea with an outfall at Lao Point	1 Construction (a) Pipeline (2 years)			45
	2 Operation and maintenance per year			41.8

Cash Flow:

Year	1	2	3–30
million Pesos	22.5	22.5	41.8
Present value	19.57	17.01	(206.51)

Present value of total direct cost	243.09

Type of environmental analysis: Full-scale EIA.
Project location: Mahaweli basin in Sri Lanka.
Type of project: Rural socio-economic development.

Brief description

The programme includes the construction of storage and irrigation facilities sufficient to supply water for the cultivation of 128,000 hectares of new lands and for the upgrading of 32,000 hectares of existing agricultural lands in the irrigation systems designated as A, B, C, and D.

Approximately 175,000 families will find permanent employment in agricultural or agricultural-related activities. New and improved cultiva-

Table 10.2 Calculation of environmental and resource cost of alternative waste-water disposal options (in Pesos)

Option 1 – Reinjection

The environmental cost cannot be estimated, although it involves: (i) possible loss of potential energy; (ii) treatment cost for dissolved solids in reinjection pipes; and (iii) additional environmental problems from chemicals used to keep the reinjection pipe from being clogged.

Option 2 – Discharge to Mahiao River without treatment

The environmental effects in this case include both the quantifiable and the non-quantifiable consequences, namely:
1 rice productivity: 4,000 ha per season serviced by BRIS;
2 river fishery: no data;
3 stock health;
4 laundry, bathing and human health; and
5 sea ecosystems.

Quantifiable effects:

Value of rice production loss:
Total rice area   =   4,000 ha

Return/ha for irrigated rice
(average 1975–8)   =   1,838 – 1,492 = P346

Annual loss if irrigation water cannot be used due to heavy contamination
                                         =   4,000 × 346 × 2 – (4,000 × 324)
                                         =   2,768,000 – 1,296,000
                                         =   P1.47 million

Present value of rice loss at 15 percent discount rate (years 3–30)
1.47 × 4.9405   =   P7.26 million

Value of fishery product loss:
assuming total loss of product currently obtained

From data on average cost and return profile of fishing operation in Leyte, the
nett return   =   6,914 – 4,918
                                         =   1,996
or   =   29 percent of gross return

Total value of fishery product in the Camotos Sea and Ormoc Bay in 1980
                                         =   P39.4 million
Annual loss of fishery product   =   39.4 × 0.29 gross return

Present value of fishery loss at 15 percent discount rate (years 3–30)
11.4 × 4.9405   =   P56.3 million

Non-quantifiable effects:
River fishery, stock health, human health, loss of water use for laundry and bathing, effects on the marine ecosystems, plus possible family dislocation.

Table 10.2 (cont.)

Option 3 – Discharge to Mahiao River with treatment

Environmental effects:
1 rice productivity unknown;
2 river fishery; no data;
3 stock health, laundry, bathing and human health; non-quantifiable but less than alternative 2; and
4 marine ecosystems; unknown.

Option 6 – Disposal at sea

Environmental effects: unknown effects on marine ecosystems.

Table 10.3 Cost of waste disposal under alternative schemes (in million Pesos)

Alternative	Direct cost	Environmental cost	Total measured cost	Non-quantifiable or non-measured costs
Reinjection	138.3	Unknown	138.3	Energy loss
Untreated Mahiao discharge	120.2	Rice 7.3 Fishery 56.5	184.0	Freshwater fishery, stock health, laundry, bathing uses, human health, sea ecosystems
Treated Mahiao discharge	359.3	–	359.3	Rice production and a lower loss on items in alternative 2 with the exception of sea ecosystems
Untreated Bao discharge	81.1	Fishery 56.5	137.6	Freshwater fishery, stock health, domestic use, human health, sea ecosystems
Treated Bao discharge	359.1	–	359.1	Less than alternative 4
Lao Point	243.1	Unknown	243.1	Non-quantifiable but high
Biasong Pt.	353.2	Unknown	353.2	Non-quantifiable but high

tion will produce more than 600,000 tons of rice and other crops annually and therefore meet the current import demand for rice as well as satisfy a major portion of future demands. In addition, the proposed reservoirs will substantially increase hydroelectric power output for the country.

Under the Accelerated Programme, the total live storage capacity of the major reservoirs is 2,555 million m^3. With full development of the Rotalawels and Moragahakands reservoirs, a total of more than 4,000 million m^3 of water will be available for irrigation and power generation.

In addition to the proposed dams and reservoirs, the major canal

(Minipe Right Bank Canal) and a tunnel will be constructed to divert water from the Mahaweli Ganga at Minipe to the Ulhitiya Oya and the Maduru Oya reservoirs for irrigation of Systems B and C. Also, a barrage (Kandakadu Anicut) may be built in the Mahaweli Ganga near Manampitiya to divert Mahaweli water to System A.

The areas which will be irrigated under the Accelerated Programme could be tabulated. These data could be compiled from the most recent estimates from ongoing feasibility studies for System A, B, C, and D. When fully developed, the Accelerated Programme will provide irrigation supplies for the cultivation of 80,800 hectares of new lands (mostly for paddy) and for the improvement of 14,350 hectares which are in existing irrigation schemes.

The proposed settlement plan for the Accelerated Programme includes the clustering of house lots into a hamlet which will be located not more than 1–2 km from irrigated allotments. Each hamlet will be comprised of about 100 settler family units, each allotted 0.4 hectares (one acre) of upland as a house lot and vegetable garden and 1 hectare for paddy cultivation. About four or five hamlets will be consolidated into a village, and four village centres will form a township. All the necessary infrastructure such as roads, schools, hospitals, etc. will be provided by the government, and it is expected that the settlers will establish other facilities such as a shopping centre, community centres, etc. through their own efforts. In addition to the present inhabitants, the Accelerated Programme area will accommodate a population of about one million people.

Pertinent reports

Two EIA reports were prepared relating to the Mahaweli project: (a) "Environmental Assessment, Accelerated Mahaweli Development Programme", by TAMS for Ministry of Mahaweli Development of Sri Lanka/USAID, Oct. 1980; and (b) "Environmental Assessment of Stage 11 of the Mahaweli Ganga Development Project", USAID, Sept. 1977.

The present study is based essentially on the former reference.

Environmental study area

The portion of the Mahaweli Ganga river basin which includes Kotmale, Victoria, Randenigala, Ulhitiya Oya, and Madura Oya reservoirs and their catchments and downstream irrigation areas, plus the Rotalavela and Moragahakanda reservoir systems as applicable.

Environmental study team

Data not included in EIA report.

EIA budget adequacy

Data not included in EIA report.

Methodology

The EIA classifies the environmental resources of the study area into three categories: (i) terrestrial environment, (ii) aquatic environment, and (iii) human environment. The human environment category includes three subcategories, "social profile", "cultivation practices" (including pest control), and "public health".

Existing environmental conditions

The EIA presents detailed information on the existing environmental conditions. Some pertinent information, according to classifications used, is as follows.

Terrestrial environment

The climate is hot and humid, with two annual monsoons of 1,650 mm rain. In the dry zones (to be serviced by the proposed irrigation system) evapotranspiration usually exceeds rain.

Over the past 25 years, community (town) areas increased from 1,000 to 4,000 ha, intensive agriculture decreased from 87,000 to 63,000 ha, and forest areas have reduced by half. Present land uses indicate chena cropping occupying 23 per cent of the land within the project irrigation service area (ISA).

About 28 per cent of the proposed ISA is forested (tropical dry mixed evergreen forest). All former forest reserves were released for development and have been largely cleared, and rapid encroachment on the remaining forest is continuing (and will be accelerated by the proposed irrigation).

The region's wildlife has been exceptionally diverse with a variety of habitat including marshes (villus) and grasslands as well as forests. Several wildlife reserves are within the project area (wholly or partly) and others are nearby. A number of the species are endemic and are threatened.

Aquatic environment

The Mahaweli Ganga is the largest river in Sri Lanka, and the project is based on utilization of this resource. Groundwater is very limited in the project area.

The water quality of project area rivers is well suited for irrigation and other human use purposes (low salinity, low sodium absorption ratios).

Most of the fish catch is from irrigation tanks (about 180 kg/ha/year). Inundation (floodplains) fisheries amount to about 50 kg/ha/year. Riverine fishing is of the subsistence type. Total annual project area catch is about 1,850 tons. In addition there are substantial fisheries on both the Maduru Oya and Mahaweli Ganga rivers. Fish farming is very limited.

Per capita fish consumption has declined from 11.4 kg in 1972 to 10.4 kg in 1978. Because this is important to rural nutrition, one project goal is to increase this to 20 kg/year. Another goal is to improve the income of fishermen families, many of whom are landless.

The wetland in the project area includes some 60 villus (marshes) ranging from 10 to 900 ha in size, distributed throughout the total Mahaweli Ganga floodplains area of about 12,800 ha. The villus are highly productive biologic communities and a high-quality wildlife habitat. They are commercially important for the grasses produced, which are enough to support 1 head of livestock per ha of villa.

Human environment

The project area is sparsely populated, and farmers are engaged mostly in rice cropping below village tanks or upland crops grown in chena cultivation. The population is predominantly Sinhalese, average family size is about 5, and "encroachers" are plentiful. More than half the families earn less than Rs 3,000/year.

In traditional villages in the project area, farmers operate usually a 0.2 to 0.6 hectare plot of lowland below the village tank, a small rainfed homestead plot, and an area of rainfed upland shifting chena cultivation. On the irrigated lowlands, rice farming is developed as a predominant monoculture, especially within the large tank systems. On some well-drained parts of the lowlands, chillies, onions, and vegetables are also grown. Paddy yields from rainfed and irrigated sources average about 2.5 tons/hectare/year. The availability of water is a major factor affecting yield levels as well as cropping intensity. Where a reliable water supply is available, paddy yields are well above 3.0 tons/hectare, occasionally reaching 4.5 tons/hectare.

On the rainfed homestead plots, various perennials and vegetables are grown along with bananas, pineapples, mangoes, papaya, and other tropical fruits. The chena cultivation focuses on annuals, mainly cereal and root crops, including pulses, millets, vegetables, tobacco, and often rainfed paddy. Most of the encroachers who have entered the project area in the past few years are subsisting on chena cultivation.

The most serious insect pest for rice in the project area is the brown planthopper. Other major insect pests include rice thrips and paddy bug. Sugarcane suffers considerable damage from shoot borers and smut. In addition, the mania and rose ringed parakeets cause an estimated 5 per cent loss to rice crops in the project area. Wild boar and elephants are also responsible for substantial crop losses.

Diarrhoeal diseases are common, due to inadequate sanitation. Of the vector-borne diseases, malaria is considered of primary project concern. However, malaria incidence has been decreasing due to anti-malaria programmes implemented over the past decade.

Significant environmental effects from project

Terrestrial environment

Watershed erosion is severe, but nevertheless reservoir siltation will not be enough to impair reservoir operations over the project design period (50 years).

Conversion of downstream forest/scrub land/chena areas to paddy will of course eliminate considerable wildlife habitat. Also, decreased river flood flows will convert much of the villus area into comparatively poor grazing area.

Increased encroachment seems inevitable both for "squatter land" and for fuel. Project implementation will also make use of new lands for irrigation some of which has been valuable wildlife habitat. However, these same encroachments seem likely to occur eventually in any case. The present project will accelerate the process.

Aquatic environment

Under the Accelerated Programme, a large amount of the water diverted from the Mahaweli Ganga will be delivered to irrigation systems outside of the Mahaweli Basin. Of the remainder, only about 20 per cent is likely to re-enter the Mahaweli as irrigation return flow. Overall, the volume of flow in the river will be reduced by about 50 per cent. Wet as well as dry season flows are expected to decrease in the Mahaweli; however, future flows during the dry months should increase slightly in the Maduru Oya due to the planned transbasin diversion into System B. Flood peaks in the Mahaweli Ganga will be considerably reduced by the surcharge storage in the new reservoirs.

With the conversion of forests to agricultural land, the future surface run-off is expected to increase. However, the effect on stream flows should not be significant, because the forested area to be cleared is relatively small in comparison with the total drainage area of the Mahaweli Basin. In addition, the increased run-off will be retained by rice paddies and eventually lost to evapotranspiration.

In a few localized areas water quality in return flows may deteriorate significantly, preventing their immediate reuse for irrigation. This may occur where salt accumulates due to improper drainage or where sonic sub-soils exist which, when irrigated, release sodium into drainage waters. However, in most of the project area, adequate drainage and the flushing action of heavy monsoon rains should limit salt build-up in soils or high sodium concentration problems.

Generally, surface water and groundwater in the project area should be suitable for livestock drinking as well as for swimming, bathing, clothes washing, and related domestic uses. However, the use of these waters for bathing or swimming and for human consumption will depend upon the provision of protected water supplies and adequate sanitation facilities.

Potential fish yields calculated for the proposed reservoirs clearly indicate that the deep up-country reservoirs are likely to be much less productive (20 to 30 kilograms/hectare/year) in terms of fish output than the shallower low-country ones (100 to 300 kilograms/hectare). Yields from the reservoirs will greatly exceed existing river yields both on a unit and total area basis. The total nett yield for the major proposed reservoirs is estimated at about 2,550 tons/year.

The presence of a series of dams on the main river will also block upstream spawning migrations of the massier. This, combined with the inability of the massier to adapt to reservoir habitats, will probably result in a significant reduction in the population of this species within the Mahaweli Ganga. Other species which may be adversely affected by interference with migratory movements include eels, two species of barbs, the endemic mountain labeo and the freshwater shrimp *Macrobrachium*.

The reduction of floodplain and associated villa areas will result in a corresponding loss to fisheries resources. The total loss in terms of fish yield is estimated at 320 tons/year. A further non-quantifiable adverse impact would be the reduction of floodplain spawning and nursery grounds for a number of fish species which inhabit rivers, streams backwaters, ponds, and tanks of the entire Mahaweli Ganga system. Overall, there will be a nett increase in potential fish yields from project area waters of about 2,140 tons, or a gross economic benefit of about Rs 8.6 million annually.

There will be a reduction in area for livestock grazing in the villus and a decrease in the villa carrying capacity from 1.0 to 0.75 animal units per hectare. The total carrying capacity for the project area villus will be decreased by more than 60 per cent, to a level of 2,880 animal units per grazing period. The decrease in floodplain villa area will result in a total loss in quantifiable economic benefits of about Rs 5.7 million annually. This includes losses to fisheries, grazing, and associated dairy production.

Any of the new reservoirs, irrigation canals, drainage systems, or paddy areas may be susceptible to aquatic weed infestation, chiefly from water hyacinth, floating ferns, or cattails. Particular areas of concern would be where eutrophication may be increased due to the accumulation of nutrients from run-off or return flows. Consequently, small downstream tanks and villus, the lower part of the Mahaweli Ganga with its reduced flow, and the shallow Kandakadu Barrage are likely to experience a continued infestation of water weeds.

Human environment

A major social impact of the Accelerated Programme will involve the transition from small isolated village societies to production-oriented large-scale colonization schemes. Implicit in the model of transition is the modernization of rural society with the attendant loss of traditional values and social cohesion within small kinship-based villages.

The population in the project area will be increased by about 1 million people. Current project area residents who are over eighteen years of age and have an agricultural background will have priority in the resettlement planning. The principal social benefits will accrue to settler families who stand to gain land and irrigation waters; this is also the major benefit perceived by project area residents as well as potential settlers from other regions who are applying for allotments.

An important attitude prevailing among future settlers is that the 1 hectare paddy land allotment, irrigated for two full seasons, will represent an improvement from present landholding. However, planning calls for traditional inheritance and kinship roles to be abandoned with respect to the mechanisms for landholding and its acquisition. This may prove difficult to enforce; studies elsewhere indicated that allotted land was leased, mortgaged, and given in tenancy to relatives within the first year of cultivation.

As in previous colonization schemes, the Accelerated Programme will also face the problem of employment for the second generation of the farmer settler families. Some of the second generation offspring can provide employment in non-farm sectors; however, not all of them can be accommodated in this manner. This may lead to fragmentation of paddy land and home plots or the further encroachment on undeveloped lands within or adjacent to irrigation blocks. Many of the present chena farmers in the area are second generation settlers from other schemes who have encroached land in order to be in a position of acceptance in the new programme.

At the proposed reservoir sites, especially Victoria and Kotmale, a total of 25,000 to 30,000 residents will have to be relocated. The affected people have accepted the inevitability of relocation, but there is a general resentment and a sense of loss of ancestral homes for those who have experienced little geographic mobility moving to nearby estates or into the Mahaweli area, which would benefit smaller landholders. However, most are concerned about how they can support themselves in the period it will take to replace their lost tree crops and paddy.

A major benefit of the Accelerated Programme will be to increase agricultural output. The main focus will be on rice production. The single rice crop intensity presently achieved per year under rainfed conditions or small tank irrigation will be increased to obtain double cropping. Approximately 8 tons per hectare of paddy will be produced from the two crops grown per year on the newly cultivated lands. Moreover, much of the existing irrigated paddy land will receive supplemental water to permit additional cropping intensity.

One constraint to the high intensity rice monoculture envisioned will be the farm labour supply. Another problem will be pest control. Since there are no geographical barriers to prevent the movement of any known insect pest or plant disease, it is anticipated that the crops proposed for the project area will be susceptible to damage from the same pests found in other parts of the island. Intensity of pest activity for the new rice growing areas is expected to be manifested by an increase of brown planthopper and sheath blight.

Extensive sections of wildlife habitat will be removed and thus eliminate a substantial amount of natural predator control. This, coupled with the increase in cultivated areas and the intensification through double cropping, will necessitate a significant increase in the use of insecticides, fungicides, and herbicides.

With the substantial increase in population which is anticipated in the project area, there will be an inevitable spread of a number of viral and parasitic water-borne communicable diseases. This will be exacerbated by the lack of basic health education combined with the cultural practices of the people. They would be expected to continue their present utilization of the same water supply for drinking, bathing, and waste disposal which would be very conducive to the spread of gastroenteritis, hepatitis, dysentery, and other water-borne diseases. This condition will be worsened if suitable water supply and sanitation facilities are not provided, or, perhaps more importantly, not maintained.

Reduced river flows and seepage from irrigation channels in the project area will enhance the formation of small pools which will increase the breeding potential of the principal malaria vector, *Anopheles culicifacies*. Malaria incidence will undoubtedly increase in the region. The present intensive control programme involves the risk of producing malathion-resistant *A. culicifacies* which could trigger an epidemic until new controls are decided. This vector has already developed resistance to malathion in India.

Among the other diseases, dengue fever, chikungunya virus, scrub typhus and bed bugs are all likely to spread in the project area. For the present, neither filariasis nor schistosomiasis would be expected to spread as a result of project implementation.

Rabies, tetanus, accidents and snake bites are also likely to increase, particularly in the early years of construction and clearing. Tetanus may be a serious problem for construction workers due to its prevalence in the project area soils. Existing health facilities in the Mahewali region will, of course, be too limited to accommodate the health needs of the additional population.

Overall, dietary patterns and nutritional quality should improve for the incoming settlers due principally to increased food availability and an increased standard of living. However, one potentially serious problem may be an insufficient supply of animal protein to meet nutritional requirements for the general maintenance of good health. The supply of dairy products to the project area may be limited since the grazing area may be reduced. On the other hand, increased freshwater fish production could contribute significantly to meet this need for animal protein.

Measures for offsetting adverse effects

Coordinating agency

Establishment of a National Coordinating Agency for Natural Resources, along with an Environmental Protection Agency, is recommended for furnishing institutions capable for follow-up implementation of needed environmental protection measures.

Watershed management/forests

A package of watershed soil conservation measures is recommended, including reforestation, establishing timber and fuel wood plantations, rehabilitating abandoned plantations by conversion to upland cropping, plus engineering measures for erosion control. The fuelwood plantations would utilize local village participation. A "Mahaweli Catchment Redevelopment Law" would be enacted for establishing a new National Forest Authority. Included in the package would be the preparation of a systematic plan for continuing logging and clearing operations.

Wildlife

New wildlife reserves are to be established in those "high quality wildlife habitat" areas not needed for agricultural purposes. In addition, to compensate for loss of habitat in the Mahaweli region, a series of six large continuous reserves/parks are recommended in and around the project area. These include the Somawathie National Park (especially important for elephants), Mahaweli Conservation Park (bird sanctuary), and Wasgomuwa National Park (endangered vertebrate species). A package of institutional improvements is recommended, including establishing a National Department of Wildlife Conservation, and authorizing a detailed study for planning the proposed new park and other reserve systems.

Wetlands and weed control

Within the context of the measures described above, the remaining villus and mangrove swamps will be preserved to the extent possible. A programme will also be developed for use of practicable methods for controlling aquatic weeds.

Fisheries development

The recommended action programmes include: (i) establishing fisheries management systems for the new reservoirs, (ii) a series of pilot project fish farms to determine the best approach for achieving markedly expanded aquaculture, and (iii) strengthening of the ongoing "tank" type of aquaculture using relatively low level technology including construction of a centralized hatchery.

Downstream water and soil management

These recommendations include: (i) establishment of a water management system in the ISA, (ii) control of land clearing operations to minimize loss of topsoil and subsequent erosion, (iii) use of contour techniques in upland areas including plantings and terracing, (iv) establishment of riverbank forest reserves, (v) use of an integrated pest management approach, and (vi) establishing a multipurpose water and soils monitoring programme including a salinity intrusion survey and periodic water quality monitoring.

Health and sanitation

The recommendations include: (i) provision of an adequate rural water supply system, (ii) control of malaria and other vector mosquitoes through strengthening of the existing programmes, (iii) immunization procedures to be used during the construction, and (iv) strengthening of primary health care resources.

Social considerations

The recommendations include: (i) establishment of a regional planning and socio-economic studies unit, (ii) establishment of a settler orientation programme, (iii) studies for developing guidelines for managing a variety of social problems, including special attention to the poorer population sectors such as fishermen's families and agricultural labourers, and evaluation of tourist potentials, and (iv) strengthening of agricultural extension services.

Land use planning

This recommendation is for preparation of an optimal land use scheme which allows maximum agricultural development commensurate with preservation of forests/wildlife, including detailed mapping of non-arable lands and associated studies including evaluation of grazing potentials.

Priorities and scheduling

A tentative scheduling is outlined, showing when the various recommendations are to be undertaken as related to the various stages of project implementation.

Environmental monitoring

While the study does not deal with the need for comprehensive environmental monitoring, it does recommend a comprehensive "multipurpose soils and water monitoring programme" in the project irrigation service area. Other monitoring is to be included under the various recommended sector programmes.

Concluding remarks

The recommendations of the EIA for achieving desired environmental protection measures as part of the overall plan are very comprehensive, so much so that implementing them will require major alterations in the existing national government structure and policies.

Case study 10.3 Tin Smelter Project in Thailand

Notes: This case study can be used by trainees to make mitigation plans and discuss post-project monitoring.

Name of the project: Environmental impact assessment for tin smelter project.

Type of environmental analysis: EIA.

Type of project: This is a metal-refining industry. The manufacturing process essentially involves heating the ore and utilizing the difference in melting point temperature (alloy formation involves slightly different methods) for obtaining the separation of the various components including the production of the tin metal of over 99.9 per cent purity from the original ore concentrate of approximately 73–75 per cent purity.

This is the only tin-smelting and refining plant in Thailand. It is capable of producing about 40,000 Mt/year of refined tin, which is 20 per cent of current total world production. A number of by-products are also produced, including tin-lead.

The industry produces three types of waste: namely liquid, solid, and gas. Domestic wastewater, laboratory wastewater and plant surface run-off are the main liquid wastes. Heavy metals such as Fe, Pb, Ta, Nb, Ti, Sn, Al, Zi, and Cn are the main heavy metal pollutants. Solid waste management does not pose any significant problem. Some amounts of toxic heavy metals, including Pb, As, Sb, and Bi, are emitted to the atmosphere. Also the sulphur present mainly in the fuel can generate significant quantities of SO_x. Thus air pollution is the most threatening hazard at a tin smelter.

Project location

The tin smelter is located at the southern promontory of Ao Kham Bay on the southeast shore of Phuket Island, which is about 6 km south of Phuket town though 12 km by road. The plant is located adjacent to the tin ore processing facility. The plant is bounded on the east and south by the sea and the west and southwest by coconut groves. The total area of the plant is 5.8 acres.

Reports on pertinent studies

See References 1–4, page 305.

Environmental study area

The study area includes the land mass within approximately a 5 km radius of the plant. This area has been determined to cover more than adequately any resources which may be significantly affected by the tin smelter operation.

EIA team

The EIA team consists of two co-managers, with one project field engineer, two air quality experts, one socio-economist, one water quality expert, and one ecologist, with support staff.

EIA budget adequacy

Adequate budget was provided.

Methodology

The methodology for preparing the EIA is that recommended by NEB (Ref. 5, p. 305). It is based on the methodology developed by the Battelle Institute/United States Army Corps of Engineers. In this methodology environmental resources are classified and evaluated in four general headings, namely: (a) natural physical resources, (b) natural ecological resources, (c) human use of economic development resources, and (d) quality-of-life values. In addition to estimating effects of the tin smelter operations on these resources, and identifying, delineating, and quantifying adverse effects, the method includes preparation of recommendations for minimizing unavoidable adverse effects and for offsetting these by positive enhancement measures.

To supplement the data from different sources, a number of field surveys were made covering all specialized environmental impacts (including socio-economics, wildlife, flora, and fauna, plus a sampling analysis of wastewaters, drinking water quality, health status of the workers, etc).

Existing environmental conditions

Background

Based on discussions with long-time residents of Phuket, it appears that prior to the construction of the tin smelter (about 20 years ago), the study area was sparsely populated, with land use including some coconut groves, rubber plantations, and secondary forest. Agricultural development coupled with population growth has resulted in increases in cultivated crops as well as coconut and rubber plantations and thus created a more densely populated agricultural zone.

Environmental concerns

During the past 20 years (the duration of tin smelter operations), several new families have moved into what was previously a sparsely inhabited area. This can be expected as a result of increased economic opportunities from the industrial development, improvements in transport/access, etc. It may also be expected that the increased population may result in increased frequency and opportunities for complaints. Complaints on record cover blasting noise and smoke.

Blasting noise from slag granulation: frequently 2–3 times/day, mostly occurring during night; continuous blasting noises (>100 times in each duration); disturbs relaxation time of surrounding people, patients, children, and babies; and caused different levels of vibration to houses depending on distances – creating damage to items, e.g. mirrors, window panes, and roof tiles.

Smoke from blasting and stacks: aesthetic nuisance (clothes and houses got dirty, bad odours); and fear of illness due to bad odours.

Environmental base map

The environmental base map (EBM) shows the plant and its environs. The EBM shows all potentially sensitive environmental resources, that is any resource which might be significantly impaired by the plant operations, including waste emissions.

Environmental effects from project

Adverse effects on physical resources

Air quality: odour and dust nuisance during certain hours on some days (though the modelling and stack emissions indicate that the tin smelter may not be the source); reduced yields from fruits from coconut plantations; and visible damage to leaves.

Noise pollution: noise has affected most of the residents of the villages.

Adverse effects on water resources

The wastewaters discharged from the laboratory and canteen without any treatment are unsightly and these waters exceed Ministry of Industry (MOI) standards for some parameters.

Adverse effects on human use values: agriculture

The smelter air emissions have caused significant reductions in yields of coconut plantations. Also the toxic effects of groundwater and soil polluted by tin dredge tailings which have been panned or stored in the coconut groves by local villagers have caused the plants to yield less.

Adverse effects on quality-of-life values: socio-economics

About 90 per cent of the respondents at Ban Ao Makhan and 100 per cent at Ban Laem Phan Wa Wee were negatively affected by noise and dust emissions.

Positive effects on human use values

Water supply: the tin smelter operations created beneficial impacts on water supply in that the smelter made arrangements for local villagers to utilize the groundwater supply developed by the tin smelter.

Mining/mineral resources: the operation of the tin smelter has an obvious beneficial impact on local, regional, and national mineral resource development and subsequent beneficial economic impacts.

Quality-of-life values: wage earning forms the major proportion of household income in the area. The smelter has created job opportunities and other related employment opportunities for the local villagers. These indicate long-term benefits for the people in the area.

Land prices in the vicinity have increased because of the presence of the industry. Economic benefits include benefits of increased earning and creation of jobs for the workers and their families as well as the gross regional product, and overall economic benefit to the nation.

Summarized projected effects

The impacts of the smelter operations are both beneficial and adverse, with the beneficial impacts outweighing the adverse. The primary beneficial impact is the economic benefit which is believed to play a major role in the villagers' good primary healthcare. In addition, the provision of water supply for many villagers is a primary beneficial impact.

The adverse impacts are related to air and noise pollution from the plant. Apprehension naturally results regarding health when one believes that air pollution is causing damage to vegetation, leaving deposits of dust at the living quarters, and may be damaging to human health. These fears may or may not be justified. The health data from the local clinic do not indicate any difference in the health condition.

Measures for offsetting adverse effects

Air quality

The cyclones, baghouses, and electrostatic precipitator are generally performing well. Consideration should be given to undertaking the corrective maintenance measures for the electrostatic precipitators (ESP) recommended by Research Cottrell as these measures will ensure a longer and more efficient operating life of the ESPs and should further reduce the frequency of tripping of the ESPs; bag replacement and maintenance should be improved, and the performance closely monitored; and consideration should be given to upgrading the old ventilated baghouses, so that the emissions are from a stack or stacks which can be monitored and also will reduce local dust deposition during calm periods.

Stack emissions from liquidator 3 resulting from dross production need additional pollution control in order to reduce the arsenic trioxide emission concentration. It has been proposed that by cooling the gas prior to baghouse filtration, the efficiency of filtration would increase. This cooling could be accomplished by installation of a medium efficiency dry cyclone with modification for air cooling in the exhaust line prior to the baghouse. It may also be necessary to install a second baghouse in series or vent the baghouse to an ESP. The approach here should be step-by-step to mini-mize unnecessary expenditures. This means that air cooling on a pilot scale should be tested first to determine the potential increase in arsenic removal efficiency of the existing baghouse. Further steps would be de-pendent on the results of the pilot testing. In addition it would be a good idea to only operate liquidator 3 on windy days to increase dispersion.

A general "tightening-up" and possibly some modifications are needed for improving shop-floor ambient air quality. This is particularly true for the electric furnaces during charging, the refining and casting area, the hardhead tank, and the area around the Al/As dross storage room and liquidator 3 (particularly during liquidating). An analysis of needs for improvement in hygiene lines, exhaust fans, protective structures, etc., is needed to enable detailed design of cost-effective facilities. A corrosion control analysis should be incorporated in the study in order to prevent further corrosion-related gas line leakage.

The baghouse and hygiene system engineering study and improvement planning is completed and detail design is underway. The construction was expected to begin in the second half of 1986.

Water pollution

The water pollution analysis shows that the only pollutants exceeding MOI effluent standards are from the laboratory and canteen. Because of the small volume of wastewater and the vast dispersion/dilution effect of the tides and currents, it is evident that the effluent does not significantly impact on the local ecology. However, the smelter could easily meet MOI standards by routing the canteen wastewater flow to a septic tank/oil trap system and pumping the laboratory wastewater to the septic tanks system rather than directly discharging to the sea. This will eliminate any direct discharge of undiluted or diluted laboratory wastewater (this is the same disposal method as is commonly used by laboratories in Bangkok).

Noise pollution

The effect of noise pollution has been evaluated by noise level measure-ments at various locations in-plant and in surrounding communities. Noise pollution was shown not to be an occupational hazard for workers. The normal plant operation does not have any significant effect on sound levels in nearby villages. However, periodically, there are explosions due to slag granulation which are reported to cause nuisance conditions at nearby residences. The smelter has been and is continuously making every possible effort to reduce the frequency of such explosions. The fre-quency has been reduced from the occurrence of explosion in 18 per cent of tappings in 1983 to 14 per cent in 1985. This results in an average of less than two explosions per week. It is possible that this is the best achievable under present processing circumstances and is thus an unavoidable impact. It is not feasible to shift processing times to ensure that the slag explosions occur during the day. The smelter is continuing to modify its processing to reduce the number of slag explosions. One of the expansion plans is a new cooling water system, for the improvement of the water pressure and water flow rate of the slag granulation system. The high pressure and the high flow rate of granulating water will reduce the chance of slag explosion and therefore reduce the frequency of slag explosion. The installation of the cooling water system is planned within 1986/87 smelter budgets.

Solid wastes

Solid waste pollution control is not a significant factor in the assessment of environmental impacts of the tin smelter because the process solid wastes are either recycled or sold as slag or dust.

Environmental monitoring

The monitoring activities are planned to provide confidence in the continuous improvements in pollution control at the smelter and to ensure that the objectives of environmental protection are met.

The plan includes monitoring of both the natural environment and public and occupational health-related parameters. The monitoring will include systematic measurement of air and wastewater discharges from the smelter as well as special periodic ambient environmental quality measurements.

The implementation of the monitoring plan will serve to provide the following:
(a) establish a database to confirm meeting applicable MOI and National Environment Board criteria and standards;
(b) ensure worker health and safety;
(c) assist in the efficient operation of the smelter by providing feedback on operation/maintenance.

The monitoring programme includes point-source sampling for all significant air and wastewater discharges and ambient air quality sampling for the shopfloor and at the two nearby villages. The monitoring programme also includes continued monitoring of drinking water quality, recording of operational problems of air pollution control facilities, recording of blast occurrences, and continuing safety/health checks. The smelter monitoring programme will commence when appropriate equipment has been identified and obtained. Periodic reports will be issued to the MOI as required.

Concluding remarks

From the overall assessment it can be concluded that, while the tin smelter operations do cause minor effects on the local environment as a result of wastewater and noise, the only significant adverse effects may be caused by air emissions. These problems can be readily overcome so that the overall adverse impacts of the smelter will be minor or possibly insignificant, especially when compared to the major social and economic benefits derived during the past 20 years of operation and which are expected to continue in the future. These benefits are enjoyed by the local population, the Upper South Region, and the nation.

REFERENCES

1 Metal Levels Associated with Tin Dredging and Smelting and their Effects upon Intertidal Reef Flats at Ko Phuket, Thailand, Coral Reef, Chapter 1, pp. 131–137, 1982.
2 Environmental Guidelines for Coastal Zone Management in Thailand/Zone of Phuket, H. F. Ludwig/SEATEC, 1976.
3 Inception Report: Environmental Impact Assessment for Thailand Tin Smelter, prepared by SEATEC Consortium, October 1984.
4 First Progress Report, Environmental Impact Assessment for Thailand Tin Smelter, prepared by SEATEC Consortium, March 1985.
5 Manual of NEB Guidelines for Preparation of Environmental Impact Evaluations, National Environmental Board, 1979.

Case study 10.4 Thai National Fertilizer Corporation Project

Source ESCAP: Environment and Development Series, Environmental Impact Assessment, Guidelines for Transport, p. 65.

Notes: This case study can also be used by trainees to develop mitigation plans and post-project monitoring.

Name of project: National Fertilizer Corporation, Eastern Seaboard, Thailand.

Type of environmental analysis: EIS.

Type of project: This project is an ammonia and phosphate fertilizer manufacturing complex. The complex will produce nitrogen–phosphorus (NP) granules, nitrogen–phosphorus–potassium (NPK) granules, urea granules with small amounts of ammonia phosphoric acid, mono-ammonium phosphate (MAP), and di-ammonium phosphate (DAP).

The NFC fertilizer complex will occupy an area of approximately 1.6

km^2 on the Gulf of Thailand, and will require an additional area of more than 1 km^2, to the east of the main plant location, for phosphogypsum storage. The complex will employ a workforce of approximately 3,000 workers during the construction stage, and approximately 700 during operation.

The complex will produce for sale a total of 670,000 tons per year of NP and NPK granules; 140,000 tons per year of urea granules; and smaller amounts of ammonia phosphoric acid, MAP, and DAP. Most of the complex output will be shipped to domestic dealers for further distribution. This quantity of fertilizer product represents a sizeable percentage of Thailand's fertilizer needs.

The complex was scheduled to begin operation in late 1987, based on the initiation of construction in early 1985.

Solid raw materials required by the complex, with the exception of filler, will be brought to the complex by ship. Products will be distributed by barge and by truck, and/or by rail. Water will be supplied from Dok Krai Reservoir, which has ample capacity to satisfy project needs. Power will be available from the new facilities of the Provincial Electricity Authority (PEA) and Electricity Generating Authority of Thailand (EGAT) which are being developed to serve the growing needs of the Eastern Seaboard Area. These and other requirements of the complex, such as transportation, port facilities, and housing for workers, have been included as part of the overall development plan for the Map Ta Pud Industrial Estate.

The processes and operations that will be used at the complex are similar to those that are presently in use at many other fertilizer plants worldwide. No new or experimental technology is utilized in the complex. The complex is planned to be a modern, environmentally sound facility that benefits from worldwide experience.

Project location

The National Fertilizer Corporation will be located on the Gulf of Thailand at the Map Ta Phut Industrial Estate in Rayong Province.

Reports on pertinent studies

See References 1 and 4, pages 316 and 317.

Environmental study area

The study area described by the EIS will include an area within a 20 km radius from the project site. Because most of the impacts caused by construction and operation of the complex will occur in the project area, this will be the only area described in depth.

EIA team

The EIS has been basically prepared for MFC by its consultants, namely TESCO (a Thai environmental consultant), Foster Wheeler International Corporation, the project management consultant (PMC), and Synco (an environmental consultant). This was a one-year study involving approximately 30 professionals with specialist inputs on physical resources, ecological resources, human use values, quality-of-life values, and project management.

EIA budget adequacy

Before the EIA process is started, one needs to ensure that adequate budget is available to collect data, analyse data available, carry out necessary research investigations, and develop any appropriate models.

Methodology

The EIS document has been prepared in accordance with information included in the manual of NEB Guidelines for preparation of environmental impact evaluations as well as the specific guidelines contained in the terms of reference (TORs) developed by NEB for the EIS on the particular project. Work in preparing the EIS has considered all studies and potential impacts identified in TORs.

The methodology for making an EIS is essentially that prepared by the Battelle Institute/United States Army Corps of Engineers for water resources development projects. Here the environmental impacts are studied in four categories: (a) physical resources, (b) ecological resources, (c) human use values, and (d) quality-of-life values.

Field studies were performed on each of these topics, and existing data were used as appropriate.

Existing environmental conditions

Background

At present, the part of Rayong Province where the complex will be located is largely rural. Cassava cultivation dominates the area, with sugarcane, fruit trees, pineapples, coconuts, and rice also occurring frequently. Rubber is also increasing as a local crop. In the immediate vicinity of the site are several small villages, including Ban Ao Pradu, Ban Nong Faeb, Ban Nong Ta Tik, and Ban Ta Kuon. At a distance of about 5 km is the municipality of Map Ta Phut, which has a population of about 7,000.

More sizeable nearby population centres include Rayong, which is about 15 km to the east, and Sattahip, which is about twice as far to the west.

Cassava processing dominates the industry of the area, with cassava pellet and cassava flour manufacturing plants the most prevalent industry by far. There are nine such plants within only a few kilometers of the plant site. A second significant industry is pineapple canning. However, the first stages of the planned industrialization of the area are already evident, namely construction of the PTT Gas Separation Plant. Also, a plastic granules facility has been built a few kilometers to the east of the plant site, in Rayong.

Since the plant site is a seacoast area, two activities usually associated with the ocean are also found, namely fishing and recreation. A small resort, Haad Sai Thong, is located at Ban Ta Kuon, about 3 km east of the plant site and 1 km south of the gypsum stack area. The resort is located near the mouth of Khlong Huai Yai, which is a stream located to the west of the gypsum stack. Some recreational house plots belonging to individuals are also found in the area.

The fishing industry is less significant to the area than agriculture, and fishing activity centres around the mouth of Khlong Huai Yai. The area is not considered a prime fishery area.

Topographically, the project area is relatively flat. The plant site is at an elevation of 5 to 10 m MSL. The land rises gradually towards the inland areas, with isolated hills at distances of 10 km or more from the plant site. Drainage is good, flowing primarily southward to the sea. Flooding is not a significant problem.

The area is not seismically active and is far from existing centres of seismic activity.

Several different types of soils are found in the area, and these are identified on a soils map presented in the report. In general, the soils tend to be sandy, well-drained, and low in nutrients.

Although agriculture is important in the study area, the methods used are not entirely efficient or modern. Fertilizer is applied to crops in many cases, but in amounts that are generally less than recommended. Therefore, especially in cassava areas, nutrients in the soil are gradually being depleted. Farm machinery is used in some cases, water buffalo and cattle in others. Water shortages have been found to be a problem, which is being addressed in part by a government programme to encourage the growing of rubber, which has roots deep enough to reach groundwater, rather than cassava.

Water and power supply to the project area have been incorporated in plans for construction of reservoirs and electrical substations to serve the area. At present, the Dok Krai reservoir provides water for irrigation. It is planned that this water will be transferred to the industrial estate. However, by the time this occurs, another reservoir, Nong Pla Lai, will have been constructed to supply irrigation water. Electrical power sub-stations are now under construction in the region to increase the availability of power for industry.

Transportation facilities of many kinds to serve future needs of the area have been planned by the responsible agencies and authorities. These facilities are at various stages of early development and include highway and road networks, a railway line, and an industrial port facility for ocean-going vessels.

Existing environmental conditions

Air quality in the vicinity of the plant site has been sampled at two locations, and has been found to be generally well within air quality standards. Particulates were found to be present at levels of 81 to 92 mg/m^3. High levels of total hydrocarbons (1,350 to 2,600 mg/m^3) were noted, but since the methane portion of the measurement was not accounted for, the values cannot be compared to standards.

The two air quality sampling stations were located at Map Ta Phut and Huai Pong, near centres of population and of industrial development. Thus, it can be expected that air quality elsewhere in the region is better than at the two locations studied.

In the immediate vicinity of the plant site, there are several perennial streams but no rivers. The streams, Khlong Huai Yai and Khlong Nam Hoo, join and flow to the sea at Ban Ta Kuan/Sai Thong. These streams also border the gypsum stack location on the east and the west, respectively.

Water samplings to date have found the water quality to be rather poor and affected by upstream discharges from industry and communities as well as by salt water intrusion. The water level was very low in both streams, and in the April sampling, Khlong Nam Hoo was found to be stagnant, due to the irrigation dam being closed. Turbidity was high, as were total solids and total suspended solids. COD was high, especially in the upper location on Nam Hoo. The influence of salt water intrusion could be seen at the lower location on Nam Hoo, since high levels of total solids, sulphate, and salinity were found.

Sea water quality is found to be affected by contaminants in fresh water discharges, with near-shore water in a state of eutrophication because of waste organic matter brought in by the streams.

Sub-surface strata in the project area generally consist of sand near the surface, sandy clay below, grading into a clay layer with very little sand at even greater depths. A bedrock of granite underlies the area. The depths and thicknesses of the individual layers vary spatially, with the region nearest the shore having the most extensive sand layer. Inland areas, namely the gypsum stack site, have more extensive clay layers.

Groundwater is high in iron, manganese, and turbidity. Low pH was also found in some cases.

Existing pollution in the area is caused primarily by the human population and by the cassava processing industry. Wastewater, consisting both of sanitary waste from residences and of effluent from tapioca plants, contributes high loadings of BOD to the local streams. Solid waste, that is rubbish and garbage, is burned, land-filled, or dumped into the sea.

Existing air emissions from industrial sources consist primarily of SO_x and particulates, and are generated by tapioca plants and other industries in the area.

In the Rayong Province, public health is generally not good, because of the combined problems of poor sanitation, lack of potable water, presence of malarial mosquitoes, and insufficient health care professionals. Malaria, although declining, is still the most common "notifiable disease", and of these diseases, causes the greatest number of deaths.

At present, people living in and around the plant site are aware that the area will be expropriated for the industrial estate. However, those living in and around the gypsum stack area are not so aware, although rumours exist. People living in the study area generally perceive the project as providing socio-economic benefits, including job opportunities and future development, although they also believe there will be increased pollution as a result.

Environmental base map

There is not any specified EBM in the report. However, a location map shows the waterways, transportation routes, pipelines, etc., in the vicinity.

Environmental effects from the project

Adverse effects on physical resources

Potential impacts to surface water quality during construction could arise from dust emissions (from vehicles and disturbance of soil cover), high suspended solids (from storm water run-off), and sanitary waste (from construction personnel).

The discharge of wastewater from the fertilizer complex, under all-flow conditions, will increase the concentration of sea water contaminants in the area near the discharge point. Sea water within a short distance from the discharge point will be hazardous to marine life. Under misoperation conditions, sea water pH will be affected in the initial dilution zone and high concentrations of fluoride and phosphate will be released into the receiving water.

The turbidity and some dissolved minerals will be increased in the groundwater. According to the hydro-geological characteristics of the project area, the major problem in the gypsum stack area is the potential contamination of shallow unconfined groundwater by leachate from standing water used in gypsum disposal.

The topography will be affected temporarily during the construction phase.

Fluoride and phosphorus pentoxide emissions from the NFC plant will lead to depositions in the soil surrounding the plant site and gypsum stack.

Construction and operation activities will generate localized sources of high noise level. During operation of the NFC complex, road trucks will be used to transport product and some raw materials. It is estimated that truck traffic volume will be 20 trucks per hour based on 6 days per week. Noise level from road trucks ranges from 82 to 92 dBA at a distance of 15 meters. Only the Haad Sai Thong recreation resort will be significantly affected by these transportation activities.

Construction activities will create additional emission sources typically associated with large construction projects. These additional sources include air emissions from construction vehicles and equipment, fugitive particulate emission from the disturbance of soil cover, water quality impacts from surface run-off, and potential impacts from the sanitary waste of construction workers.

Adverse effects on ecological resources

Construction activities at the phosphogypsum disposal area will impact fresh water ecology in the two streams since the area is very close to the streams. There will be an increase in total dissolved solids and turbidity of the water from erosion and run-off. Sedimentation from erosion and surface run-off will also affect living conditions such as respiratory processes and feeding habits of benthic organisms and some fishes. The dominant benthic organism in Khlong Huai Yai was *Chironomus* sp., which will be affected by sedimentation.

High concentrations of some chemicals in the NFC plant wastewater will be a hazard to marine organisms within 3–5 m from the discharge point along the plume trajectory. Any possible adverse impact from the fluoride will be limited to a 5 m radius around the diffuser and then it will only affect very sensitive species (*Perna Perna*).

Adverse effects on human use values

The NFC will change the existing land use pattern in the project area from agricultural areas, villages, etc., to the fertilizer plant and gypsum stack. Houses and the crops in the plant site will be removed and the land owners will have to find a new place for settlement.

Two unpaved roads located in the plant site area and used by local commuters will be eliminated by plant construction. Traffic volumes will generally increase near the project area.

Fluoride emissions from the operation of the NFC plant will cause some localized impacts on existing agricultural vegetation. An area of approximately 140 ha, generally north of the gypsum stack, is exposed to annual average fluoride concentrations above 0.25 $\mu m/m^3$. Plants sensitive to fluoride may be affected in this area. Thus the unknown susceptibility of the majority of crops (cassava, coconut, paddy rice, and rubber) needs a threshold examination.

Examination of the monthly ground level fluoride air concentrations reveals areas that receive a two-month average above 0.33 $\mu g/m^3$. Forage materiais are subject to fluoride accumulation and if it exceeds 40 ppm (less than 0.33 $\mu g/m^3$), cattle may suffer fluorosis. But the areas of potential forage contamination are not in the pasture, and constitute a maximum of 1.4 per cent of the study area. However, there is an increased percentage of susceptibility.

Contamination of the streams with increased phosphates and ammonia will increase the aquatic plant biomass. This will change the ecosystem and thus affect fisheries.

A small number of swimming crab fishermen may have to move from the fishing ground adjacent to the project site to fish in other areas. Some adverse effect of the discharge (fluoride and phosphate) on the larval stage of fishes and invertebrates may be expected.

Construction of the NFC complex will require resettlement of villagers who are presently living on portions of land to be devoted to the project.

Some impact is anticipated at the black sand beach mine at Nong Baeb. It will depend upon conflict resolution between the mining company and the government during expropriation for the Map Ta Pud Heavy Industrial Estate project development.

Adverse effects on quality-of-life values

Impacts will occur from plant construction and operation due to the number of workers moving into the area. Plant operation will create an area around the gypsum stack having impacts from fluoride emissions. The majority of the villagers are aware of possible water and air pollution. During certain operations, ambient concentrations of contaminants can be expected to increase. An ammonia spill would have a significant impact on public health.

Measures for offsetting adverse effects

The mitigating measures of the project plan that will offset the potential impacts are described as follows.

(a) Siting of the complex in an area where many of the existing environmental resources/values are not of prime importance. The project site: (1) does not contain any valuable ecological resources (either terrestrial or aquatic), (2) does not contain any items of archaeological significance or historical importance, (3) is not subject to floods or seismic disturbances, (4) is not heavily populated, (5) is not the location of significant mineral resources or mining activities, and (6) is not a prime area for tourism, recreation, or aesthetic pursuits. The project will also not compete with local industry for raw materials, or workers with similar skills.

(b) Procedures in the construction period will involve: preferential use of local labour to minimize the number of workers who migrate to the area; establishment of construction camps by subcontractors for migrant workers; use of dust suppressant spraying to minimize fugitive dust during construction activities; use of temporary dams to control erosion and promote settling of particles from stormwater run-off to prevent damage to surface waters (fresh and nearshore) and aquatic ecosystems; provision of sanitary waste facilities for workers; and cooperation with local and provincial public health authorities.

(c) Use of air emission control equipment that limits emissions of pollutants, including SO_x, NO_x, hydrocarbons, acid, mist, ammonia, carbon monoxide, and volatile organic compounds, to levels that result in ambient concentrations well below applicable air quality standards. Emissions from the plant will also not create any harmful synergistic effects with each other (i.e., ammonia with CO) or with other existing emission sources in the area. Deposition rates are low enough that they will not adversely affect soils.

(d) Siting of the gypsum stack area over a thick layer of naturally occurring, low permeability clay to serve as a liner that will prevent seepage of cooling pond water from reaching groundwater or surface water.

(e) Constructing very low permeability dikes around the gypsum stack down to the underlying clay layer to provide safe lateral containment for the gypsum pond water and to restrict the potential impact on neighbouring groundwater to insignificant levels. Analyses show that conservatively projected seepage rates are so slow that the time required for contaminants to escape the gypsum stack area exceeds the life of the plant by more than a factor of four.

Use of on-site wastewater treatment to treat effluent from the complex, followed by use of a well-designed, submerged diffuser 2,000 m from shore to discharge the effluent to the ocean at a depth of 4 m. Analysis shows that the sea water quality beyond about 10 m from the discharge point will be only minimally altered and that no significant impacts will occur on marine ecosystems or fisheries.

(g) Plant operational procedures that utilize evaporation from the gypsum cooling pond to minimize wastewater discharge from this source, restricting it only to part of the rainy season (about 3 months per year).

(h) Stacking of phosphogypsum in the gypsum stack area using well-established techniques that involve double-diking to minimize the chance of leakage or spillage of slurry water from this area.

(i) Application of noise criteria that will meet United States Occupational Safety and Hygiene Association (OSHA) standards for occupational noise within the plant boundary. Any equipment not meeting noise control standards will be subject to attenuation, and ear protection equipment will be provided if necessary. Attenuation of plant noise by distance beyond the boundary will reduce noise impacts on human receptors in the area to insignificant levels.

(j) Commitment by the project to conduct environmental monitoring activities during construction and operation of the complex so as to verify the protection of the health and welfare of workers, nearby population, and the surrounding environment. Monitoring activities will be performed at locations both within the complex and around it. Significant sources of emissions and effluents have been identified and will be monitored. The monitoring programme will cover: (a) sources within the plant, (b) air quality and meteorology, (c) surface water quality, (d) sea water quality, and (e) groundwater quality. Selected ecological studies may also be made. The early results obtained will be used to modify details of the monitoring programme as necessary. To the extent desirable, the monitoring programme will use the same sampling stations and parameter lists as in the baseline programme. The monitoring results will be compiled and reported periodically to the appropriate authorities.

(k) Commitment by the project to perform an occupational health and safety monitoring programme covering employees of the complex, so that any concerns can be identified, addressed, and countered by the proper remedial action.

(l) Project plans to investigate alternative commercial uses for phosphogypsum to eliminate the need to stack it over the life of the plant. These commercial uses could include: (a) being a raw material for manufacture of plasterboard or cement, or (b) application as a soil conditioner (possibly with lime) to supply calcium and sulphur to soils. These kinds of uses for phosphogypsum are being demonstrated in Japan and the United States.

In addition to the potential impacts summarized above that are mitigated by the project design, by regional circumstances, or by the location of the site, several other potential adverse impacts were identified that will be mitigated by plans or activities to be developed and undertaken by the project. The topics involved in these impacts are: (a) fluoride emissions from the gypsum stack and resulting fluoride impacts on nearby agriculture, livestock, flora, fauna, and people; (b) relocation of villagers living in the gypsum stack area; (c) socio-economic and public health issues associated with low probability "worst case" emissions or discharges from the complex; and (d) cooperation with local, provincial, and governmental authorities on infrastructure and facilities planning so that growth in the area can be adequately managed.

Environmental monitoring

The project will have an environmental monitoring programme during both construction and operational phases to provide continuing assurance that the planned environmental protection measures are working adequately.

During construction, environmental monitoring will be conducted on: (i) particulate emissions from traffic, earth moving, and debris, and surface water quality effects associated with construction area run-off at both the plant site and gypsum stack area. During operation, major sources of air emissions and wastewater discharge will be monitored at the plant. In addition, ambient air quality surrounding the plant will be monitored, along with meteorological conditions. Water quality monitoring will include both surface and groundwater. Surface water sampling stations on inland streams and in the ocean will be the same as those used in the baseline study. Groundwater monitoring will occur both up-gradient and down-gradient from the gypsum stack in shallow wells. Occupational health and safety of workers at the plant will be monitored on a continuing basis.

Concluding remarks

The EIS study conducted for the ammonia and phosphate fertilizer complex was conducted in accordance with the study plan developed with and approved by the National Environment Board (NEB) of Thailand. The EIS report produced as a result of the study is compatible with both the

NEB's guidelines for the preparation of the environmental impact evaluation and the terms of reference prepared by NEB for the NFC project.

Potential environmental impacts associated with constructing and operating the project were evaluated for a total of 28 separate topic areas in 4 major subject categories (physical resources, ecological resources, human use values, and quality-of-life values). This evaluation represented a comprehensive investigation of how the project might affect the environment based on present plans for its construction and operation.

In the analysis, emphasis was placed on evaluating those impacts affecting the sensitive receptors that were identified in the project area. Both routine and non-routine operating conditions for the complex were considered, including several low probability "worst-case" conditions. For some topic areas, no sensitive receptors, issues, or impacts were identified. These areas received correspondingly less emphasis.

Because of the commitment by NFC to design the plant using modern, environmentally sound control technology and to take advantage of favourable existing conditions in locating plant facilities and defining plant operating procedures, the EIA revealed that many potential impacts had already been effectively mitigated.

For example, locating the plant in a major new industrial estate (i.e., at Map Ta Pud) that has been the subject of extensive planning and analysis by several private and governmental bodies, allows NFC to benefit from the planned infrastructure development already completed. Utilization of land for the plant site that is within the territory expropriated by IEAT simplifies many land use and socio-economic impact questions.

The complex will also benefit from development projects planned in the Map Ta Pud area for transportation (highways, railway line, and deep-water port), water supply (from Dok Krai Reservoir), power supply (by PEA and EGAT), natural gas supply (PTT), and housing (new town – Ban Chang). The effect of this previous planning is to reduce impacts in these particular topic areas to levels of no consequence. NFC will coordinate with these other projects to assure their timely development and compatible schedule.

The overall conclusion is that by using the planned mitigation and control measures, the NFC project can be constructed and operated without significant impact on the environment.

REFERENCES

1 Preliminary Report of EIS Study of National Fertilizer Complex, July 1984.
2 C. Tharnboopha and N. Lulitanon, *Ecology of the Inner Gulf of Thailand*, Marine Fisheries Laboratory Technical Paper No. 4/1977 (in Thai).

3 C. Tharnboopha, *Water Quality off the East Coast of the Gulf of Thailand*, Marine Fisheries Laboratory Technical Paper No. 10/1979, 1980 (in Thai).

4 *Study of Pollution Control Measures and Impacts of the Development of Chemical Fertilizer Complex and Integrated Steel Industry*, Mahidol University, Volume IV, Environmental Status and Impacts on the Development of Chemical Fertiliser Complex and Steel Industry on the Sea-Coast in the Eastern Region of Thailand, 1983.

5 *The Directory of Industrial Factories in Changwat Rayong*, Rayong Provincial Industry Office, Ministry of Industry, 1982.

6 S. Khetsamut, *et al.*, *Benthic Animals off the East Coast of the Gulf of Thailand*, Marine Fisheries Laboratory Technical Paper No. 11/1979, Dept. of Fisheries, 1979 (in Thai).

7 *Report on Initial Evaluation on Major Industry on the Eastern Seaboard*, Environmental Working Group, National Environment Board, Volume 1, March 1981.

8 *Development Document for Effluent Limitations Guidelines and New Source Performance Standards for the Basic Fertilizer Manufacturing Point Source Category*, United States EPA, March 1974.

9 *Guide to Pollution Control in Fertiliser Plants*, United Nations Industrial Development Organization, Monograph # 9.

Case study 10.5 Map Ta Phut Port Project

Note: This case study can be used to generate an impact network diagram.

Name of the project: Environmental impact statement of Map Ta Phut Port Project, by Industrial Estate Authority of Thailand, August 1985.

Type of environmental analysis: EIS.

Type of project: This is the development of a commercial port or multi-user zone. Within this area, the following will be established: a port operations centre, bulk commodity storage areas and berths, general cargo storage facilities, and bulk liquid berths. Marginal reclamation along the shoreline will also be incorporated.

The site of the Map Ta Phut port was fixed during the earlier feasibility study (JICA 1983) relating to the establishment of a major heavy industry and residential zone in Rayong province. Concerning berth requirements, construction of Map Ta Phut port is intended to proceed in phases to provide facilities supporting progressive growth in industries adjacent to the site. Thus three development stages are considered.

(a) Short-term development: required before 1992 for loading raw and finished products of NFC, MPC, etc.

(b) Interim operations: specialized facilities for handling hazardous flammable liquids.

Table 10.4 Work force – port personnel

	1995	2000
General cargo berth	157	300
Liquids berth	26	40
Utilities	43	60
Customs & immigration	50	60
Port administration	47	60
IEAT personnel	40	45
Harbour operation – marine	84	130
Harbour operations – engineering & administration	69	80
Other facilities – gatehouse, weighbridge, fire, medical, canteen, etc.	98	130
	614	905

(c) Interim operations: specialized facilities for handling hazardous flammable liquids.

The port will have all the basic facilities as following: (1) harbour craft requirements – tugs, pilot launches, work boats, buoy maintenance; (2) road and rail; (3) work force (see Table 10.4); (4) water supply, drainage, and wastewater collection and treatment; (5) solid waste management; (6) emergency services; (7) power supply; (8) port traffic; and (9) cargo handling and storage.

Project location

The Map Ta Phut port project is located in Rayong province in the eastern seaboard area and the site is exposed to the Gulf of Thailand.

Reports on pertinent studies

See References 2 and 3, page 329.

Environmental study area

The port will occupy approximately 2 to 8 km of shoreline and an off-shore area within the break of about 4.75 km. The dredged shipping channel will extend to approximately 4 to 5 km from shore. For the purposes of the EIS the port has been defined to include all offshore works, the commercial port area, and the berths and loading/unloading areas for specific uses (tapioca, fertilizer, raw materials, and products).

EIA team

Not provided with the report.

EIA budget adequacy

Not provided with the report.

Methodology

The methodology basically follows the procedure laid down by the National Environment Board. First of all an initial environmental examination was made in January 1985, for which comments were received from IEAT and the National Environment Board, after which this EIS report was made. The EIS follows an "item to item" impact description.

Existing environmental conditions

See the relevant section from Case Study 10.4, pages 307–310.

Environmental effects from the project

The network of potential impacts of the proposed port is divided into main parts: (i) the construction phase and (ii) the operational phase.

Adverse impacts: aquatic

Dredging and reclamation will result in formation of plumes of suspended sediment around the dredgers, reclamation outfalls, and dumping ground. The coastal waters at Map Ta Phut are at present unpolluted and have low levels of suspended sediments.

Small areas (at most 3.5 km^2 mostly about 0.5 km^2) will be affected sufficiently by increased turbidity and deposited sediments to affect marine biota and productivity, in some cases causing total loss of photosynthetic activity. This will necessarily have further implications in the food chain of the coastal environment. The impact in the context of biotic and fishery resources of the Eastern Seaboard is not considered to be significant, although local fishermen will be forced to fish elsewhere. There is little inshore fishing activity at Map Ta Phut compared with elsewhere along the coast and the coastal waters are not considered to be a significant spawning or nursery areas compared with waters further to the east.

Disturbed sediments will have a more significant impact on recreational resources at the Sai Thong beach resort just to the east of the port site, reducing the quality of inshore waters for contact and non-contact recreation during the construction period.

Disturbed sediments will also damage the remaining corals on the islands of Ko Saket, but these have been evaluated as low in significance as an ecological or touristic resource in comparison with other colonies occurring along the Rayong coastline.

The sediments that will be released have been tested to determine their polluting potential. It is concluded that the sediments are unpolluted and that the potential for uptake of dissolved oxygen or release of nutrients affecting biological productivity is negligible.

Maintenance dredging during operations will not have significant impacts on the marine environment.

Other sources of water pollution in the area at present are tapioca-processing plants and communities. These result in poor quality in streams flowing through the area (high BOD and low dissolved oxygen) but there is no evidence of their having adverse effects on coastal water quality. Monitoring of coastal waters and sediments indicate that the marine environment is largely unaffected by land-based sources of pollution.

Sources of water pollution include: run-off during construction and quarrying; sanitary wastewater during construction and operation, including shipboard wastes; and oily wastewater and tank washings.

The impacts from run-off, sanitary, and oily wastewater will not be significant in relation to other sources which will occur as the area develops, provided appropriate measures are taken to collect, treat, and dispose of wastewater.

Quarrying and transport of quarried materials also have the potential for water pollution by dust, but this is not expected to be significant at any of the proposed sites.

Construction of the port could affect dispersion of effluents from the proposed outfall from the National Fertilizer Corporation's plant on the industrial estate. This impact has been evaluated and the impact is not considered to be significant.

Adverse impacts: atmospheric

Sources of air emissions during construction will include: dust from traffic, site clearing, and construction activity; emissions from vehicles bringing materials to the site and from construction equipment; emissions from burning of waste materials; and dust from quarrying.

These emissions are expected to result in degradation of air quality, primarily in the working environment affecting construction employees. Dust and other emissions from on-site are unlikely to spread sufficiently to affect homes and other properties around the site.

Dust and emissions from vehicles carrying materials, particularly quarried rock and aggregate to and from the site, are expected to generate dust nuisance in communities along their routes. This will only be significant if the Khao Bandai Krit East site is selected as the routes from other sites do not pass close to communities.

Dust from quarrying itself will affect communities and farm fields in the immediate vicinity of sites. It will be significant at Khao Bandai Krit East and Khao Noen Krapok where it will affect cassava fields and orchards adjacent to the quarry sites. There are no houses within 500 m of any sites, except for worker housing at Khao Chi Chan. Dust will be generated within the quarry working areas and measures will need to be taken to protect workers.

The existing air quality at the site is high and there are no major sources of air emissions. Development of the industrial estate will inevitably change this situation. Emissions and resulting air quality resulting from ships using the port and other port activities have been predicted. Emissions from the port are unlikely to cause significant deterioration in air quality compared with NEB standards.

Dusty cargoes present risks to workers on site and to people and property from dust nuisance generated during handling and dust explosion hazards.

Handling tapioca is likely to be the greatest source of nuisance in surrounding communities, although there may be some visual impact, as is evidenced from tapioca-handling facilities elsewhere on the Inner Gulf.

Adverse impacts: noise and vibration

The noise environment at Map Ta Phut is typical of a quiet rural area. There are no significant sources of noise in the area at present. Sources of noise during construction and operation will include: construction equipment and activity; vehicles; cargo handling equipment; and ship and port PA systems and sirens.

The working environment will be subject to significant noise levels and measures will be required to ensure that Labour Department standards for occupational noise levels are met.

After development of the industrial estate, the numbers of people living close enough to the site to be affected by noise from port operations will be very small and this impact is not considered to be significant.

Adverse impacts: land and other resources

The coastal strip which will be affected by development of the port and the associated industrial estate is low lying. About 40 per cent of the area is used for farming – growing orchard fruits, coconut, cassava, and other crops. There are 5 houses and several groups of fisherman's huts along the shoreline. There is also a picnic area. Two houses and one group of fishing huts are actually within the area to be occupied by the port.

Outside the boundaries there are numerous shelters and huts, a private resort area, and 1.5 km to the east a small beach resort (Sai Thong) with a capacity of about 150 persons.

All properties and land uses within the site boundaries will be lost, but the impact of the port in isolation from that of the industrial estate will be compensated. Fishermen using the shoreline are mostly not land owners and will not therefore be entitled to compensation. Many of them have moved to the area within recent years to avoid overcrowding elsewhere.

Construction of the port will change patterns of littoral sediment drift causing build up to the west of the port and erosion to the east. This would have a significant impact on the beach at Sai Thong unless provisions can be made to replace the eroded material.

The port development will place only a small demand on water and power supplies and the transportation network compared with the industrial estate. Its impact is not therefore considered to be significant.

Black sand mining for extraction of tin has been carried out on a small scale along the foreshore at Map Ta Phut. Access to the resource will necessarily be foreclosed by port construction.

The value of these resources has never been estimated but the fact that no mining has been undertaken in recent years suggests that the resource is not of major commercial significance.

The potential impact on Sai Thong beach resort was noted above. The island of Ko Samet is also being developed for tourism. The port is unlikely to reduce the level of use of these facilities, it may in fact increase it; but it is likely to change the visitor population from non-local visitors to visitors associated with the port and industrial estate \workforce and supporting populations. The area is not considered to be of regional or national significance for tourism.

Adverse impacts: visual impacts

The port and industrial estate development will have a major impact on the immediate visual environment, replacing an undeveloped coastline with large industrial buildings, cranes, warehouses, and other structures.

The main impact will be on those people living adjacent to the site or using the island of Ko Samet for recreation. The horizon is close owing to the low-lying wooded terrain and the port is not expected to be visible from the resort buildings at Sai Thong but the eastern reclamation will be visible from the beach. Until such time as major structures are built on the eastern reclamation, the port is unlikely to be obtrusive from the beach. Ships entering and leaving the port may be considered as a positive attraction.

People using Ko Samet will have a clearer view of the commercial port area and the industrial estate. The impact will therefore be much greater.

Adverse impacts: solid waste disposal

Wastes will be generated during construction, by the construction workforce, by the permanent workforce, by cargo handling operations, and from ships discharging in port.

The daily waste generation during operation is estimated to be about 3 tonnes per day. Waste generation during construction and operation is unlikely to cause adverse environmental impacts provided appropriate measures are taken for collection, treatment, and disposal.

Adverse impacts: accidental

Accidents may be caused by incidents on-board ship, fire, explosion, occupational accidents, collision between vessels, and grounding, on the shore or on the gas pipeline to the west of the port.

These accidents may result in loss of life or injury, damage to property, and pollution by spills. The risk has been quantitatively assessed on the basis of presently available data; however, it is our view that the risks are such as to require strict control over shipping movements.

Risks from explosions caused by dusty materials are discussed above (Adverse impacts: atmospheric–page 320). Other risks to people and property may arise from handling of dangerous cargoes: vinyl chloride monomer, hydrocarbon gases, chlorinated hydrocarbons, caustic soda. Details of hazardous cargoes to be handled at the port are not available, but if such cargoes are to be transhipped, the appropriate preventive measures and emergency provisions should be established.

Adverse impacts: socio-economic and public health impact

Development of the port and industrial estate will have a very major impact on local socio-economic conditions, changing the area from a rural area with low population density and relatively low income, to an industrialized area with a large new population and opportunities for significant creation of wealth.

The impact of the port alone is unlikely to be significant in isolation from the complete development, as the port workforce will be 900–1,000 compared with an estimated total of over 15,000 for the industrial estate. This could lead to an induced population increase of as much as 70,000 by the time the estate is fully developed. A new town will be built to house the majority of this population and a separate EIS is being prepared for this development.

Two houses and a group of fishing huts lie within the port boundary and will be demolished in the early stage of construction. Several other properties lie within the industrial estate boundary. At present it seems that the affected families and fishermen are not aware of the proposed development and are making no plans to relocate.

The main employment sectors that will be affected by the port development are inshore fishing and tourism. The number of families relying on fishing for part or all of their income is believed to be about 20. 70 crab and shrimp nets are in operation in waters adjacent to the port and there are several squid fishing boats. Incomes of these families vary from season to season very substantially, but are generally low compared with industrial and agricultural workers.

It is expected that some fishermen will take up employment associated with the port; others will move elsewhere and provisions may have to be made to facilitate this to avoid family and social problems.

Employment in tourism, at the Sai Thong beach resort and Ko Saket, is expected to increase as a result of the port development. There will also be substantial increases in employment opportunities in sectors servicing the large new population.

It is likely that unless strict controls are exercised, illegal development will occur around the plot boundary, with consequent problems of water supply sanitation, public health, waste disposal, and unsightly development.

Public health impacts may include an increase in communicable disease incidence caused by the influx of workers and foreign sailors and disposal of shipboard waste; an increase in disease through poor sanitation in camps, new housing areas, and squatter settlements; and stress on available medical facilities caused by a large increase in population.

Measures for offsetting adverse effects

Aquatic impacts

The following mitigation measures have been proposed for dredging and reclamation. Construction of the western breakwater and silt basin should be a priority to minimize sediment release from the reclamation. Reclamation of the eastern area should be as far as practicable, awaiting construction of the eastern revetment, to minimize impacts on the Sai Thong beach resort. The eastern reclamation should be drained into the port, not outside the eastern revetment, to minimize impacts at Sai Thong. Best practicable technology and operating methods should be used to minimize sediment release from dredging and barge loading. All operations should be properly supervised and a regular programme of equipment maintenance carried out. Overspill from loading barges should be kept to a minimum, consistent with achieving an economically viable load, while loading barges should be regularly checked and maintained to prevent leakage from bottom seals. Spoil should be dumped only within specified boundaries and a pattern of dumping should be adopted to minimize repeated dumping in exactly the same spot. These same general conditions should also apply to maintenance dredging where relevant. It is not considered that further physical measures to control fine sediment release are necessary.

The following monitoring measures are proposed. Bottom conditions should be inspected and recorded by divers at intervals before and during construction and operation and if possible a photographic record kept. Turbidity in waters at Sai Thong should be measured at monthly intervals over the construction period to monitor aesthetic and water quality impact on recreation. Dissolved oxygen, ammoniacal nitrogen, and other nutrients should be measured at intervals during construction to determine whether water quality changes have occurred as a result of dredging. Records should be kept of any evidence of algal blooms and of the conditions under which they have occurred. If it can be arranged, a serial photographic record of sediment plumes around dredgers, barges, reclamation drains, and dumping sites should be made, principally for reference in assessment of similar developments in the future.

Mitigation measures for other impacts on water quality. Temporary bunds should be constructed to contain surface run-off from the land sites. Collected run-off should be passed through retention ponds to collect suspended solids, before discharge. A treatment system should be provided at the construction camp. This should be either a package plant or septic tank. Consideration should be given to two possible alternatives for treatment of sanitary wastewater during port operations: either an anaerobic pond followed by facultative and polishing ponds discharging to a near-shore outfall; or an anaerobic pond discharging to an offshore outfall. A conventional activated sludge sewage treatment plant is not considered to be appropriate for port operations owing to fluctuations in the volume and quality of loads. Sanitary effluents should not be discharged into the harbour itself. There may be some merit in providing a combined outfall with NFC, provided construction can be scheduled appropriately for both developments and operational arrangements organized. All sanitary provisions should be in accordance with the Memorandum on Guidelines for Incorporating Sanitation Parameters into Planning Design of Ports and Harbours in Developing Countries including Thailand. Oily wastewater (from fuel storage tanks, maintenance shops, ship bilgewaters, tank washings) and run-off from dirty areas of the port (vehicle marshalling, parking, and fuel storage areas) should all be collected and passed to an oil–water separator before discharge. Oily run-off may be returned to the stormwater system after treatment. Reception facilities for oily wastes from ships should be provided and their use enforced by monitoring and penalties for oily discharges in or approaching the port.

Regular monitoring of water quality should be carried out within the port and in adjacent waters during operation, to identify adverse environmental changes.

Atmospheric impacts

Mitigation for general emissions. Good housekeeping practices should be adopted to control dust from construction operations, quarrying, and transport of quarried materials. These may include periodic water spraying dusty areas and shielding of dusty areas, maintenance of road surfaces, ventilation of enclosed areas, cleaning of equipment and vehicles as well as adoption of proper operating methods. Unpaved access roads which may lead to dust problems in communities should be paved. Burning of waste materials should be avoided.

Occasional monitoring of air quality should be carried out by the appropriate government agencies in Map Ta Phut village, Sai Thong, and the new town, and in the working environment of the port.

General housekeeping measures to control dust emissions as described above, should be adopted when handling dusty cargoes. Recommendations on handling dusty cargoes to minimize dust nuisance in the occupational and external environment and to reduce the risk of explosion, should be adopted, and laid down by the Port Authority as conditions for private operators. Occasional monitoring should be carried out by the Port Authority to determine dust levels in the occupational environment within the port.

Noise

Noise specifications for construction equipment should be laid down in contracts for construction work in accordance with Labour Department standards for the occupational environment.

Occasional measurements of sound levels in the occupational and external environment should be made to monitor noise. Records of complaints should be kept.

Land and other resources

Mitigation measures. Compensation will be provided for land owners as required by existing schemes. Several fishermen who have no legal status will be displaced and consideration may be given to giving them financial and other assistance in finding alternative employment or alternative locations at which to keep their boats and equipment. Strict boundary regulations should be enforced to prevent overspill of activities beyond the port and industrial estate and to prevent illegal squatter settlement. The boundary should be securely fenced and regularly inspected. A programme of excavation of sand accumulated on the west side of the port and transported to the Sai Thong beach should be adopted, to mitigate the adverse effects of erosion at Sai Thong and provide an improved beach resource.

It would be useful to monitor use of the Sai Thong beach resort, if the owners agreement can be obtained, to provide information on the implications of this type of development for coastal recreation.

No special provisions are considered to be necessary with regard to power, water and other resources.

Visual impacts

Special measures to mitigate visual impacts at Map Ta Phut are not considered to be necessary. However, normal standards of good design and maintenance should be adopted to avoid visual clutter caused by port structures and equipment.

Solid waste management

Contractors should be required to make proper arrangements for disposal of wastes arising during the construction period. Dumping on the foreshore or in the sea and burning of waste should not be permitted. Dumping of wastes from ships approaching the port or into the harbour should be prohibited by harbour regulations. Provisions should be made for reception of shipboard wastes and for their safe disposal if any risk is presented to public health. Arrangements should be made with the Municipality for collection and proper disposal of solid wastes. Charges may be levied on private operators and ships generating waste for disposal.

Accidental impacts

Port approaches and operations should be regulated in accordance with international navigational standards regarding pilotage, anchorage, ship movements, etc. A prohibited anchorage should be defined within 1 km of the gas pipeline and established by international agreement. Local regulations should be issued prohibiting passage of deep draft vessels in the vicinity of the gas pipeline in waters less than 15 m deep. Handling of hazardous cargoes should be subject to approval by the Port Authority. When application for such approval is made, information should be required to enable an evaluation of the risk and the adequacy of the preventive and emergency provisions to be made. International standards on handling of dangerous cargoes should be adopted. A first aid unit, properly equipped, staffed, and trained, should be established by the Port Authority. An emergency response system should be developed in cooperation with local fire, police, and medical services, and regular exercises should be carried out to test preparedness. Port workers should be regularly informed and trained in safe working methods and emergency procedures.

Socio-economic and public health impacts

A programme of actively informing residents of the port area about the proposed development should be undertaken as soon as the decision to proceed has been taken. This will enable the population to make plans in reasonable time for relocation, new employment, schooling, etc. An orderly relocation of population would be in the interests of preventing illegal settlement. Some residents may benefit from assistance (financial or other) in relocation where they are not entitled to compensation.

To minimize public health impacts: arrangements for quarantine of vessels should be made in accordance with international practice; temporary and permanent workers should receive medical examinations and necessary treatment before starting work; facilities for first aid should be provided at the construction site and camp, and in the port; and proper sanitation should be provided during construction and operation to minimize the spread of disease.

General recommendations

Necessary conditions to achieve mitigation of impacts during construction should be stipulated in contracts for construction work and site policing: inspection should be carried out. Where activities not under the direct control of the Port Authority are to be carried out (e.g., transfer of hazardous materials from tank storage to the industrial estate), all operating methods and equipment should be subject to evaluation and approval by the Port Authority. An environmental control division (or officer) should be appointed for Map Ta Phut Port. The duties of this division should include: evaluation and approval of activities occurring in the port not under the direct control of the Port Authority; maintenance of the water supply and wastewater treatment system; collection and disposal of wastes from ships and onshore; monitoring and enforcing pollution prevention regulations affecting vessels; and carrying out regular monitoring to identify adverse environmental changes caused by pollution. The model proposed by Poston may be used as a guideline for establishing the environmental control division.

Harbour regulations should be drafted to control: discharge of liquid or solid wastes from ships approaching or moored in the port; use of reception facilities for sanitary wastewater, oily wastes, and solid wastes from ships; conditions of operation for handling dusty cargoes to minimize nuisance in the occupational and external environment and the risk of explosions; piloting, anchorage, ship movements, cargo handling; information to be provided by vessels approaching the port; conditions of approval for handling hazardous cargoes to minimize risks of fire, explosion, toxic release, or other hazard.

Environmental monitoring

The required monitoring programme for each impact has already been described, along with the mitigation measures for the convenience of a continuity of the explanation.

Concluding remarks

The EIS report is prepared in fulfilment of the requirements for preparation of an EIA of the Map Ta Phut Port Project. This study addresses the environmental impacts of the port alone; however, the overall development of the area comprises an industrial estate, an urban area, and associated infrastructure and services as well as the port.

The EIS report lacks a number of items found in formal presentation, such as the environmental base map, beneficial impacts from the project, the professionals or EIA team involved in the study, etc. Without these, the EIS really looks a bit handicapped and poses problems to the researchers. The organization of the report is not sequential and looks poor. But the analytical work is envisaged to depth, and thus the technical work is appreciable. This is one of the very few EIA case studies regarding the port development done in the region.

REFERENCES

1 *Manual of NEB Guidelines for Preparation of Environmental Impact Evaluations*, National Environment Board (NEB), Bangkok, April 1979.
2 R. J. Hofer, Water Quality Management Plan for the Raoyong Map Ta Phut Development Planning Areas, Office of National Environment Board.
3 JICA, The Study on the Development of the Industrial Port on the Eastern Seaboard in the Kingdom of Thailand, Final Report, 1983.
  Source: Strengthening Environmental Cooperation with Developing Countries, pp. 100–128.

Case study 10.6 EIA at Work: A Hydroelectric Project in Indonesia

Philip Paridine, Canadian International Development Agency

The proposed Lake Sentani hydroelectric development is located in the province of Irian Jaya in the extreme northeast of Indonesia. The site is near Jayapura, some 20 km from the border with Papua New Guinea. Sentani is a natural lake with an outflow through the Jafuri River eventually reaching the Pacific Ocean. By closing off the Jafuri outlet and diverting the flow through a series of channels and tunnels to Yautefa Bay, it is possible to generate hydroelectricity.

The main environmental features of the project are therefore a reduction of the Jafuri flow, manipulation of the lake water levels, input of extra fresh water into the marine system of Yautefa Bay, and terrain disturbances along the flow diversion corridor.

Sentani Lake is surrounded by 22 small villages whose residents live a traditional lifestyle. In the Yautefa Bay area fishing is practised while the diversion corridor is currently designated for high intensity development. The Sentani culture is very old and is traditionally orientated towards the lake with houses constructed on stilts in the water. This factor became a key aspect of the impact assessment.

When the Canadian-based consultant firm Acres International became involved in the Sentani Lake project in 1982, several studies had already been completed. In 1977 Tata consultants did a feasibility study which developed the flows through channels. The Tata study proposed a 10 MW plant and would have raised the lake level by 2 m, requiring relocation of the Sentani people. Subsequently, a 1975 feasibility study was performed by NEDESCO and SMEC. That consortium, also funded by the Asian Development Bank, examined the Sentani proposal and redefined it to increase the installed capacity. As in the previous study, no environmental assessment was included in the terms of reference.

Form of the assessment

In 1982 when the Canadian International Development Agency (CIDA) became involved in the project, Acres was asked to re-examine the situation. A proposal for a feasibility study and environmental reconnaissance was funded and work subsequently progressed to the design phase, during which a full EIA was conducted. An interdisciplinary environmental team worked with the designers to develop alternative scheme and integrate mitigation measures directly into the project proposal. The local population was directly consulted and the lifestyle of the lake-dwellers will continue to be possible after project development. The proposal submitted to decision makers involved a 12 MW project and decisions are now pending on construction.

Content of the assessment

There has been a growing awareness of the necessity to increase energy in this part of Indonesia. National policy is to promote development of some of the less populated areas of the country, thus creating the need for energy to supply the projected growth. The projected population increase and associated industrial activity within the Japurá region over the next four years requires an increase in the generation capacity of the existing electrical system. The most economically attractive alternative involves use of the outflows from Lake Sentani as a potential hydroelectric supply. This would substitute for expensive diesel-generated electricity and permit supply to the provincial capital and surrounding region.

Scoping of studies of the existing environment

The environmental reconnaissance level study involved the fielding of a team which was on-site for six to eight weeks. The team consisted of a civil engineer, a hydrologist, a scientist, an economist, and an energy systems planner. The team operated interdependently through daily meetings. Based on an understanding of hydroelectric projects in general, and a limited database from previous studies, a generic list of impacts was established. The reconnaissance was intended to verify the database and scope issues for further studies.

The team's first priority was to establish contacts with local government, residents, the university, and anyone else who could provide baseline information and help identify the issues of importance for the local population.

During the environmental reconnaissance, the project concept became very important as it was obvious that the original 2 m water level increase would entail major impacts. The effect of alternative lake operating levels was determined as a critical area for further study and subsequent environmental information gathering was scoped accordingly.

Food availability for the Sentani people is directly related to the lake levels. Not only is the lake used for fishing, but the nearby marshes are harvested for sago. In addition, the shoreline behind the houses is used for the planting of vegetable gardens, so that lowering of lake levels during the farming season would be beneficial.

Farming was also potentially affected along the proposed corridor where rice and vegetable plots could be subject to disturbance by the construction of channels. Another aspect of the food availability issue concerned the tribes along Yautefa Bay, where traditional fishing lifestyles are followed. Possible disturbance by the sudden overflow of lake water into the marine environment was of concern.

An anticipated issue concerning lake water levels that was identified during the reconnaissance phase was that of public health. As the Sentani people use the lake as a latrine, too low a water level could spread disease, while too high a level would contaminate the shore.

Along the corridor, local planning objectives had to be considered.

Ridges and swamps alternate continuously along the route. Areas that are dry and suitable for housing are limited, and estrangement of prime potential housing lots was to be avoided. Lack of land registration was of concern and projected urban growth had to be taken into consideration. National planning objectives were also of importance, since a proposed transmigration area exists south of Sentani Lake and along the Jafuri. The impacts this project would have on the water supplies and land uses for the transmigrants had to be considered.

On the basis of issues identified in the field, a scope of work was prepared for the environmental assessment and alternatives proposed for operational lake levels.

Study of alternatives

During the preparation of the environmental assessment, local people were extremely important in providing site-specific information. Although the team spent four months working on the Sentani Lake, statistically significant information could not be collected in such a short time. Where necessary, the collective memory of the Sentani people was used in lieu. Information on historical lake levels, resource utilization, and fishery in particular, was gained from the local population. Cultural information was an integral part of the data collection.

The major alternative examined during the environmental assessment was the lake level rate curve, which is the constraint governing manipulation of the water level during operation. A computer model of Sentani Lake was prepared to try various operating scenarios. The lowest constraint was dictated by sanitation levels while inundation of floorboards was the upper constraint.

For fishing, it is preferable to raise the lake level during the spring to allow the fish to spawn in their natural areas, with the water being kept high long enough for the fry to hatch and move down into the lake (thereafter drawing the lake down as fast as possible to allow people to plant their gardens).

Often a computer model is used to optimize the energy production without integrating environmental impacts. However, in this case, it was possible to achieve the same amount of energy while staying within all the environmental parameters.

As for the corridor alignment, values were placed on all of the relevant structures, so that every time a change was made, it was possible to recalculate how many houses, people, or hectares of crops would be impacted. Through land-use planning, it was possible to avoid cemeteries or schools and avoid cutting transportation paths. Hence, the corridor alignment was, in the end, quite different from that which had originally been proposed. In fact, the corridor was actually diverted considerably, to avoid land that was slated for future housing. It was also essential for the design to include safety considerations with regard to the canals.

As described above, real alternatives were considered in project design using information obtained during the environmental assessment. This resulted in some improvements being predicted for the project area including: improved fishing areas on Lake Sentani for people of Yoka near the approach channel; more recreation areas or islands in the lake from generally lower lake levels throughout the year; improved sago stands and access to swamps around Lake Sentani from generally drier conditions resulting from lower lake levels; and improved conditions in Yautefa Bay for milkfish and other estuarine species.

Environmental impacts

Despite these improvements, a number of anticipated impacts remained. Potential mitigation measures and proposed compensation were therefore summarized in the environmental assessment as follows. Construction of the hydro corridor and powerhouse will affect between 448 and 593 people, 67 to 97 structures, 30 to 45 ha of land (purchased or leased), and 25 to 145 ha of crops, depending upon the alternative chosen. The village of Puay will be the most seriously affected community on Lake Sentani as a result of weir construction on the Jafuri River. Fish resources of the upper Jafuri River will be lost and a decline in fish catches on Lake Sentani near Puay is likely. The latter is expected due to anticipated water quality degradation in this end of the lake when the natural outflow to the Jafuri River is blocked by the weir. The drying up of the upper reaches of the Jafuri River will also adversely affect Puay's accessibility to agricultural lands and wildlife (and, hence, hunting) along the river. The people of Lake Sentani will be inconvenienced by having to adapt their fish cages to a greater annual range in lake-level fluctuations. The people dependent on Yautefa Bay fisheries are likely to be adversely affected in the short term by a reduction in fish harvests until marine resources in the bay adapt to an estuarine environment. The virtual termination of lake flows to the Jafuri River will reduce mean annual flows in the Sunggrum River, although these are estimated still to be adequate for irrigation requirements currently forecast.

Mitigation measures

A number of proposals for mitigation were presented to alleviate impacts. The people currently occupying or owning lands along the hydro corridor and at the Jafuri River weir site should be compensated for buildings, lands, and crops lost or damaged as a result of the project. The people of Puay and Sekanto should receive sufficient compensation to enable them to continue their lifestyle with adequate fish resources and without the need to relocate their village. Families with fish cages around Lake Sentani prior to operation of the hydro project should be provided with screening materials to eliminate potential problems associated with a greater annual range in lake-level fluctuations. Families who regularly fish Yautefa Bay as their primary resource base should be provided with additional gill nets to off-set a possible reduction in fish harvests following construction and operation of the hydro project. Footbridges with railings across the tailrace channels in the vicinity of the fishponds and at the tailrace outlet to Yautefa Bay should be constructed to allow people continued access to both sides of the channel in these areas. Efforts should be made to restore the environment as far as possible following completion of the project, through grading, contouring, and planting.

Results of the assessment

While the project has not yet been completed, the substantial changes in design without power loss already indicate the value of the environmental assessment. Detailed actions have also been suggested for appropriate government agencies to take before construction of the project. Ensure no further development occurs on the corridor easement, including a 30 m buffer zone on either side. Provide careful inspection when staking out the easement in detail as discrepancies between technical drawings and site conditions can easily occur. Organize preparation of compensation payments for building, land, and crops, and ensure consistent and equitable treatment of individuals (including compensation for lands temporarily disrupted during construction). Planning for relocation of people and structures should begin well ahead of construction, and the affected populace should be included in the process. A reasonable schedule for relocation should be determined, and the people affected should be notified well in advance. Keep local residents well informed of project activities so they may adjust their own activities accordingly. Appoint a responsible individual to manage compensation awards for the people living around Lake Sentani, the Jafuri River, and Yautefa Bay who are expected to be impacted by the disruption to fishery resources.

During construction, it is important that a safety and environmental inspector be employed as part of the construction management contract to ensure that all necessary safety precautions are in place and that environmental recommendations contained in this report pertaining to construction activities are followed. This should include supervision of daily reporting of fish catches in the villages of Puay and Sekanto and in villages around Yautefa Bay, since these data are vital to any subsequent monitoring programme following project implementation.

Monitoring following construction

Approximately three months following project operation, a survey of Puay, Sekanto, and Yautefa Bay fisheries should be undertaken to determine impacts and assess whether further mitigation is warranted. This should be undertaken by the safety and environmental inspector. Approximately one to two years following commencement of hydro operations, it is strongly recommended that a comprehensive environmental evaluation be carried out to compare post-project conditions with impact predictions. The need for further mitigation based on the above assessment should be documented as part of the monitoring programme. Further environmental monitoring is recommended five years after hydro operation using a similar programme to that outlined above.

Constraints

While some government authorities in Jakarta were initially skeptical about the environmental assessment, attitudes changed as the results started to be known. It became evident that the project design and operation could change without affecting the cost-benefit ratio of the project. Government agencies, locally and in Jayapura, provided the study group with information requested, although constraints on horizontal coordination limited the ability of the team to discuss the project with various ministries.

Unfortunately, the university and environmental studies centre could not provide the group with technically skilled personnel. Although keen to assist in any way, the resources were not available to offer. Ultimately, however, a useful baseline study was completed. Fortunately, local people were always willing to give information about their lives and priorities and this compensated somewhat for the lack of technical knowledge.

One specific constraint was a requirement that local people not be told about the proposed hydroelectric project. Therefore, questions had to be formulated in an odd manner, which tended to make them suspicious.

To sum up, the Sentani project demonstrates the value of incorporating environmental factors early in the planning process, such as during reconnaissance. Because of this, key decisions were made early to allow changes to the project before designs were set. The value of scoping a list of issues to consider was also demonstrated. It allowed focusing on the right questions and eliminated costly and delaying studies.

Integration of the environmental team with the overall project team allowed a major impact, potentially involving the relocation of 60,000 people, to be avoided. It also permitted optimization of resource utilization in the proposed project operations.

Because of effective communication with local people, the study was able to obtain information that was not available as published baseline data. This made a critical difference to project design. The involvement and cooperation of local agencies was also essential.

Finally, the importance of monitoring must be emphasized. It is impossible to quantify everything, especially with so little reference material on which to base some key predictions. Thus monitoring is absolutely necessary to make sure that the study and design are correctly verified and implemented, and that the mitigation measures that were proposed actually work.

Case study 10.7 The Greater Cairo Wastewater Project

Mohamed Talaat Abu-Saada, Cairo Wastewater Organization, Egypt, and Stephen F. Lintner, US Agency for International Development

Note: This is an example of a case study where environmental aspects have not been costed.

The Greater Cairo Wastewater Project, undertaken jointly by the Arab Republic of Egypt and the United States, is an excellent example of how environmental assessments can be used to assist host countries and donor organizations in the evaluation of phased implementation strategies for major projects, the selection of technology, the evaluation of operation and maintenance issues, and in the identification of complementary projects to assure sustainable performance of the project. This experience can be helpful when preparing environmental assessments for other projects in developing countries.

In 1976, the Arab Republic of Egypt embarked on a massive undertaking to improve the wastewater collection, treatment, and disposal systems for the capital city of Cairo. The objectives of the project were to improve wastewater collection, conveyance, treatment, and disposal in the metropolitan region. The implementation of this undertaking has been assigned to the Cairo Wastewater Organization (CWO), while the operation of the system is the responsibility of the Cairo General Organization for Sewerage and Sanitary Drainage (CGOSD). The project involves not only extensive rehabilitation of existing facilities, relief pump stations and force mains, but new construction as well, including major wastewater treatment plants and disposal systems. Additional project activities will provide extensive support for institutional development and training programmes. In addition, the Ministry of Health will conduct water quality monitoring on a regular basis.

The city is geographically divided into two banks, East and West, by the River Nile. The East Bank, the oldest portion of the city, has an extensive wastewater system dating back to 1906. The West Bank wastewater system, which was constructed in the 1930s, is not as extensive, and as a result, the West Bank has a higher proportion of its population living in unsewered areas.

During the planning stages for the Greater Cairo Wastewater Project, consideration was given to these various structural differences and the varying needs of the areas. As a result, East Bank improvements focus on the construction of a major conveyance system, to carry existing and future wastewater to a new treatment plant at Gabel el Asfar. Construction activities for the West Bank are more extensive. They include the expansion of basic collection and conveyance facilities in the extensively unsewered areas, rehabilitation and expansion of the Zenein wastewater treatment plant, and the construction of a greatly expanded wastewater treatment plant at Abu Rawash.

The need for the project

Cairo, like many capital cities in the developing world, has been faced with the problem of supplying wastewater services to a population which is growing as the result of both rapid natural population growth and high rates of rural–urban migration. The 1985 population of the metropolitan region was estimated at approximately 8 million and is projected to reach approximately 13.6 million by the year 2000. In serving a population that is increasing at a rapid rate, the Cairo wastewater system, which was originally designed for a population of less than 1 million, had become seriously overloaded and deteriorating to a point where unsanitary conditions were developing throughout much of the city. Inadequate investment in maintenance, especially for pump stations and sewers, further reduced the efficiency of the system. In addition, many areas around Cairo have never been sewered, even though many had been supplied with piped water.

Presently, about 66 per cent of the population is served by the existing sewerage system and 34 percent reside in unsewered areas. The reliability of collection in the sewered areas is reduced due to the general overloading of the system and inadequate pumping capacity. In the unsewered areas, populations rely on a combination of public and private services for the collection of wastewater from vaults below or adjacent to houses. These devices frequently overflow or become inoperable, resulting in the large-scale flooding, ponding, and pollution of entire neighbourhoods. The high cost of commercial collection of wastewater in the predominantly lower income unsewered areas, discourages all but the most essential use of the sewage disposal pits in these areas and promotes a variety of improper disposal practices. Because of these conditions, studies have shown that the rate of illness is higher in the unsewered urban areas of Cairo than in most rural areas in Egypt.

Approximately one half of the sewage collected receives partial wastewater treatment prior to disposal. The remainder, including that collected from unsewered areas, is disposed directly into open drains originally constructed for agricultural purposes which have become an element of the urban wastewater infrastructure. These drains eventually discharge into the Nile delta resulting in local degradation of water quality. Wastewater from industry and thermal power generation is not a significant problem in Cairo due to the concentration of these facilities to the north and south of the city outside the service area of the system.

The negative impact of this situation on environmental health and water quality is recognized by the Government of Egypt, which has given top priority among infrastructure investments to the Greater Cairo Wastewater Project. The project has broad recognition of the need to make improvements in the system. This attitude has been important as there has been considerable local disruption of traffic and business during the implementation of the project.

Donor support

The Government of the United States acting through the United States Agency for International Development (USAID) and the Government of the United Kingdom acting through the Overseas Development Administration (ODA) have provided capital and technical support for this project, as well as private British banks. Assistance is also being provided by the Federal Republic of Germany and Japan. Local currency costs are being provided in part by the Government of Egypt. A major element of technical assistance has been supported for the design of both the rehabilitation and new construction phases of the project by a jointly financed British–American engineering consortium named AMBRIC. AMBRIC works in collaboration with a consortium of Egyptian firms.

The total project cost is expected to be more than $3 billion. Supplemental studies, including environmental assessment, tariff studies, unsewered area studies, environmental health review, etc., cost $1.5 million and were funded by USAID.

Rehabilitation phase

The existing wastewater system includes over 400 km of common sewers, 82 pneumatic ejector stations, 95 conventional pumping stations, and approximately 120 km of major collectors, in addition to five wastewater treatment plants. Due to excessive deterioration of the system, a multifaceted rehabilitation programme was implemented between 1980 and 1986.

The work supported under the rehabilitation phase of the project consisted of major and minor repairs, structural and equipment modifications, debris and grit removal, and general cleanup of the system. Work was conducted on five major system elements: collectors and sewers, ejectors and ejector stations, pumps and pump stations, force mains, and treatment plants. This phase provided for a substantial improvement in the performance of the existing system.

The rehabilitation phase not only reduced the problems associated with the wastewater system, that is, flooding and ponding of sewerage, but it also provided a foundation for developing most of the detailed plans and construction specifications for expanding and improving the system to serve the population of Greater Cairo.

New construction phase

On the East Bank, a major conveyance system is planned which will carry wastewater from the existing sewer collection system to a major tunnel pumping station at America, which will have installed a centrifugal pump. From America, a new 15 km culvert conveyance system will transport wastewater northward to two plants, a new locally designed treatment plant at Shoubra el Kheima and a major new activated sludge treatment plant at Gabal el Asfar. The Gabal el Asfar wastewater treatment plant will be a non-nitrifying activated sludge plant with thickening and drying facilities.

Construction activities on the West Bank have been designed to improve and expand the wastewater system and to assure its proper management. To meet these design criteria, construction will include deep collectors to allow the elimination of 12 existing pumping stations, steep gradients to assure an adequate scouring velocity where incursion of sand is a problem, and simple archimedean screw-type pumps for major pump stations. With regard to the expandability of the system, primary collectors will have the capacity not only for current volume, but for extension of services to present unsewered areas and to adjacent developing areas.

Besides providing sewerage services to unsewered areas, additional activities focus on construction of a new treatment plant at Abu Rawash. The plant is a non-nitrifying activated sludge design and is expected to treat flows reaching 400,000 m^3 per day. The design minimizes both energy cost and maintenance. Based on the examination of the system, the Zenein plant was the only treatment plant considered suitable for retention in the system. The plant will undergo extensive modifications during this phase, which will result in an operational capacity of 300,000 m^3 per day.

Operational assistance and training

In order to assure the reliable performance of the Cairo wastewater system, the Government of Egypt and USAID have started implementation of a series of institutional development and training programmes in operation and maintenance. The programme has focused on the development of improved institutional capabilities in administration, planning, and financial management. Extensive support has been provided for the "training of trainers" in a wide variety of professional, administrative, and technical skill areas. Special attention has been given to critical problems such as the management of grit accumulations in the sewers, sewer cleaning, pump station operation, and wastewater treatment plant operations.

The West Bank environment assessment

USAID is required by United States law (22 CFR 216 "USAID Environmental Procedures") to prepare environmental assessments for all projects which are anticipated to have a potentially significant impact on the environment. All major water and wastewater projects are specifically required under this legislation to have an environmental assessment prepared to ensure that they are planned, designed, and implemented in an environmentally sound manner. The Arab Republic of Egypt, although not specifically requiring the preparation of environmental assessments, requires that proposed projects be reviewed for compliance with a variety of laws and regulations concerning the environment.

Under USAID regulations, an environmental assessment is defined as a detailed study of the reasonably foreseeable significant effects, both beneficial and adverse, of a proposed action on the environment. The objective of an environmental assessment is to identify potential environmental consequences of a proposed project to ensure that the responsible decision makers in both the host country and USAID make an environmentally informed decision when reviewing and approving a proposed project and implementation plan. Included in the assessment is a detailed evaluation of alternatives to the proposed project and the identification of mitigation actions which might be adopted to eliminate or reduce unavoidable negative environmental impacts.

It should be understood that under the USAID approach, environmental assessments do not recommend a specific course of action, nor do they determine whether a project should or should not be undertaken. These decisions are reserved for resolution by USAID and host government personnel during the process of project design, review, approval, and implementation. This is important, as it makes the assessment a "dynamic" tool to ensure environmental soundness, rather than a "completed" document prepared to assure compliance with a regulatory requirement. The value of an environmental assessment in the USAID system is that it provides information concerning key environmental issues, an analysis of alternatives and reviews potential mitigation actions. This information is then evaluated with other detailed analyses relating to engineering, economics, management, training, and financing to provide an effective and environmentally sound project design and implementation plan.

An agreement was reached early in the design of the Greater Cairo Wastewater Project that the Government of the United States would provide assistance for capital construction on the West Bank of the Nile and the Government of the United Kingdom would provide assistance for capital construction on the East Bank of the Nile. Initially, it was anticipated that the AMBRIC model used for design of the system could be extended to joint USAID–ODA preparation of a detailed environmental assessment. However, for a number of reasons this did not prove possible and USAID proceeded to fund the preparation of a detailed environmental assessment for the proposed West Bank construction programme.

Preparation of the environmental assessment

CWO and USAID recognized the need for the preparation of a detailed environmental assessment from the earliest stages of project development. An element of the initial design studies prepared by the AMBRIC Consortium included a preliminary environmental review of the project. The Washington-based Environmental Coordinator of the Bureau for Asia and Near East of AID made preliminary site visits to the project area and held discussions with representatives of CWO during April 1979 to review the proposed new construction programme on both the East and West Banks of the Nile. The scope of work for the environmental assessment was prepared by the environmental coordinator with the assistance of CWO during visits to Egypt during November 1980 and March 1981. The environmental coordinator returned to Egypt to supervise the initial phases of field data collection with representatives of the consulting firm retained to prepare the assessment and in October 1981 to participate in the CWO sponsored "scoping session". The planning visits to Egypt allowed for the advance collection of a variety of data and for coordination with the AMBRIC and Egyptian consortiums.

The environmental assessment was prepared for the General Organization for Sewerage and Sanitary Drainage and the Organization for Execution of the Greater Cairo Wastewater Project CWO by American and Egyptian consultants. The total cost for preparation of the assessment was approximately $270,000, which was grant-financed by USAID. It was prepared over a 12-month period which included significant periods for the review of draft versions of the document.

The study was prepared by a 12-person interdisciplinary team of experts from the United States and Egypt which included specialists in agricultural engineering, agronomy, economic analysis of capital projects, economic analysis of natural resources issues, environmental engineering, Egyptian law, industrial pollution control, public health, soil science, social science, and wastewater systems operations and maintenance. The assessment was prepared in two volumes: an executive summary (in Arabic and English) and a main report (in English with an Arabic summary and table of contents).

Preparation of the environmental assessment for the Greater Cairo Wastewater Project included the conduct of the first environmental "scoping session" held in Egypt. A requirement under USAID environmental regulations, a "scoping session" is a meeting of knowledgeable and potentially affected parties to review the proposed scope of work of the environmental assessment and to provide advice concerning the preparation of the study.

The session for the project was hosted and chaired by CWO and had 31 participants. These included representatives of Ain Shams University, AMBRIC, Ministry of Agriculture, CWO, General Organization for Physical Planning, Ministry of Health, Ministry of Irrigation, National Committee on Environment, University of Alexandria, and USAID. The preparation of the assessments benefited significantly from this session which allowed for the improved targeting of field efforts, identification of key sources of data, and the establishment of high level contacts with senior representatives of major governmental and technical organizations.

Major issues reviewed in the environmental assessment

The environmental assessment focused on the review of the current environmental conditions in the greater project area, an analysis of the causes of these problems, an analysis of alternative wastewater management plans, a review of wastewater collection and conveyance alternatives and their environmental impacts, and a review of wastewater treatment and disposal alternatives and the environmental aspects of the following issues: alternatives for the sequence of facilities construction; alternatives for wastewater treatment; and alternatives for effluent disposal.

Each of the alternatives was reviewed with regard to its cost, its reliability under local conditions, the associated environmental health benefits, and its institutional requirements, and social acceptability in the Egyptian context. The assessment emphasized the evaluation of alternatives with regard to both the impact of new facilities as elements of a well conceived and well run system, but also those impacts which could result if portions of the system do not function as intended. It also analysed constraints to efficient operations such as inadequate tariffs, non-enforcement of sewer use ordinances, and inadequate resources for spare parts.

The project design of the Government of Egypt and USAID made extensive use of the environmental assessment in the development of a strategy for phased investment. Based on the assessment, first priority was given to collection and conveyance investments, with second priority given to treatment disposal investments. The environmental assessment was also used to justify the need to identify and obligate significant additional funding by both governments to assure successful implementation of the complete project.

It was recognized that the emphasis on collection and conveyance would provide for rapid and significant improvements in environmental health for large numbers of residents in areas which were either unsewered or subject to routine flooding due to inadequate conveyance. However, it was understood that this decision would continue on an interim basis, the long standing practice of discharging untreated wastewater to agricultural drains.

It should be noted that the analysis included in the environmental assessment showed that while this would temporarily result in a minor negative incremental impact to water quality, the benefits obtained from construction of permanent facilities for the removal of untreated wastewater from densely populated areas justified this decision. In addition, the risk associated with this investment strategy was limited due to the small amounts and restricted range of industrial pollutants discharged into the West Bank collection system.

Lessons learned about environmental assessments

Timing is all important

The experience of the Greater Cairo Wastewater Project demonstrates that environmental assessments for major capital development projects can be prepared in a cost-effective and timely manner when they are prepared at an appropriate point in the course of project development. CWO and USAID believe that the funds spent to prepare the environmental assessment represent an effective expenditure of $270,000 to support the approximately $1.4 billion of new construction for the West Bank section of the Greater Cairo Wastewater Project.

USAID experience is that environmental assessments of major capital projects are best done following the preparation of the preliminary feasibility study, which allows for a clear identification of the proposed project and alternatives. The environmental assessment, to be an effective tool in decision making, should be available for concurrent review with the feasibility study. USAID does not recommend that any project be authorized to go to final engineering design and/or construction prior to the preparation, review, and clearance of a detailed environmental assessment.

The costs of environmental assessments can be minimized if selected data collection needs are identified early and are included in the basic data collection programme for the engineering feasibility study. Savings can also be achieved by requiring the engineering consultant to allow the environmental assessment team to use base maps, system plans, technical data, and cartographic drafting bases.

EIA should be an on-going review process

The experience of the Greater Cairo Wastewater Project illustrates that the initial environmental assessment is only one element of a continuous environmental review process which should be used by host countries and donors in the planning, design, implementation, and operation of a major capital development project.

It should be noted that the Greater Cairo Wastewater Project was actually subject to a series of field-based environmental reviews by USAID environmental personnel: (a) prior to the preparation of the detailed environmental assessment, (b) during the technical review of final engineering designs for selected elements of the project, and (c) through periodic field reviews.

Most important in assuring sound project implementation are the annual reviews of the water and wastewater sector which are held by the Governments of Egypt and the United States. These sessions allow for the routine assessment of progress, the timely identification of problems, and the joint resolution of issues. This continuous process is critical to assure that a project is planned, designed, and implemented in an environmentally sound fashion as opposed to only being subject to the preparation of a detailed environmental assessment as a legal or policy requirement.

EIA can help establish phased investment strategies and technology selection

The experience of the Greater Cairo Wastewater Project demonstrates that environmental assessments can be designed to provide insight into complex project design decisions such as the selection of phased investment priorities and technology selection in a large-scale project. The environmental assessment was an important tool for the CWO and USAID in making the difficult decisions on the sequence of construction elements, in order to optimize environmental health benefits in a project with an implementation period of over a decade. The environmental assessment assisted in the selection of technology for wastewater collection, treatment, conveyance, temporary disposal, and permanent disposal.

The usefulness of the environmental assessment in the project design and implementation process was enhanced by the fact that the analysis of all technical alternatives and mitigations proposed in the environmental assessment included an evaluation of their capital cost (foreign and local currency), recurrent cost (foreign and local currency), institutional development and training requirements, and the identification of the responsible implementing organization. This information proved critical to decision-making as it provided information on the cost and managerial implications of various options.

EIA should provide an integrated analysis for programme planning

The experience of the Greater Cairo Wastewater Project demonstrates that an environmental assessment can influence the decisions of host country and donor officials identifying major problems requiring resolution, providing a basis for policy, review, and serving as advocacy documents to obtain support for project funding. The environmental assessment identified a series of issues which represented generic problems in the management of wastewater in Egypt. It reviewed the problems of institutional development, operation and maintenance, system reliability, and the financing of recurrent costs. By providing an integrated and objective analysis of the current status of wastewater services on the West Bank of Cairo and an assessment of the potential human health impacts of this situation, the assessment served as an advocacy document for justifying the provision of support for complementary project activities in institutional development, operation and maintenance, and training.

A major outgrowth of the assessment is the Water and Wastewater Institutional Development Project approved in 1985 with joint Government of Egypt and USAID funding of $420 million. The assesment brought to the attention of the host government and donor organizations the serious negative environmental impacts which can occur when systems fail to operate as planned due to inadequate design, poor construction, or improper operation. It stressed the critical role played by properly prepared institutions and trained personnel in assuring that the environmental objectives of the project are achieved on a sustainable basis.

The importance of "scoping sessions"

The experience of the Greater Cairo Wastewater Project demonstrates the utility of conducting "scoping sessions" as part of the process for the preparation of environmental assessments. The USAID environmental procedures require that "scoping sessions" be conducted as an element of the environmental assessment preparation process. However, the experience in the Cairo study, and other studies, indicates that the sessions provide an important mechanism to assure widespread knowledge of the proposed project, the potential environmental impacts, alternatives, and possible mitigation activities.

Scoping sessions provide a forum for the participants, the project sponsor, and the assessment team to interact to obtain a consensus on such things as the critical environmental issues which should be reviewed, the critical organizations and individuals to be contacted, and location of the important sources of data. It also provides a means for establishing contacts to ensure that senior level personnel instruct their staffs to provide assistance to the team and logistical support for field visits. CWO and USAID attribute much of the $78,000 in savings which was realized by the consultant in the preparation of the assessment as attributable to the contacts made at the scooping session.

The advantages of a "joint team" approach

The experience of the Greater Cairo Wastewater Project demonstrates that the use of joint teams comprised of personnel from the host country and international consulting organizations is a technically sound and cost-effective practice. The preparation of the environmental assessment benefited from the use of an Egyptian private sector consulting organization as a subcontractor which provided both professional personnel, support personnel, and logistical assistance. This association increased the efficiency of the personnel provided by the international consultant and provided direct access into the well developed Egyptian consulting community. It also reduced the time required by CWO and USAID to support the field operations of the international consultant.

The "joint team" approach provided the Egyptian subcontractor with an opportunity to expand their area of expertise and to develop a potentially long-term relationship with a firm from the United States. USAID has continued to use this approach for the preparation of environmental assessments throughout the Asia and Near East Region. For example, a major Pakistan–USAID environmental assessment was prepared recently by a joint team which included five experts from an American consulting firm and five experts from an associated Pakistani firm.

Host governments and donors should recognize, however, that the use of joint teams requires the adoption of a policy which promotes collaborative preparation of consultant studies. USAID believes that the joint preparation of environmental assessments is an effective technique for the transfer of this methodology when this is a planned objective of technical assistance and provisions are made in the consultant contract to assure this will occur. It is recommended that when joint teams are proposed to prepare environmental assessments the scope of work should include a provision for the international firm to review the objectives and methodology of the environmental assessment with the local firm. The scope of work for the local firm should include provision for review of local customs, laws, regulations, and institutions with the international firm.

The need for a flexible review and comment process

The experience of the Cairo Wastewater Project demonstrated the need to adopt a flexible approach to the review and comment process for environmental assessments. In most countries, developed and developing alike, personnel in governmental and non-governmental organizations are limited in their ability to review and comment on the large amounts of material which are routinely submitted to their offices. The traditional system used in the United States of soliciting formal written comments in response to a draft assessment is not an efficient way to obtain comments in the Near Eastern context. For a number of reasons, it is difficult for many organizations to provide written comments in a timely fashion (60 to 90 day review and comment period). After a major extension of the review period, CWO and USAID conducted visits to a number of key individuals to obtain their comments. This proved to be a satisfactory although informal means of obtaining responses to the draft and final assessment.

As the result of this type of experience in Egypt and other countries in the Asia and Near East Region, USAID has adopted a mixed approach to review and comment on assessments which includes formal written comments, small group meetings to review draft documents, and consultations with key individuals. USAID has found that the preparation and distribution of independently bound executive summaries greatly assists in providing senior level personnel, who do not have the time to review the complete assessment, with an opportunity to review the major findings and recommendations of the study.

Index